THE ROAD TO
SAN DONATO

THE ROAD TO SAN DONATO

FATHERS, SONS, AND CYCLING ACROSS ITALY

ROBERT COCUZZO

MOUNTAINEERS
BOOKS

MOUNTAINEERS BOOKS is dedicated to the exploration, preservation, and enjoyment of outdoor and wilderness areas.

1001 SW Klickitat Way, Suite 201, Seattle, WA 98134
800-553-4453, www.mountaineersbooks.org

Printed in the United States of America
Distributed in the United Kingdom by Cordee, www.cordee.co.uk
22 21 20 19   1 2 3 4 5

Copyeditor: Amy Smith Bell
Cover and book design: Jen Grable
Cartographer: Lohnes + Wright
All photographs by the author unless credited otherwise
Cover photograph: *The author's father, Stephen Cocuzzo, standing next to his first bicycle in Brighton, Massachusetts* (Cocuzzo family photo)

Library of Congress Cataloging-in-Publication data is on file for this title at
https://lccn.loc.gov/2019008875 (paper) and
https://lccn.loc.gov/2019980532 (ebook).

Mountaineers Books titles may be purchased for corporate, educational, or other promotional sales, and our authors are available for a wide range of events. For information on special discounts or booking an author, contact our customer service at 800-553-4453 or mbooks@mountaineersbooks.org.

♻ Printed on recycled paper

ISBN (hardcover): 978-1-68051-244-1
ISBN (ebook): 978-1-68051-245-8

An independent nonprofit publisher since 1960

FOR VIENNA SAVOY,
while your mother was making you,
I was making this.

AUTHOR'S NOTE

This book principally chronicles a cycling trip that I embarked on with my father, Stephen Cocuzzo, in Italy in March of 2017. A second research trip to Italy was taken in June of 2018. For the sake of the reader and the cohesiveness of the story, some research, interviews, and scenes from the second research trip were consolidated and integrated into the telling of the *first* trip with my father. In this book, dialogue is based on recorded interviews, journal entries, extensive notes, and my best recollections.

Although most of the Italian translations herein were provided by Delia Roffo, I was also helped by Stefania Cocuzzo, who translated my interview with her father, Fulvio Cocuzzo, which was conducted via Skype. I'm indebted to the fine work of many other authors and researchers, most notably Aili and Andres McConnon for their exquisite telling of Gino Bartali's life in their 2012 book, *Road to Valor*, referenced in a number of chapters. Their work served as invaluable inspiration during the journey—both on the bike and off.

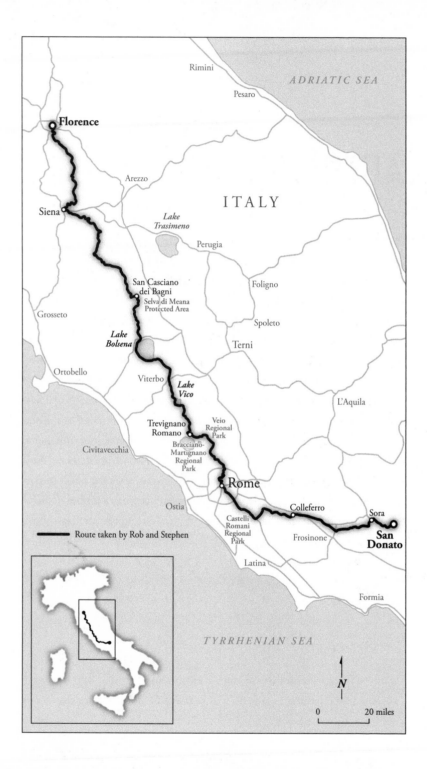

Rimini

ADRIATIC SEA

Pesaro

Florence

Arezzo

ITALY

Siena

Lake Trasimeno

Perugia

San Casciano dei Bagni

Selva di Meana Protected Area

Foligno

Lake Bolsena

Grosseto

Spoleto

Terni

Ortobello

Viterbo

Lake Vico

L'Aquila

Trevignano Romano

Veio Regional Park

Civitavecchia

Bracciano-Martignano Regional Park

Rome

Ostia

Colleferro

Sora

Castelli Romani Regional Park

San Donato

Frosinone

Latina

Formia

—— Route taken by Rob and Stephen

TYRRHENIAN SEA

N

0   20 miles

INTRODUCTION

I t was never my intention to write such a personal book, certainly not at the age of thirty-two. After all, my story was not wildly different than most of the kids I grew up with in my middle-class neighborhood outside of Boston. Sure, I carried my fair share of psychological and emotional baggage, but the traumas of my life weren't all that traumatic. Raised by loving parents who supported my dreams, I never wanted for much of anything. Beyond the normal run-of-the-mill growing pains associated with love, loss, and identity, there was no real struggle in my upbringing.

Yet when my father and I embarked on a cycling trip through Italy in search of our family's roots, I began pulling on the thread of my life and found something surprising at the other end. A pervasive silence hung over my family history. Although I was raised by storytellers, so much of my story was hiding from me in plain sight. From generation to generation, details had been lost amid the onslaught of everyday life, leaving me with only a cursory understanding of where I came from.

This silence weighed especially heavy over my relationship with my father. Our bond was stronger than most, forged by a shared love of adventure sports that we spent countless hours doing together. Whether bicycling through the city, skiing icy slopes, or climbing rock walls, we developed a unique partnership that required us to depend on one another. We pushed each other faster, harder, and higher in those endeavors. We communicated without speaking—pointing out debris in the road, anticipating the next turn down the mountain, and instinctively readying the rope to catch the other person when he was about to fall.

Perhaps because of this almost telepathic communication, we didn't see the need to delve deeper into our personal lives. My father was without question the most eccentric person I knew. Nothing about him was conventional. Not his appearance, his profession, his passions, or even his diet. His mode of thinking was entirely his own—for better and for worse. Throughout my life I'd never taken the time to truly understand what motivated who he was and how he thought. Instead, I'd shrug my shoulders and say, "Oh yeah, they definitely broke the mold after they made my old man."

When my father and I set off on a two-week cycling tour through Italy, we were both at inflection points in our lives. My father was downshifting, easing into a pseudo retirement and pondering how to spend the rest of his days with my mother. Meanwhile, I had the throttle pegged, accelerating from one objective to the next, gearing up to launch into married life with my longtime girlfriend. The dynamics of our father-son relationship were about to change dramatically, and this bike ride symbolized the last hurrah as the team we'd been for most of my life.

Before the trip, I believed my father and I had plenty of time to understand one another. The many questions I had for him would eventually be answered, and the secret parts of myself would gradually be revealed. However, the folly of my shortsightedness came into harsh focus when my grandfather—my father's father—fell ill. His life was drawing to an abrupt close, and in the chaos of trying to thwart the sickness that consumed him, there was little time to resolve everything left undone. I didn't get the chance to glean the ultimate wisdom I hoped to inherit from my grandfather. Watching him rapidly wither away, I could easily imagine the same outcome with my father. I pictured myself at his bedside, hastily trying to learn what I could within the little time we had left together.

Although we never discussed it, the bike ride became my opportunity to get at the core of who my father was. As I meditated on our relationship over hundreds of miles pedaling through Italian countryside, I realized there was so much more I needed to learn from him. The older I got, the more of him I saw in myself, but I hadn't figured out how to manage the impulses we shared. My father had the owner's manual, and this bike ride gave me the chance to tear out some key pages and throw them in my back pocket.

The truths of our relationship and family history transcended the two of us, stretching back generations of fathers and sons. When Dad and I reached the tiny village where our family name first took root, the dramatic history we discovered brought a fuller appreciation of our past and provided new tools for navigating our future.

Somewhere during the writing process, many authors ask themselves: *Is this even worth reading? Why would someone care about my story?* For me, that question echoed most loudly during early morning writing sessions when I'd dredge up my most intimate reflections and dare to bare them on the page. *What's the point of all this?* I thought. *Why am I throwing my dirty laundry out there for people to pick apart?* Sometimes these questions of doubt blared so loudly in my mind that I stopped writing entirely for weeks on end.

What brought me back time and time again was the belief that everyone can relate to the journey that unfolds in this book. In one way or another, we're all on a quest to better understand ourselves and the people closest to us. So little time is spent unpacking the twists and turns that delivered us to our present. That's especially the case with our most immediate relationships.

Some of the most mysterious relationships in our lives are the ones directly in front of us. Time has a way of layering on memories that leave the deepest truths of those we love most hidden from sight. Too often, we don't take the time to discover the essence of family and friends before it's too late.

This book is intended to sound the alarm for readers: make haste and begin that journey as soon as possible. When you strip away all the layers, you discover the foundation upon which your own life is built.

CHAPTER 1

Twenty years from now you will be more disappointed by the things you didn't do than by the ones you did do. So throw off the bowlines. Sail away from the safe harbor. Catch the trade winds in your sails. Explore. Dream. Discover.

—Attributed to Mark Twain

I could practically smell the coffee on his breath through the phone. Just past eight in the morning, my father was already heavily caffeinated. As with every day for the past twenty-seven years, he had risen at 3:30 in the morning, downed a pot of cheap coffee, threw a handful of punches at the heavy bag hanging in the basement, brewed another pot of coffee for my mother, climbed onto his bicycle, pedaled thirty miles in the frigid cold for fun (and another five miles to work), showered, grabbed another coffee at the convenience store, and then dialed me up as he waited for his first client to arrive at his hair salon. Dad didn't wait a second to launch into his grand plan.

"I got the idea for your next book," he said breathlessly. "Let's bike across the country."

My father was known for these flights of fancy. When he got something into his mind, he didn't so much put his foot on the gas as break the knob right off the throttle. Casual jogging back in the late 1970s led to him running twenty-two Boston Marathons. "Dieting" for my father consisted of consuming nothing but water and black coffee for seven straight days. One tiny tattoo during a midlife crisis cracked open the floodgates to nearly full sleeves of ink, including an ill-advised tattoo of a mermaid with a serpent wrapped around her shoulders that very nearly shattered my parents' marriage. My father not only executed on an idea—he executed to the absolute extreme.

However, this proposition to bicycle across the United States was different. Dad fantasized about embarking on a long-distance bike ride like working stiffs talk about selling off all their worldly possessions, buying a boat, and sailing into the sunset. He'd been talking about it for years but never actually put the plan into motion. Just savoring the thought of setting out on a long, *long* bike ride gave him a certain satisfaction that was almost as good as actually going on the ride itself.

For twenty years my father had been addicted to running, logging nearly a hundred miles a week to and from work. His running kick began back in high school when he played football and earned the nickname "the Galloping Guinea" for sprinting around the field. By the time he was in his early fifties, the pounding on the pavement had blown discs in his back that left him crippled with pain. That's when he rediscovered bicycling and went from an occasional pleasure cruiser to a full-blown zealot. His life now revolved around bicycling. When he started shaving his legs, my family knew this wasn't another passing fascination. "It helps the sweat run off my legs easier," he explained after revealing cleanly shaven calves. "And for, you know, being more aerodynamic." Except we knew the truth: he'd gleefully given himself over to the cult of hardcore cycling. The shaved legs were a sign of this covenant.

In the years since, cycling had become my father's greatest joy and indulgence. He didn't drink, smoke, or even eat meat anymore. At the ripe age of sixty-four, his highs came from cranking through city traffic every morning and evening like a bat out of hell. On the weekends he clipped into his prized possession, a seven-thousand-dollar road bike—by far the most expensive thing he owned—and pedaled for sixty, seventy, sometimes a hundred miles or more. He was a raging endorphin junkie, and the hours on the saddle provided the mental balance that kept him sane. Better still, it kept our whole family sane.

Growing up, I knew that if my father didn't get his cycling fix, he could be a miserable, short-tempered bastard. So my mother never gave him any grief about leaving her with me and my brother when he pedaled off on a long ride. Upon returning he obsessively washed every square inch of the bike's frame, every link of the chain, all the cables, brake pads, and every single spoke. He let it drip dry before wielding a hair dryer to get into all the nooks and crannies. His love of his bicycles bordered on a clinical condition. They hung neatly in our basement like books on a shelf, each telling a story from his life. He owned at least six bikes at any given time, and I often caught him in the basement just staring at them adoringly.

Despite my father's penchant for executing zany ideas and his love for the road, a truly long-distance cycling tour had eluded him. Perhaps it was because he was also one of the most stubborn creatures of habit to ever walk the green earth. He thrived off routine. Apart from the all too frequent bike accident, his days ticked along predictably for years on end. He wasn't much for switching tracks. The mere suggestion that he would kick off from work, pack up a backpack, and hit the road into the wild unknown prompted a long, exaggerated eye roll.

Except this time was different. This time, he'd asked me to go with him. I lived for pulling the trigger on an adventure. I'd spent years backpacking around South America, pinballing around Europe, and driving across the country. The past five winters I'd schlepped to remote mountain towns around the world for a book project about an extreme skier. Maybe it was out of a lurking fear that I inherited the same wont for routine and creature comforts as my father that I forced myself to shake up the Etch A Sketch of my surroundings whenever the lines started getting particularly thick.

When Dad called with his idea for this bike ride, I had just turned down my dream job at *Outside* magazine to stay back in my native Boston with my longtime girlfriend, Jenny. I was working up the nerve to ask for her hand in marriage. Moving to the magazine's headquarters in Santa Fe would not have boded well for our relationship, so after much deliberation I begrudgingly passed up the position. Though it was the best personal decision, turning down the job cut against the grain of my modus operandi. The decision had a ripple effect. I began flaking out on one adventure after the next. My failures to commit rattled my sense of identity. I felt creatively constipated and tumbled into a deep depression. I desperately needed a kick in the ass.

When my father called, I knew that the rough-and-tumble times of pedaling hundreds of miles across the country would do just that. But more important, this bike ride offered an exceedingly rare opportunity to spend time with my father, just the two of us. Growing up, I was Dad's adventure partner. He put me on skis when I was three. By the time I was ten, we were scorching down icy double black diamonds together in New Hampshire. He introduced me to rock climbing when I was eleven. By fourteen, I hung upside down from a sixty-foot ceiling with him on the other end of the rope. And, of course, there was cycling.

My father had me on a bike before I could walk. He built a baby seat out of scrap wood and mounted it to the back of his road bike, taking me out on long weekend rides when my mother went to work as a nurse. Little did she know that he wasn't taking me on leisurely cruises around the neighborhood. He buzzed down steep hills, weaved through traffic, and raced people on the bike path—all the while I kicked him like I was a jockey, screaming, "Faster faster!" He was once zooming downhill when a lady spotted me on the back of his bike. "Are you crazy?" she yelled out her car window. "I'm calling the cops!" Dad probably flipped her off and peeled away before the light turned green.

As I grew into adulthood, adventures with my father had become fewer and farther between. We rarely got a chance to rock climb together, and my skiing had taken me to bigger mountains beyond his ability. Yet as cyclists, we were still fairly matched in ability and strength, so I thought this trip offered an ideal context for us to reconnect. The trip would undoubtedly create memories that would appreciate exponentially in time. So much had been left unsaid between us since I moved out of my parents' house after high school and catapulted into adulthood. This trip would give us hundreds of miles to say it all.

"Let's do it," I told him. There was a long pause on the other end of the phone. "Take a month off," I said, "and do it."

"Yeah?"

"Yeah, talk to Mom. I'll start plotting a course."

MY JOB AS THE editor of a seasonal magazine gave me the winter and early months of spring free from office duties. Dad and I circled March for the target month for our cross-country adventure. I researched the Southern Tier, a 3,100-mile route beginning in San Diego and ending in Saint Augustine, Florida, that would allow us to embark in early spring. None of the stops along the route were particularly intriguing to us: Tempe, Arizona; Del Rio, Texas; DeFuniak Springs, Florida. The allure was in covering the distance between each destination. We didn't really care *where* we were riding as much as how *much* we were riding—and riding all those miles together.

Dad penciled himself off for the month, the longest stretch he'd ever taken off work in his life. He was the owner of a hair salon, and the hiatus came at the perfect time for him professionally. After twenty-seven years owning and operating the salon, he was considering closing the business. The rent was too high and his business partner wanted to move on. But Dad felt responsible for his longtime employees and grappled with the question of whether to open a new shop or retire and let them fend for themselves. This trip would give him an opportunity to get out of the grind, away from his employees, where he could meditate on the next stage of his life.

And so we started training, planning, and mentally preparing for the miles ahead. As our departure date approached, each of us waited for the other to blink and call the whole thing off. But neither of us did. Sometimes we all need a catalyst—someone to insist that our audacious dreams aren't so audacious. A person not to push you but to grab your hand and jump with you. Dad and I were each other's catalysts. We held each other to it and prepared to leap.

CHAPTER 2

Every book is a quotation; and every house is a quotation out
of all forests, and mines, and stone quarries; and every man is a
quotation from all his ancestors.

—Ralph Waldo Emerson

My grandfather looked like he could crush another man's skull with his bare hands. He was a mammoth of a human being who possessed mesmerizing strength. When a five-hundred-pound tree limb fell in my parents' backyard a few years ago, Papa drove right over and cut it into pieces using a rusty handsaw, then hauled it away in sixty-pound logs.

Now in his eighties, he still mowed lawns, trimmed hedges, and dragged bags of leaves off properties he'd been caretaking for decades. At eighty-four, Papa painted his entire house—the *outside* of his house—using a single brush. Neighbors gawked at him through the curtains, holding their breaths as this spritely, two-hundred-plus-pound old man balanced precariously on the last rung of the ladder to paint every single shingle. Eventually one of the neighbors couldn't bear to just watch anymore. He marched across the street, got to the edge of Papa's driveway, and yelled, "Hey, Joe, . . . how much for my house?"

Papa was the first of his family born in the United States and possessed the same bootstrap sensibilities of his Italian immigrant parents. As with just about everyone in his neighborhood, they had come to the United States from a tiny village in southeastern Italy called San Donato Val di Comino. With only a few lire in their pockets, they chiseled off their own hunk of the American dream by laboring hard with their hands. While his family's roots dug deeper in American soil, Papa clung to his Italian heritage with an intense pride. He spoke about the Old Country with a fondness and whimsy that made it seem like part of him was back in that village, waiting for his return.

Despite Papa's might, he had an Achilles' heel. Prostate cancer had festered in his body for years, kept at bay with various treatments that our family never really discussed. When the cancer finally broke through his doctor's defenses, the disease spread throughout Papa's body like a flash flood. His bull-like strength vanished nearly overnight. He lost seventy pounds and struggled to care for himself. When he slipped and fell in the shower and my grandmother couldn't help him to his feet, the fire department was called. Picturing the man of all men shivering naked and helpless in the bathtub, waiting to be rescued by a bunch of strangers, broke my heart.

As Papa's decline steepened, my family's focus turned to caring for him. Dad and I stopped talking about our cross-country bike trip. Both of us assumed the trip was off until further notice. Instead, we made regular visits to my grandparents' home in Cape Cod, where Papa took to sleeping most of the day. For the first time in his life, he depended on others to perform even the most menial tasks. In the blink of an eye, this man who could singlehandedly hang a ceiling of sheet rock now couldn't open a can of soda. The sense of helplessness snuffed out his spirit. We kept up an optimistic facade that he would rebound and return to his virile self, but we knew this was probably the beginning of the end.

A month or so after my Dad pitched the idea for our bike adventure, I drove down to the Cape to visit with Papa. He sat at the kitchen table, flipping through old black-and-white photographs. "Hey, Papa!" I called out, slipping my hand into his and reaching down to hug him. His bony shoulders felt like rungs on a coatrack. "What are you looking at?" I asked.

"I was looking for some papers and I found this manila folder with these snapshots," he said. I pulled up a seat next to him and watched him scan through the images. Each photo looked like a postage stamp in his still-massive hands. "This one was taken at Blackmore, down in Myrtle Beach. The golf course that Gary Player designed," he said, adjusting his glasses with thumb and index finger. "There were twenty of us in the group. I think that was a dozen years ago." He studied the photo, scanning his eyes across the faces. "All these guys are dead," he concluded with a sigh. "All them passed away. I've lost a lot of friends. But anyway, life goes on . . . "

Papa examined one photo after the next, tossing each onto the table like he was folding a hand in poker. He leafed through another stack, then paused on a photo of a younger version of himself standing in front of a white convertible. Bare-chested with a bronze tan and a full head of thick black hair, he had a white cloth in one hand like he had just dried off the last drops of water after washing the car. "I loved that car," he told me. "Ford convertible. A '59. Had a rumble seat—you pull a lever and the rumble seat opened in the back. It was a gorgeous car. Black . . . black with a white top. It was a sharp car. I loved that car."

"What happened to it?" I asked.

"My father sold that car on me."

"What?"

"He sold it. That bastard. I was coming back from being aboard a ship in the Coast Guard and he sold it while I was gone. Not only did he sell my car, but he kept the money." Papa placed the photo on the table. "I never had much love for my father."

Papa was usually slow to anger, but this photo struck a painful nerve from his past. The raw emotion in his voice was sharp and unfamiliar, and made me realize just how little I knew about his early life. "Why?" I asked. "What was your relationship like?"

"He wasn't much of a father to me," Papa said bluntly. "He was a mean bastard, a drinker. I never got a nickel off my father from the day I was born. But I put that aside because I didn't want to be like him." He sighed. "Some things you just don't forget. I still live with it. To this day, I'm very bitter toward him."

I saw my grandfather as the Italian patriarch who had always sat at the head of the table. The man who could cut down a sycamore as easily as he could slice up a crusty loaf of bread. The details of his life before I was born existed in my mind like these scattered photographs: disjointed stories with little unifying context. I didn't know the burdens he had faced. He'd always hidden them from me. I knew next to nothing about his father, the man who brought our family name over to the United States from Italy. I wondered, *Why was their relationship so toxic? What was the sorrow about?*

"Would you look at that?" Papa said, picking up another photo. He bellowed out a wheezy laugh. "This is from Italy . . . the Colosseum." In the picture he looked two hundred pounds heavier—but a jolly two hundred. Under his arm was my little grandmother and two friends, each in sweatpants and fanny packs, all four beaming.

"Where'd you go?" I asked.

"Rome," he said. "We . . . ahh . . . we took a cruise and ended up in Sicily."

"That must have been nice."

"Oh yeah, it was wonderful, Robbie. Really wonderful." I asked if he visited San Donato, the village where his family was from. His smile softened. "No, we never made it there," he said, placing the photo on the table. "I'm upset that we never got a chance to go there."

Never got a chance to go there? I thought. *How is that possible?* I'd heard about this fabled village for my entire life. The place was practically a living character in our family lore. How on earth had my grandfather never ventured there to see it? For years, he'd talked about this mythic place nestled in the mountains. I assumed he'd been there.

"I would have loved to see it," he said, shuffling the photos and slipping them back into the envelope with the others. "Even just once."

I gazed out the kitchen window to the Italian flag flapping off the backyard shed. For decades, Papa had gone in and out of that shed, fetching tools, tying up bags of trash, cleaning the blades of his lawn mower. Routine had taken over his life—like it does for all of us when we're not watching. With the end in sight, the costs of that time gone by were crystalizing with regret. He had never been to the village—and he never would. In his regret, I found my own: *Why am I only now coming to know this person who has been with me my entire life?*

DAD PICKED UP THE phone on the second ring: "Yo!"

"I got it," I said.

"Got what?"

"Our cycling trip—let's go to the village."

He knew exactly where I meant. "Papa's village?"

"Yeah. Let's fly to Florence and pedal to the village. It will be, I dunno, five hundred miles or so."

Silence. It was one thing for my creature-of-habit father to cycle through towns that spoke his language and served his food and quite another to put an ocean between him and the safety of his routine. I had no idea when he'd last left the country. Chances were, neither did he. But there was something therapeutic about this idea of pedaling through Italy together and discovering the village Papa never got a chance to see. Here we were helpless, watching my grandfather fade day after day. But over there, we could live for him and check that big empty box on his bucket list.

"We'll go for Papa," I said. "We'll pedal to the village, take photos, meet any family we can find there, and come back and tell him all about it."

"We'll kind of go in his honor?" Dad said, now on board.

"Exactly."

Sitting at the kitchen table with Papa that day, I'd had a vision of my own father. I could picture us sitting at a similar table years from now, flipping through old photographs and sharing regrets of the things we never made time to do together, places we'd never seen. The window of Papa's life was rapidly closing, with so many things left undone, not the least of which was reconciling with his own father. I didn't want that to happen for me and my father. Dad's dream was to pedal across the country. I was going to make sure that we did that—except we'd be pedaling across the Old Country.

I BOOKED OUR FLIGHTS to Florence for late March and researched a cycling route to Rome. Papa's village of San Donato was around a hundred miles south of the capital city, so I figured we'd be able to piece our way there from Rome. There was a litany of questions to consider. Do we ship our bikes to Italy, or do we rent? Do we use saddlebags and panniers to carry our luggage, or do we simply travel ultra light wearing backpacks? But of all the questions, one reigned supreme: with the tickets booked, would my father stay healthy enough for us to take this trip?

Yes, he was in peak physical condition, probably fitter than most of my friends who were half his age. But my father had an addiction that put his life on the line every single day. It wasn't an addiction in the traditional sense. As crazy as it might sound, most of my family thought my father was addicted to risk-taking. No matter how hard we pleaded with him, he flat out refused to give it up.

CHAPTER 3

There he goes. One of God's own prototypes. A high-powered
mutant of some kind never even considered for mass production.
Too weird to live, and too rare to die.

—Hunter S. Thompson

My father had been hit by a car twenty-one times. Or more accurately, while riding his bicycle, he'd been hit by sixteen cars, four buses, and a Dodge Ram pickup truck. And these weren't just superficial sideswipes. He'd been launched into windshields, T-boned at intersections, and driven into the cold, hard pavement with enough force to crack his helmet in half. When the pickup truck hit him, the driver accidently punched the gas instead of hitting the brake and proceeded to run over my father's bicycle, instantly turning it into carbon fiber kindling. Luckily for Dad, he rolled out of the way milliseconds before the truck's tires crushed his rib cage.

Part of the problem was that Dad's bike didn't have any brakes. He rode what is known as a fixed-gear, or fixie—the weapon of choice for most city bike messengers. What makes the fixie unique is that the bike's chain is on a single track connected to a cog on the back wheel that does not spin freely. On a regular bike, when you stop pedaling, the back wheel spins freely, allowing you to coast. But on a fixie, if you try to coast, the pedals continue to turn in unison with the back wheel, forcing your legs forward whether you like it or not. This direct connection between the wheels and the pedals makes going down hills, swerving around potholes, and stopping short extremely difficult. To stop, Dad had to essentially pedal backward, resisting the bike's forward momentum, until it slowed to a halt.

Part of the machismo associated with riding a fixie is to strip off the bike's hand brakes and rely entirely on the strength of your legs to stop the bike. "Its beauty is in its simplicity," my father would tell people, after they exclaimed, "You don't have any *brakes*!?" Stripping the hand brakes opened him up to disastrous scenarios. For instance, if he was going downhill and picked up too much speed, the pedals could spin wildly out of control, dragging his legs through the rapid rotations until his feet were thrown from the pedals. Or if he was speeding along a flat and his chain broke, he'd have no way to stop but to put his feet down and drag them along the pavement. Pedaling a fixed gear through gridlock traffic was a bit like rock climbing without a rope—every move needed to be perfect.

My dad was hard-wired for the fixie. His attitude on a bike might best be described as punk rocker meets Hells Angel. Like a lawless bike messenger, my father weaved around cars, ran red lights, and swerved around pedestrians on one of the most trafficked streets in Boston. Massachusetts Avenue was littered with ghost bikes, bicycles painted all white and chained to street signs that served as makeshift memorials to cyclists who had been killed there. Fatalities were common on Mass Ave. One morning in 2015, I got a barrage of calls from friends when local news reported that an unidentified cyclist had been crushed to death by an eighteen-wheeler on Mass Ave. I frantically dialed up my father's shop, only to find him casually sipping coffee on the other end of the line. He rode by these ghost bikes twice a day, but they never seemed to give him much pause.

Instead, on a street that called for defensive driving, Dad was always on the offense. He flipped off motorists who cut him off, spit on their windshields, and screamed obscenities fiery enough to singe your eyebrows. Perhaps not surprisingly, the combination of no brakes, chaotic traffic, and my father's *Mad Max* mentality made collisions in traffic a common occurrence. The aftermath was always the same. Horrified pedestrians would swarm my father, who, if not unconscious, would try to get up and shake the glass and grit from his jersey. Blood would stream down from his old elbows as he clicked and clacked on the sidewalk in his cycling cleats. In the old days, before he gave up swearing, he'd be spewing a colorful string of expletives. With his long blond hair, black goatee, and patchwork of tattoos covering his compact build, Dad was a sight to see even when he *hadn't* just been slammed across an intersection by a school bus, so onlookers were always quick to collect.

The driver would be next on the scene, phone pressed to his ear with 911 on the line, his jaw dragging on the ground behind him. "Are you alright? God, I didn't even see you. Are you alright—Jesus, I didn't see you." Dad would no doubt be more concerned about the condition of his bike than his own body. "I'm fine," he'd say. "Really, I'm fine." But then the ambulance would pull up with lights and sirens screaming. The gloved EMTs would check his wounds, shine a flashlight in his eyes, and insist that he come to the hospital to get checked out. So into the ambulance Dad would go, bike and all—or what was left of it. He'd sit there on the gurney, waving goodbye to the driver who almost killed him, completely neglecting to get any contact information.

"You have to talk to him," my mother once insisted outside the hospital room. I was nineteen at the time, back home visiting from college. "He can't go on like this," she pleaded. "It's not fair. He has a family to provide for. I'm not taking care of him if he's a vegetable. You have to talk to him." My parents made for a curious couple. On the one hand, there was my father, looking like a swashbuckling pirate who just stumbled out of the Bermuda Triangle. On the other hand, there was my mother, a smartly dressed lady who practically ran the Catholic church in our hometown. They loved each other intensely and were the definition of opposites attracting, but my mother's patience for my father's frequent brushes with death was long gone. She once caught him blasting down Mass Ave. without a helmet. The only thing buffering his skull from the pavement was a thin painter's cap. She slammed on the horn when she saw him, but he couldn't hear her because he was wearing earphones that were no doubt blasting AC/DC.

"He won't listen to me," she insisted outside the hospital room. "He'll listen to you. *Please.* Talk to him." I entered the room and sat on the edge of my father's hospital bed. He was waiting to be taken into surgery to have a screw drilled into his broken ankle. This latest crash hadn't been with a car.

Instead, he had been racing another cyclist early in the morning. Sprinting neck and neck—as Dad told the story—he was about to overtake the other cyclist when he had to swerve out of the way of a car and rammed into a cement median, shattering his ankle into bits.

"I *had* this guy," Dad said.

"Forget about the guy," I said. "You have to chill out. Mom is really worried."

"I know. I know. It's fine. It's *fiine*. Don't worry."

"It's not fine," I said, doubling down. "You have to take it easy. You're fifty-two years old, for god's sake."

The surgeon entered the room, trailed by my mother, and picked up Dad's chart from the end of the bed. "Mr. Cocuzzo, any medical history we should know about?"

"No, Doc," he proudly reported. "I'm perfectly healthy."

My mother shot him an exasperated look. "Actually, he has three coronary stents." Four years earlier, Dad almost had a heart attack when three of his arteries nearly closed while he was running to work. Despite his being a strict vegetarian for the past thirty years, hereditary heart disease had clogged up his arteries. He now had tiny plastic tubes in his heart and swallowed a cocktail of pills every day to keep the blood flowing.

"Other than that, I'm pretty healthy," my father said.

"Do you smoke?"

Dad shook his head.

"Drink?"

"Haven't had a drop in thirty-plus years," he said.

"How 'bout caffeine? How much coffee to do you drink?"

"You know . . . a couple cups."

"A couple cups?" my mother chimed in. "Stephen, you drink a pot a day!"

The doctor closed the file. "Alright, Mr. Cocuzzo, a nurse will be in shortly to get you ready for surgery."

With the doctor gone, I continued to make my case. "It's unfair to Mom," I said. "She doesn't want to see you end up dead. And what about Mark and me? You owe it to us. You have to slow down."

He nodded. Truth be told, I didn't believe the words coming out of my mouth. It wasn't that I didn't want him to slow down and be more cautious—I did. But his all-or-nothing attitude was who he was and who he'd always be. I didn't fully understand it, but my father held a primal devotion to his athletic endeavors. Cycling, being physical, was more than an addiction—it was a way of life. I didn't actually expect him to stop. And, honestly, I admired him for it. Dad had one gear and one gear only: *GO!*

AS I PLANNED OUR trip to Italy, the thought of leading my collision-prone parent down Italian back roads and through the Tuscan countryside simmered anxiously in my mind. If I've learned anything from my years traveling, it's that you can absolutely count on the shit hitting the fan spectacularly. I just hoped that any catastrophes we encountered in Italy didn't involve me pulling a Fiat hood ornament out of my father's forehead.

That was, of course, if I didn't kill him myself. This would be the longest uninterrupted time my father and I had ever spent together. Our relationship had benefited significantly from us not living under the same roof over the past thirteen years. Before I left home for college, we were like two bull elks circling a small watering hole. Our horns locked often. Spending every waking hour together, navigating hundreds of miles on unfamiliar roads, and encountering the normal, run-of-the-mill inconveniences of international travel would be a challenge for any two human beings. The thought of doing all that with a man who had a penchant for danger and a Rubik's Cube of idiosyncrasies made me anxious. I was absolutely certain that we would reach a breaking point. The only question was how broken that fight would leave us. Would we find strength to come together, or would it drive us further apart?

"DAD, YOUR PASSPORT IS expired."

"Wha—?"

"I'm looking at it right now," I said over the phone. "We need to get you a new passport. Pronto."

"You gotta be kidding me," he said. "We're leaving next week."

"We are?" I deadpanned. "Listen, go down to CVS and have them take a passport photo of you. I'm coming to get ya." Thirty minutes later, I pulled up to my childhood home in Arlington, Massachusetts, a suburb outside of Boston. My parents had lived there my entire life. Despite Dad and Papa renovating the house over the years, the two-bedroom was now dwarfed by all the new McMansions rising up on our quiet residential street.

Waiting at the door, Dad spotted my car through the rain and darted across the front lawn, which he had converted into a Zen rock garden a few years back. "Thank God we checked, huh?" he said, climbing into the car. He was wearing ripped jeans, a pair of beaded moccasins, a tight white undershirt inside out, and his fanny pack across his chest like a seat belt.

"Yeah, now let's just hope we can get a new passport in time for the flight."

Dad drew quiet. Situations like this, the lack of control, were exactly why he hated air travel. To him, the whole process was daunting. On the *extremely* rare occasions we flew anywhere when I was younger, well before the post-9/11 scrutiny of TSA security, Dad had the family encamped at the airport a full four hours before our flight. So I guess it shouldn't have come as much of a surprise to learn that the last time he used his passport, Reagan was in office.

Luckily for him, this wasn't my first time getting an emergency passport. While backpacking through Europe during college, I had my passport, along with my student visa and all my credit cards and money, stolen in Amsterdam. Earlier that day I had checked out of my hostel and set off on a psychedelic romp through the pot capital of the planet. Lost in a haze, I left my backpack with all my possessions on the floor of a coffee shop. With no money to book another hostel, I ended up sleeping on the floor of the train station before reporting to the US embassy the next morning. At the embassy a line stretched around the gates, each person neatly dressed, with their applications organized and ready to be presented. Meanwhile, I looked like a piece of dryer lint stuck to the skirt of reality. At 8:30 on the nose, a big Hawaiian opened the gates and called out, "Are there any Americans in line?" I was the only one to raise my hand. "Okay, come to the front." I had a new passport by the time the closest cannabis cafe opened.

By contrast, the passport office in Boston's City Hall looked like Noah's ark. All walks of humanity sat on the edge of their seats, praying they had the proper combination of paperwork to beat the flood. Dad took a seat and pulled his readers out from his fanny pack to fill out his passport renewal application. I watched him scan the instructions with the tip of his pen before jotting his first name in the box designated for last.

"Dad, last name goes there."

"Ugh—"

"It's cool," I said, trying to keep him calm. "It's cool. I'll grab you another." As I fetched him a fresh application, I considered what the road ahead held. Ninety-nine percent of my traveling abroad had been done alone, where I was only responsible for myself. I could go where I wanted, do what I wanted. Traveling with another person would be a continual negotiation, pleading a case of where to stay, when to eat, and what to do. That type of travel was completely foreign to me. And now I was about to experience it with the most travel-phobic person I knew.

"Here you go," I said, handing him a new application.

"Alright, let's see." I held my breath as he scanned the instructions again. *You got this, Dad*, I thought. *You got this.* But then I wondered, *Do I got this?*

I DROPPED MY FATHER back home and returned to my apartment in Boston. "How'd it go?" Jenny asked.

"Well, we got it," I said. "Passport should be ready for us to pick up by Monday."

"Oh good," she said.

I returned to the kitchen table, where I had begun whittling down the bare essentials for the trip. Camera, tubes, tires, wrench set, patch kit, and a myriad of other items were scattered along the table. "What's that?" Jenny asked, pointing to a couple of little orange baggies.

"Oh, those are emergency sleeping bags," I said. "Just in case we get caught out in the middle of nowhere for the night."

She shot me a look. "You're kidding me, right?"

I snickered. "You never know."

"Yeah, I don't even want to know," she said, shaking her head. "You guys are crazy."

Emergency sleeping bags aside, Jenny had supported this trip since the beginning, even when the initial idea was for a monthlong cross-country tour. She wasn't looking to get rid of me; rather, she viewed this trip as an opportunity for me to shake out the last bits of my restlessness, a chance to finally hang up my bachelor boots. For most of our relationship, I'd been a flight risk, jetting off for weeks or months at a time to hunt writing projects around the world. We'd been dating on and off for five years, and with both of us wanting a family, we needed to get started soon. Jenny hoped this time away would sufficiently scratch my adventure itch and allow me to finally settle down and get married.

As I giddily checked the emergency sleeping bags off on my packing list, I wondered if that would ever be possible.

CHAPTER 4

Whatever you can do, or dream you can, begin it.
Boldness has genius, power, and magic in it!

—Goethe

Papa was sitting in his recliner when I arrived. The volume to the television was cranked, booming the murmurs of a golf analyst through the house like the voice of God. Papa was as good as deaf. A lifetime of pushing lawn mowers without ear protection had left him with tinnitus, a constant ringing in his ears that at one point was so maddening he considered "buying a gun," as he put it. Thankfully, my uncle Joe finally convinced Papa to get hearing aids, which mercifully reduced the tinnitus. And yet the TV remained loud enough to drive a terrorist out of hiding.

"Hey, Papa!" I called out.

He turned to me and his face lit up. "Hey, guy! How ya doin'?" He fumbled with the remote. "Let me turn this damn thing down."

He looked painfully frail. His skinny legs were crossed, and even in baggy sweatpants I saw how bony they'd become. He looked as wispy as old grass clippings, a shell of his former self. All that was left was his big head and catcher's mitt hands.

"How you doin', Papa?" I asked, plopping down on the couch across from him.

"I'm still here," he said.

"Well, that's good."

"It's like I told the nurse the other day. I says, 'I feel very fortunate. I'm eighty-six years old. I've lived the better part of my life. I'm beyond expectancy. The only thing is that if I would happen to go all of a sudden, I would miss my family . . . '"

"How's the nurse?"

"Oh, she's a *big* girl. Probably throws manhole covers around like they're nickels. Gave me a shower the other day. Oh, was she rough! For Chrissakes, you'd think she was washing down a mule or something."

His comedic timing was still impeccable. "You look good, Papa."

"Well, I'm down to 175 now. I'm trying to put a few pounds back on, but I just can't do it . . . With the medication I'm taking, everything tastes like sawdust. I can't get the food down. Outside of soups and cereal. Ah well, what can you do?"

That seemed like the greatest indignity of Papa's decline. As if his physical deterioration wasn't enough, the cancer had also robbed him of the simple satisfaction of eating with his family. While we gorged on my grandmother's legendary eggplant parmesan, stuffed peppers, heaping plates of pasta, and antipasti, Papa spooned mouthfuls of cold, soggy cereal that he could barely choke down.

For the past five or so years, I'd flipped on my voice recorder whenever my family sat down at the dinner table with my grandfather. He was the consummate storyteller, and I had hours of tapes of him regaling us about his Italian neighborhood in Boston called Buggs Village. The neighborhood originally got its name from an Irish contractor, John "Buggs" Behan, who gave masonry and bricklaying jobs to Italian immigrants in the early 1900s. Over the years, discrimination toward Italians caused people to forget about the neighborhood's namesake, and they assumed that the area might as well have been called something equally vulgar, such as "Guinea Town" or "Wop City."

The vast majority of the Italians who came to Buggs Village, including my grandfather's family, were from the remote village of San Donato. Papa's grandfather, Giuseppe, immigrated to the States with his eldest son, Loreto (Papa's father), and got a job as a dynamiter. Blowing up tunnels for highways and railroads in Boston, Giuseppe saved up eleven thousand dollars to buy a small plot in the neighborhood and built a compound of triple-deckers that became known as "Cook's Yard," where his entire extended family—grandparents, uncles, aunts, and cousins—lived together. Papa was the eldest child in his family of five, but often told me he didn't enjoy any of the special treatment typically reserved for the first born. He didn't even have his own bed growing up—he slept on the living room couch. There was never enough money, so Papa would collect his father's empty wine bottles and return them to the store for a penny a piece.

His mother was a fashionable lady who dressed with the flair of a Roaring Twenties flapper. She wore high heels and red lipstick while tending to her house and baking Italian pastries. She and Papa's father were known to squabble when he got home from work, and occasionally she would hurl one of her pies at him from across the room. Although she adored her eldest son, whom she called "Joe-Joe," she rarely hugged or kissed him because his father forbade it.

What companionship he did find was in the streets of Brighton, running around with a terrific cast of characters who went by names like Jumbo, Jingles, Jopa, and Fats. Every afternoon they'd line up outside Pew's Soda Shop, smoking cigarettes, talking about cars, and catcalling women, one of whom became my grandmother. Although she made eyes with him outside the shop, my grandmother formally met my grandfather when her family ordered a couch that he delivered to her house. Papa came wearing a leather jacket and his olive-black hair perfectly coiffed. They married a few years later and moved into the Yard to start their family. My father, their firstborn, was gleefully passed around by the extended family, where love was expressed in food. When my father became tubby from all the cannoli and pasta, my grandmother draped a sign around his neck that read: *Non darmi da mangiare*. ("Don't feed me.")

My grandmother joined the ladies kibitzing beneath the grapevine in the Yard, while the men worked as mechanics, masons, and landscapers. Papa went into the landscaping business with his uncle, maintaining properties in the surrounding towns. At the end of each day, he and his neighborhood cronies funneled into the Brighton Elks Lodge, where Papa was a charter member and pulled beers behind the bar. The guys would play poker, drink Canadian Club, smoke cigars, and talk about the Old Country. The lodge was converted from the old Egyptian Theater on Washington Street in Brighton Center. To commemorate the opening, someone had the bright idea of bringing in the circus to perform during the week of Thanksgiving. "CIRCUS COMING TO BRIGHTON," the headline read in the local newspaper. "Lions 'n' everything."

Indeed, the show boasted five lions, five elephants, and a famous clown named Balloono. Everything was going to plan when suddenly one of the lions, a five-hundred-pounder named Eloise, broke out of her cage and rushed the crowd. Four hundred men, women, and children screamed to the exits, trampling a few unlucky souls. Papa and five of his buddies crammed into a phone booth. One woman locked herself in the ticket counter and refused to let anyone else join her. With the crowd funneling out the exits, the lion turned her attention to the elephants. She leapt onto the back of one of the elephants, which abruptly hurled the cat to the ground with its mighty trunk. Someone ran to the Brighton Police Station and alerted the cops, who screeched up to the theater guns drawn. When they arrived, the lion tamer had subdued Eloise with a stool and a pistol full of blanks. "The populace of Brighton enjoyed Thanksgiving Dinner, happy that they had avoided being one," read the minutes in the Elks' logbook in November 1962.

THAT WAS THE WORLD my grandfather regaled me with in his stories, a sepia-toned past of Italian-American life. Some of his friends worked as bookies, or made careers as gamblers. A few were in the mob. One was a hit man. But above all, they were a hardworking class of bootstrapping immigrants, working tirelessly to drive stakes into their own plot of American soil. I reveled in Papa's tales and never tired of hearing stories that I already knew verbatim. These stories made me want to become a writer.

Coming to grips with the fact that he was nearing the end of his life, I realized that I was missing critical information despite all the hours of recordings. I desperately wanted him to pass on some life lessons. I had interviewed hundreds of people over the course of my career, but no matter how many questions I asked or how I asked them, my grandfather tiptoed around the meat of his memory. I wanted him to bestow his wisdom on me. Wasn't that the most valuable inheritance?

"So you guys must be leaving soon?" he said.

"Yeah, this Friday."

"Oh, that's wonderful, Robbie. Just wonderful. I'm so happy you guys are going."

"Yeah, Papa, should be a hell of a trip. We'll say hi to all your old cronies in the village," I told him.

His dimples pinched his hollow cheeks. "San Donat," he said, clipping the O as he always did. "Can't believe you guys are going."

"I know—it's going to be something else."

"And you're biking?"

"Yep, from Florence." Like most of us, Papa had long since given up trying to understand my father's obsession with cycling—all the miles and crashes.

"You'll take care of your father, won't you?" he asked. "He's not a young man anymore, you know."

"I will. And we'll get back here to tell you all about what we found in Italy."

"That'd be nice," he said. "I'd like that."

I leaned forward on the couch, toward him. "Papa . . . what would you say is your greatest accomplishment?" The question seemed to take him aback.

"The family," he finally said. "I'm proud of the family."

I pushed a bit further. "What about it?"

"You know . . . I wasn't the best husband . . . but I was a good father."

"You were. Yes, you were."

"I did my best to take care of everyone. You know, if your father needed anything. Or Uncle Joe, or Aunt Nancy and Jodi—if I had a few bucks, I gave it to them. I tried to help however I could. Doing work over at your father's. I built that deck for Joe. When Nancy's kids were sick in California, we tried to be there. And Jodi, living in the place in Brighton. I did my best."

I could tell he wanted to move on, but I wanted more. "What would you say was your philosophy on being a good father?"

"I don't know . . . I just did it," he said. "I did my best to keep the family together. That's what you need to do: keep the family together."

"Keep the family together," I repeated. I reached for his hand to shake. I tried to hold the moment in my mind, knowing that this could very well be the last time I saw him alive. I wanted to tell him just how much he meant to me. I wanted him to know that he represented everything it was to be a stand-up guy, a true patriarch in my mind. But I couldn't. Papa hadn't given up hope yet, and I wasn't about to betray him by revealing that I already had.

CHAPTER 5

Ever since childhood, when I lived within earshot of the Boston and Maine, I have seldom heard a train go by and not wished I was on it.

—Paul Theroux

We weren't even across the Atlantic yet and Dad already looked like death. In the middle of our overnight flight to Florence, I woke up to find him pale and glistening in a cold sweat. He had his thumbs inside the waistband of his sweatpants, keeping the pressure off his abdomen. "What's up?" I whispered.

"My stomach," he groaned. "It's acting up."

Dad had suffered from these gastrointestinal attacks for about ten years now. A section of his large intestine becomes kinked, causing extreme nausea and excruciating pain. He was rushed to the emergency room several times over the years, but doctors couldn't figure out exactly what caused these episodes and offered no long-term cure. Instead, my father was left to develop his own remedy for unkinking his intestine. He discovered that he could make the pain subside by lying in the fetal position and rocking back and forth. This would often take place on the kitchen floor or in the back hall of his hair salon. But many times these attacks seized him while he was on a long ride, forcing him to get off his bike to crawl behind a Dunkin' Donuts or into an alley to lie down and rock in desperation.

Once he had to lie down in a graveyard. "A group of kids showed up," he told me later, laughing. "Probably walking back from school or something . . .

Scared the crap out of them for sure." One could only imagine the deep psychological scarring of witnessing a stranger, decked out in full spandex, moaning and rolling in pain on top of somebody's grave.

Now in the throes of a full-blown attack, Dad desperately needed to assume his rock-and-roll position. Without saying a word, he lifted the armrest between us, lowered his head into my lap, and began to rock. I scanned the plane. *This must look absolutely insane*, I thought. *Here I am with some long-haired head bobbing in my lap in the middle of a transatlantic flight.* Your mind didn't need to be in the gutter to imagine the worst.

Slithering out of my seat, I let Dad's head fall gently to the armrest, then retreated to the back of the plane. "May I have some water?" I asked the flight attendant, who was reading by an overhead light. She handed me a water-filled plastic cup and returned to her book. Sipping the lukewarm water, I watched my father's unruly blond hair spill into the aisle as he rocked in what looked like delirious pain. *Shit*, I thought. *Have I underestimated this whole thing? Could I really take care of him?* My default setting was to assume things would magically work out, but what were the realities of our situation? I was totally winging it. I had no idea whether I was physically prepared to pedal the distance ahead. I'd never cycled more than fifty miles at a time, and I was embarking on this ride with little more than optimism fueling my tank.

THE PLANE TREMBLED AS it descended into bands of clouds that rose up like icebergs in the cerulean sky. The ground gradually came into view, a jigsaw puzzle of light green grass, dark green trees, and arid brown dirt. The landscape became more detailed during the descent, with the green blocks turning into vineyards dotted with perfectly placed cypress trees, obtuse triangles of red becoming towns of stucco roofs, and handsome villas sprouting prominently from the hilltops. Apart from one main highway, the landscape seemed removed from the twenty-first century, as if we had flown back in time. Ahead on the horizon, I spotted it, with the emerald-green Arno slithering through the stone city like a serpent.

"Yo, Dad, check it out . . . Florence."

After disembarking, we didn't have to wait for checked luggage because we simply didn't have any. Everything for the next two weeks was strategically stuffed into two tiny backpacks little larger than a calzone. Each held a cycling kit, a light down jacket, a light rain jacket, two pairs of socks, and a toothbrush; our helmets hung from the packs' straps. I also carried a saddlebag, which I planned to attach to the seat post of the rental bike to hold my camera, six spare tubes, patch kit, bike pump, extra battery pack, and two emergency sleeping bags, which, God willing, we'd never have to use.

For our time off the bike, we'd each packed a pair of light pants, a shirt, and minimalist street shoes. Before the flight from Boston, Dad had insisted that he knew the perfect footwear for us. "They'll fold up into nothing," he claimed. "Don't worry. I'll pick you up a pair."

When I showed up at my parents' house later that morning, he presented them to me proudly. "Dad, these are women's shoes."

"What do you mean? No, they're not."

I snapped a photo of them and texted it to Jenny. "Those are espadrilles," she confirmed.

"Dad, they're *freaking* espadrilles."

"So?"

"*So* what did you pack for pants . . . *capris*?"

Dad was never one to adhere to the norms of fashion. He had a freewheeling sense of style that boasted leather pants, earrings, stacks of necklaces, and flowy dress shirts that he unbuttoned like a pirate. When I was little, I idolized his rockstar ways and begged my mother to let me get my ear pierced just like him. When my father chaperoned one of my grammar school field trips, all of my friends and perhaps some of my teachers thought he was my older, much cooler brother. "Nope, that's my Dad," I proudly told them.

As I got older, however, Dad's clothing choices—or lack of clothing, in some cases—could be truly cringeworthy. Once while I was playing lacrosse in high school, I found my teammates pointing and chuckling at something in the stands. "See that guy?" one of them asked me, gesturing to the grassy hill set behind the stands. I looked up to find my father basking in the sun in nothing but a tiny pair of running shorts that he had hiked up his crotch like a Speedo. "Wow," I said, taken aback. "Who is that basket case?"

Despite the many times he strutted into parent-teacher conferences like he'd just stepped off the stage at an Aerosmith concert, I admired my father's unwavering self-confidence, especially as I entered adulthood. Everything about him defied conventionality. He was here to make an unmistakable mark, and he didn't give a damn what anyone thought. If you called his outfit into question, he only doubled down, popping off another button and adding another necklace. So when Dad stepped off the plane onto Italian soil, he did so wearing a pair of black flats that he insisted were "ninja shoes."

"WE SHOULD GRAB SOME cash before we get out of here," Dad said. His stomach pain had mercifully subsided just before landing, and color had returned to his face.

"I have my credit card," I said. "So we're good."

"Yeah, I know, but we should really have some cash on us, you know, just in case." He pulled out a thick wad of bills. "Here, let's change this."

My brother, Mark, and I could always count on my father for cash. He'd slip us a twenty spot whenever we saw him. "Here, grab yourself a six-pack," he'd kid. He never used a credit card. *Not once.* Nor had he ever taken money out of an ATM or personally written a check to pay a bill. In fact, beyond paying his taxes every year, there was hardly any paper trail to prove my father's existence. Which was exactly how he liked it, under the radar. The last time he'd cashed a check at the bank was before he married my mother. Since then, she handled all of the family's finances—buying and paying off two homes, putting two kids through private high school and college, and setting aside a modest retirement nest egg. Money was never discussed. Dad happily turned over all his paychecks to her and lived off the cash tips he received from his clients after each haircut.

The arrangement suited him perfectly, especially since he never wanted for anything. Not a thing. Apart from his bicycle collection, he was completely disinterested in material possessions. His cars were always two-toned jalopies, the most recent of which he'd purchased at a junkyard from one of

Papa's old friends. "Fifteen hundred bucks," he announced after sputtering into the driveway. "Can you believe it?"

Yes, we could.

He loved getting a deal and took infinite pride in his ability to stretch a buck. "Ninety-nine cents—can you believe it?" he told my mom after pulling out a bunch of bruised bananas from his backpack. "They were practically giving them away. I mean, *hello?*"

He had an old Yankee sensibility of making things last, dutifully sewing zippers back on to jackets, patches on to pants, and buttons back on to shirts. He scorned owning anything new. We bought him expensive cycling kits for years, but he never wore them. Instead, he kept them in the plastic like a prized collection of comic books while he sewed the zipper off an old pair of jeans to fix a worn-out cycling jersey. Throwing anything away physically pained him. "I hate waste," he said whenever he found an abandoned can of soda with a couple sips left in it. "*Hate* it." Then he knocked back the rest of the can himself, no matter how flat it was.

Frugality was going to be *de rigueur* over the next two weeks. For Dad, that was all part of the challenge. Like sneaking microwave popcorn into the movie theater, he relished the thrill of saving a few bucks. As much as I hated to admit it, I was right there with him. Though I regularly poked fun at my father's stinginess, I couldn't deny that I was becoming more and more like him. Over the years I had developed my own bizarre penny-pinching habits while traveling. Sleeping in airports or on trains to save on the cost of a hotel room. Taking several layovers instead of flying direct for a cheaper plane ticket. Subsisting entirely on all-you-can-eat breakfast buffets. That type of behavior had become far less feasible with Jenny in my life, but for the next two weeks it was just Dad and me. The arithmetic for our trip would be how much we saved, not how much we spent.

I SLID THE WAD of cash through the currency exchange window. The woman behind the glass counted out a stack of euros and handed it back.

"It's like Monopoly money," Dad said. "You hold on to it."

We walked out into the glaring afternoon sun and motioned for a taxi. I scribbled the address to our hotel on the back of my plane ticket and showed it to the driver. Despite repeated claims that I was going to study up on the native tongue, I hadn't picked up more than a few words in Italian. "We want to go *here*," I said, tapping my chest and then the piece of paper.

"Yeah, no problem," the cabbie responded in perfect English. "Twenty euros." He pulled around the airport's roundabout and zipped us through the outskirts of Florence. The scenes panned across Dad's wraparound sunglasses. Walls of graffiti. Vespas buzzing by with their drivers carrying oversized loads. Children kicking a soccer ball around a cement court. This was my father's first glimpse of Italy. Everything was new, and he stared out the window with guarded curiosity.

The cab entered the grips of historic Florence, where stone buildings passed inches from the window as the driver deftly darted around pedestrians. We jostled over cobblestone streets and down tight alleys until we popped out onto a pedestrian-only street. "That big door," the driver said. "That's you."

"Alright, Pops, let's do it." We scrambled out of the taxi. I handed the driver twenty-five euros and waved off the change. I was never sure what the tipping policy was in Europe. We shouldered our bags to the hostel, then I pressed the bell, prompting the giant wooden door to click open and reveal a tranquil courtyard with a small palm tree in the center.

"This is dynamite," Dad said, as the wooden doors closed behind us.

I'd found our lodgings online—a steal at only thirty-five euros, including breakfast. Circling around the palm tree, we found a staircase and climbed up four flights of marble steps that had been worn down over generations. "I read online that this place was built in the sixteenth century," I told Dad. "The architect was some big-time Renaissance master." He nodded approvingly.

The innkeeper met us at the top of the staircase. He had thinning salt-and-pepper hair and a graying mustache and goatee that framed his smile. "Ecco, per favore," he said, directing us to follow him through the big apartment to his check-in desk. "Passaporti, per favore."

I handed them over.

"Your brother?" he nodded to Dad.

"No, no. I'm the father," Dad said, chuckling. "He's my son."

"Thanks for adding that detail, Pops."

The innkeeper grinned, finished the paperwork, and stood up, gesturing for us to follow him through the narrow, dimly lit hallway until he turned a corner and opened up a room for us. "Prego."

There was a good reason why this room cost only thirty-five euros a night—it had a single twin bed. I glanced at my father, who didn't have any issue about sharing the bed, especially not for thirty-five euros. For that price, he'd happily spoon with me on a bath mat.

"Excellent, thank you," Dad said to the innkeeper, before slinging his mini backpack on the mattress and pulling open the thick drapes. He could sleep anywhere. He often conked out on the hardwood floor of the kitchen near the heating vents. Growing up, I thought nothing of stumbling upon him sleeping under the dining room table. There was a stretch of time when my father insisted on sleeping in the uninsulated vestibule of our family's house—during the dead of winter.

"It's like camping," he told my mother while rolling out his sleeping bag.

"What if the neighbors see?" she pleaded.

"Forget the neighbors." Mark and I gawked at him through the window as he slithered into a thin, old sleeping bag. Plumes of his frozen breath fogged the glass.

"Don't you ever tell anyone about this," my mother said. "Your father is nuts."

A FEW HOURS LATER, Dad and I were lying shoulder to shoulder in bed. There wasn't even enough space for a pillow barrier between us. Thankfully, of all my father's quirks, sleeping in the buff wasn't one of them.

Settling in, I pulled out my iPhone. "What's that?" Dad asked, peeking at the screen.

"Our route."

"You got the route on that thing?" he asked. "That's wild." Dad's burner flip phone was a couple of years away from having its own exhibit at the Smithsonian. He watched me zoom in and out on the digital map from the corner of his eye, trying to hide his fascination.

We were starting from Florence, which if Italy is seen as a long boot, was high on the shin. The first day would take us to Siena, which was due south. From there, we'd pedal southeast into the heart of Tuscany for three days until we reached Rome, which was only 144 miles as the crow flies from Florence. Of course, we weren't flying—I planned to link together a complex string of back roads, thoroughfares, and highways that would effectively double that distance. Beyond Rome, I had no idea how we were going to find the village of San Donato, our ultimate destination.

"How's it looking?" he asked.

"We'll be biking forty-nine miles on the first day."

"Oh, that's a piece of cake," he said.

"Uphill. Forty-nine miles . . . *uphill*," I said. "There's 6,183 feet of climbing on the first day."

Rolling onto his side, he groaned sarcastically. A gentle breeze wafted in through the hostel's heavy curtains. Voices echoed up from the courtyard below. Dad's breathing got heavy and rhythmic. I stared up into the darkness. *What's Papa doing right now?* I wondered. *Hell, he's probably curled up in bed, worrying about us.*

"Can't believe we're here right now," Dad said, breaking the silence. "We always talked about it, talked about the village and all, but I never thought I'd actually be going."

"I know," I said, "it's pretty surreal. It's crazy that Papa never went on his own, back to the village."

"I know, I never got that," Dad said. "Maybe it had something to do with his father. Who knows."

"What was your grandfather like?" I asked.

Dad rolled back around and thought about it for a second. "He was really good to me," he said. "He always came to all my football games growing up. No matter what, I'd look to the stands, and there he'd be."

I'd heard that anecdote from him before, but I wanted to know what my great-grandfather was actually like as a man. He was so one dimensional in my mind. What was his personality?

"Well, he didn't have much of a sense of humor," my father explained.

This statement demanded follow-up. "What do you mean by that?"

"He was a serious guy. He went to church every single morning, then after mass he'd go up to the barroom in Brighton Center and have a shot and a beer and then he'd go to work." Dad described his grandfather as a functioning alcoholic, a deeply religious man whose greatest regret was he didn't enter the priesthood. "Pretty sure that haunted him," he said. "He'd come home drunk and basically preach about the Catholic Church."

"Really?" I asked.

"Yeah, he went to mass every single morning, then he'd go to work." Dad's grandfather worked just over the Charles River in Cambridge at a Ford dealership where he was a mechanic. I wondered why he was so religious. "I don't know," Dad said. He thought it might have something to do with him growing up in San Donato. "I mean, there's like four churches there. But, yeah, he and his brother were really religious."

When he was a little boy, my father basically lived with his grandparents in the Yard, the makeshift compound they erected when they first immigrated to the United States. "We all lived together there in Brighton, back then," he said. "Papa's parents, his uncle and his family, all the nephews." He described his grandfather as an unhappy man with a temper. "I mean, he never hit my grandmother or anything like that, but there would be these shouting matches where the police would show up."

"Did this happen often?"

"It didn't happen all the time," Dad said. "Maybe I'm blowing it out of proportion. But even if it happened just once, it had such an impact on me that it seemed like it happened more—but it may have not." He sighed. "He and Papa didn't have a good relationship at all."

"I know, why was that?" I asked. I had tried to talk about this directly with Papa, but he wouldn't really go into it with me. Dad explained that his grandfather was a jealous man.

"Jealous of Papa?"

"Yeah, well . . . " My father paused for what felt like a long time, weighing something in his mind. "There's . . . a . . . a number of things—I got this from, I actually don't remember who told me this, but it wasn't from him . . . Papa believed that his father thought he wasn't legitimate."

"What?" I asked, trying to piece together that statement, although the intent could not be more clear: my great-grandfather thought Papa wasn't his son. After a few moments, I asked my father if that was possible.

"No, it's baloney!" he said. "They looked so much alike." Despite that, for whatever reason, my great-grandfather never treated Papa like one of his own kids. Growing up, my dad told me, Papa didn't have his own bedroom. He had to sleep on the couch in the parlor, while his siblings had rooms. "They loved their father. Idolized him and thought he was like a god, but Papa basically had to fend for himself."

According to Dad, Papa couldn't wait to move his family out of the Yard. "When he finally bought a house, apparently my grandfather walked up to him on the front porch and said something like, 'I guess you think you're some kind of big shot, now, huh?'" Dad wasn't sure how much they saw of each other after that. "Papa never really forgave him. But nothing he can do about it now."

My father turned back onto his side, facing away from me. His breathing got heavy again. I squeezed my eyes shut, knowing that if I didn't fall asleep soon, I'd be up against the full wrath of his snoring. I tried to settle the pigeons of thought pecking at my mind about my grandfather's toxic relationship with his father. How heavy that must have been to carry all his life. How did he handle that void of love? How did it impact who he became as a father? Why could they never reconcile? And why had my family never talked about it? That troubled me most. Why hadn't my family addressed this trauma from Papa's past?

My father started snoring. *Ok, sleep. Just sleep,* my mind pleaded. *There will be plenty of time to ponder all these questions . . . about five hundred miles' worth.*

CHAPTER 6

I have realized that the past and future are real illusions, that they
exist in the present, which is what there is and all there is.

—Alan Watts

M y father met the heart of historic Florence like a child walking into
kindergarten for the first time. He was cautious but curious. We took
a right out of the hostel courtyard and joined the stream of people surging down the street. A neatly dressed man wearing a skinny tie pedaled a
rickety antique cruiser that clinked over the cobbles like a ring of keys. A
church bell tolled hollowly in the distance while an ambulance screamed
down a nearby side street. We glimpsed into gelato bars, cafes, and leather
shops that smelled like freshly oiled baseball mitts. Just ahead, through the
telescoping buildings, we could make out the hulking archway of the Piazza
della Repubblica.

"When was the last time you were in Europe?" I asked.

"Guess it must've been before you were born," he said. "So what's that,
thirty-one years ago? Mom and I went to Paris and London back in the
eighties for a couple weeks. I loved Paris."

"Why didn't you ever go back?"

"Once you came along . . . everything changed."

We entered the piazza, where the crowd swirled in a giant eddy. Panhan-
dlers pinballed from person to person, begging for money. Tourists trailed
closely behind their guides with cameras swinging from their necks. Artists

sketched caricatures under umbrellas while onlookers lingered behind their easels. A musician plucked at a guitar. At the center of it all was a carousel, spinning this pulsing scene into a mesmerizing frenzy that shook me out of my jet lag.

A decade earlier I traveled here during college. Back then, I was utterly green to backpacking and rarely strayed from the well-worn tourist trail. I clung desperately to my *Lonely Planet* guidebook. I once spent an entire day in a stiflingly hot bus in search of a fabled nude beach that I'd read about in *Lonely Planet*. When I arrived with visions of bare naked beauties dancing in my head, the closest thing I found to a nude beach was a homeless man crapping in the sand. Alas, I hadn't yet discovered that the most memorable moments while traveling are stumbled upon when you're not looking for them.

We continued across the piazza until the Duomo stopped Dad dead in his tracks. "Wow . . . what's *that*?"

The Duomo—formally known as the Cattedrale di Santa Maria del Fiore—was such an arresting sight, all at once massive and painstakingly ornate. We fell in line with the thousands of others, heads cocked back and mouths agape. We were all technically tourists, but my father and I didn't feel that way. We couldn't relate to the flocks of people trailing tour guides with flags in their hands from their respective countries. Nor did we see ourselves in the families bumbling around with selfie sticks, their backpacks worn across their chests and passports stapled to their bodies. We were on a mission here in Italy. We were here to find our roots, to honor my grandfather, and to understand how the history of this place fit into our family lore. Nevertheless, the Duomo forced us to forget about all that for a moment and simply marvel at its grandeur.

We passed by cafe tables with their bright umbrellas and around to the towering town hall of Palazzo Vecchio, and then up to the Loggia dei Lanzi with its graphic sculptures of beheadings, rapes, and clubbings. Dad studied the replica of Michelangelo's *David*. It was impossible not to think about the history of this city. It wafted off of every square inch of architecture and lurked around every corner. Though the Medicis, Michelangelo, and the Old Masters of the Renaissance came to mind, I also thought about the darker history that unfolded on these streets not so long ago.

Almost exactly eighty years earlier, Benito Mussolini courted Adolf Hitler in hopes of making him an ally. Il Duce, as Mussolini was known, saw his Italian countrymen as the chosen race and wanted to bring about the second coming of the Roman Empire. To do so, he thought he would need the backing of German might. So in May of 1938 he threw Hitler a parade, leading him into this piazza in a grand celebration. Before leaving the States, I had pulled up footage of this infamous spectacle online. In the black-and-white newsreels, tens of thousands of Italians lined this piazza, cheering wildly as Hitler waved from a convertible. Mussolini had spent months turning Florence into a Nazi tribute. Bridges, buildings, and historic landmarks were laboriously restored by teams of high-profile architects. Nazi banners were hoisted up every flagpole and hung from almost every building.

How unthinkable it was, swastikas hanging from these regal edifices. And yet the history that ultimately unfolded in these streets was infinitely more tragic than an embarrassing parade. All this was fresh in my mind, thanks to a book my father gave me before the trip.

A FEW MONTHS BEFORE our departure, my father rang me up with a request. "Can you order a poster for me?" he asked. "It's a cycling photo from the forties called 'The Bottle,' or something like that. You should be able to find it on your computer. I want it for my man cave."

Since my brother and I had moved out of our parents' house, my father had transformed the basement into a cycling shrine. Old helmets, tattered bike seats, warped wheels, and dented water bottle cages were mounted to the basement walls like modern art installations. The centerpiece was a dilapidated fixie that my father had pedaled so hard for so long that the teeth to the chain ring had been literally worn away by all the torque. "Wait till you see this picture," Dad said. "It's going to look dynamite down there."

When the poster arrived, I slipped it from its tube and unfurled it on my desk. Even without any context, the dated, black-and-white photograph instantly told a story. Two cyclists, faces twisted with fatigue, are in the throes of a grueling climb. The heat of the day radiates off their sweaty, bronze skin and soaked black hair. The scene looks so hot that the dirt on the road appears to be sizzling like spices on a skillet. Although the two men are competitors, they share a bottle of water, as if they are no longer battling each other but doing everything they can just to survive.

"Got that poster," I told Dad over the phone. "So who are these guys?"

"Oh, *man*, those are two of the greatest cyclists ever," Dad said, his voice on the edge of exasperation. "Definitely the greatest Italian cyclists. Fausto Coppi and Gino Bartali."

"Never heard of them," I said. "Course my knowledge of cyclists begins and ends with Lance."

"Oh, man, no. Forget Lance. This was the golden age of cycling. You gotta read about these guys."

A couple of weeks later, when I had a chance to meet up with my father to give him the poster, he handed me a tattered paperback in return. "This book will blow your mind," he said. "I've read it twice. This will get you pumped for our trip."

"*Road to Valor* by Aili and Andres McConnon," I said, reading the cover. "Alright, I'll check it out." I always took my father's book recommendations with a giant grain of salt. His most recent literary fascination was about a guy called "The Iceman" who trained himself to withstand arctic temperatures through intense meditation and breathing techniques. A few days after he took that book out of the library, my mother walked into the kitchen to catch him standing outside in his underwear in the dead of winter.

Road to Valor appeared more promising. I recognized the man on the cover from the poster: Gino Bartali. The other man in that photograph, I learned, was Angelo Fausto Coppi. The two cyclists first met when Bartali brought Coppi onto his cycling team for the 1940 Giro d'Italia, Italy's version of the Tour de France. But when Bartali hit a dog on the course and crashed, Coppi pedaled away with the other leaders and claimed victory. From that point on, a fierce rivalry was born between the cyclists that later split Italy into two groups of fans: the Coppiani versus the Bartaliani. For fifteen years the two cyclists traded podiums—a golden era for Italian cycling that my dad raved about.

As I got sucked into the McConnons' enthralling book, Bartali's life off the bike held my fascination most. He grew up four miles outside of Florence. His father was a laborer, working in the quarries or laying brick in the city. Bartali and his brother Giulio grew up racing friends around the streets of Florence on old clunkers. Not much of a student, young Gino got a job working as a bike mechanic in a shop in Florence after the sixth grade. All he ever wanted to do was become a racer, but his father forbade it. He thought competitive cycling was far too dangerous.

On casual rides with his bike shop's owner and his cronies, Bartali's raw talent, even as a young boy, was undeniable. The owner pleaded with Bartali's father that his son should compete; Bartali's father reluctantly agreed. By the time he was twenty-two, Gino was one of the most celebrated cyclists in all of Italy. He dominated the Giro d'Italia three times and nearly became the first cyclist to win the Giro and the Tour de France in the same year. A year after his first tour loss, Bartali returned to win in commanding fashion. With a prominent Roman nose, wavy black hair, and a square jaw that looked like it could take a punch, Bartali became the era's most famous face in all of cycling.

As his star was rising, his beloved younger brother Giulio entered the racing scene and was on track to become a champion in his own right. But while competing in a race outside of Florence in June of 1936, Giulio was hit by a car while speeding downhill in the pouring rain. He died a few days later in the hospital, with his older brother holding his hand. His father's worst fears had come true. Devastated by the loss of his brother, Gino turned to the Catholic Church for comfort. He banished himself to a cabin by the ocean and considered quitting cycling altogether. When he returned to the bike a few months later, Bartali wore his devotion to the Catholic Church on his sleeve, earning him the nickname Gino the Pious.

BY THE FALL OF 1936, Fascism's hold on Italy took a maniacal turn. Mussolini signed an alliance with Hitler, known as the Rome-Berlin Axis agreement, linking the two countries militarily and politically. This culminated in the Pact of Steel in 1939. Seizing on Italy's downtrodden workers, Mussolini had come to power in the 1920s with a populist, nationalistic message, becoming prime minister in 1922 and dismantling the country's democratic institutions. He declared himself dictator in 1925, taking the title "Il Duce" ("the Leader").

Mussolini wanted Italy to be ruled by an elite class that would seize more land. He touted Italians as being a superior race and wanted the world to see that superiority on full display. Obsessed with physicality and athleticism, he made Italian athletes prized pawns in his grand propaganda plan. In the 1932 Olympics in Los Angeles, Italy took home thirty-six medals—second only to the host country, the United States. Two years later, Italy's soccer team won the FIFA World Cup in the National Stadium of the National Fascist Party in Rome. Mussolini seized on every athletic achievement and exploited it for political gain. The propaganda press churned out story after story of Italian athletes dedicating their victories to Il Duce.

Beyond feeding his insatiable ego, Mussolini thought that if he could secure the public devotion of the athletes, the fans would be quick to follow. But he wasn't going to leave that to chance. Mussolini and his minions controlled the athletes, telling them which races they could participate in. Corruption was rampant. If the athletes didn't fall in line, they were reprimanded. Italy's cycling scene had the most compelling cautionary tale.

Before Gino Bartali, the biggest name in Italian cycling was Ottavio Bottecchia, the first Italian to win the Tour de France. Bottecchia was victorious in back-to-back years, 1925 and 1926. At the time of Bottecchia's first win, Mussolini had consolidated his power to become full-fledged dictator. Bottecchia wasn't a fan, however, and said as much during an interview with a French journalist. A year later he was dead.

Bottecchia's death remained shrouded in mystery for years. He was killed while on a training ride in northern Italy; his body was found with a cracked skull and a broken collarbone. His death was said to be the result of a crash, but no real investigation was conducted. Many people, including the priest who administered Bottecchia's last rites, concluded that the Fascists had assassinated him. Decades later—on their deathbeds in the United States—two Italian immigrants, one of them the farmer who had found Bottecchia, confessed to having killed him. Regardless of who actually committed the murder, Bottecchia's death cast a dark shadow over Italian athletes, reinforcing the fear that if you fell out of line with Mussolini and his regime, you could end up dead.

Mussolini wanted the great Gino Bartali. With the face of a bricklayer and the strength of an ox, Bartali embodied Italian might. His dominating wins in the Giro caught Il Duce's eye, and the dictator envisioned him riding into Paris in the Tour de France wearing the yellow jersey in honor of Fascist Italy. But Bartali personally rejected Fascism. His father, a socialist who resisted the rise of Fascism when Bartali was a boy, had also witnessed his employer murdered at the hands of the Fascists. This sowed a deep distrust of Fascism in his son. Gino's devotion to the Catholic Church trumped his political interest. Despite the ominous cloud of Bottecchia's death, Bartali refused to wave the Fascist banner as other athletes did so readily.

Still, Il Duce wielded his control over the Italian cyclist. After failing to become the first to win the Giro d'Italia and Tour de France in the same year, Bartali had his heart set on accomplishing the feat the following season. But Mussolini, intent on putting Italy prominently on the world stage, demanded that Bartali forgo the Giro in 1938 to focus entirely on the Tour. The champion cyclist protested adamantly but ultimately conceded to this demand. After winning the Tour de France, Bartali did not even mention Mussolini in his remarks during a radio interview, let alone dedicate the win to the Fascist regime. When Bartali arrived back home in Italy, there was no parade, no grand spectacle marking his victory. In fact, there wasn't anyone at all waiting for him at the train station. If you turned your back on the regime, the people felt compelled to turn their back on you.

Two months before Bartali's win in the Tour de France, Mussolini welcomed Hitler to Italy. Il Duce did everything but kiss the Führer's boots in his effort to gain an ally in executing his own version of the Nazi's *lebensraum*, or space for the master race. After parading Hitler through Florence, Mussolini capped the day off at the Piazzale Michelangelo overlooking the Arno River and the city. "From now on, no force on earth will be able to separate us," he was said to have gushed to Hitler. But beyond throwing the Nazi parade, hanging swastikas from Rome to Florence, and even naming a street in the capital city in honor of the Führer, Mussolini poisoned Italy with anti-Semitism. Six months after Hitler's visit, he published *Manifesto della Razza* (Manifesto of Race), which appeared in major Italian newspapers. The manifesto declared Italians as Aryan descendants and stripped Italian Jews of their rights, laying the groundwork for what was to come.

Jews had lived in Italy for more than two thousand years and were fully integrated in the patchwork of Italian society. Numbering around fifty thousand in the 1930s, many Italian Jews were fiercely patriotic even after Mussolini embraced anti-Semitism as a tenet of Fascism. In November of 1938, Mussolini made anti-Semitism the law of the land through Leggi Razziali, racial laws that targeted Italian Jews. Jews were thereafter forbidden to marry gentiles. They were kicked out of schools, government jobs, and military service. Foreign Jews were arrested and sent to internment camps in the mountains. In the lead up to World War II, thousands of Jews fled Italy for the United States. Those who stayed behind lived in terror. Many hid in the shadows in Florence, Rome, and other major Italian cities. When the Nazis occupied the country beginning in September of 1943, the Gestapo arrested and deported ten thousand Jews to concentration and extermination camps in central and Eastern Europe. Thousands were murdered at Auschwitz.

THE STORY OF GINO Bartali offered a window into this grim period in Italy that I hadn't fully understood. Reading about this history in the McConnons' book left me feeling conflicted and, at times, ashamed. *Was it possible to have pride in my Italian heritage when Italy was so complicit during the most vile chapter of the twentieth century?* Inevitably the past distills into heroes and villains, and, apart from the cycling lure around Bartali, I had not identified any Italian wartime heroes. The country had literally rolled out the red carpet for the worst villain of them all.

As I delved deeper into Italy's role in World War II, my curiosity about my family's immigration story increased. Although my great-grandfather had left Italy by the time Mussolini welcomed Hitler to Florence, I had so many nagging questions about my heritage. As my father and I prepared to embark on this tour into the heart of the countryside, I wanted to better understand this history and reconcile it with my own identity as an Italian American.

CHAPTER 7

Everyone in their life has his own particular way of expressing life's purpose—the lawyer his eloquence, the painter his palette, and the man of letters his pen from which the quick words of his story flow. I have my bicycle.

—Gino Bartali

When I was growing up, a bicycle represented absolute freedom to me. From as early as I can remember, my buddies and I cruised around our neighborhood like a rowdy pack of stray dogs. We pedaled up into the woods by the old water tower, where we could find empty beer bottles to chuck against the rocks. Or sometimes, if we were really lucky, we'd come across an old waterlogged nudie magazine. My oh my, what joys these two wheels could bring a curious kid!

We were totally reckless. Helmets were for "losahs." We screamed down steep hills in my neighborhood, egging each other on not to touch our brakes, as we raced toward busy intersections to beat a red light. One time, my buddy Dooley blasted right through oncoming traffic while chasing me and my best friend, Wally. In my memory two cars spun out like in the movies as Dooley miraculously threaded the needle. We didn't even stop. We kept on pedaling, laughing hysterically and buzzing with that same intoxicating adrenaline we got from pelting a police car with a snowball.

We obsessed about our bikes, squirreling away money from raking leaves and shoveling snow to buy shocks, disk brakes, mag-rim wheels, clipless pedals, and (if we were really going for broke) a full-suspension frame.

When it came to bikes, the major difference between me and my friends was that when I went home, the obsession didn't end—my father stoked it. Dad gave me my first fixed-gear bicycle after I graduated college. Gleaming black and yellow, the aluminum-framed Schwinn was a thing of beauty. Dad had his mechanic switch out its traditional drop handlebars to a pair of bullhorns wrapped in camo tape. He had the back brake stripped off, so the rear wheel slid through the frame freely.

"But you have to keep the front brake," he told me.

"Why? You don't have a front brake."

"Your mother would kill me," he said. "Plus, you got more to protect up there." He tapped his head.

"Fine, but I'm not going to use it."

He smirked. "We'll see about that."

Dad took me on fixie rides through the city. We'd rip up tight alleys, jockey through traffic, and chase down every cyclist we saw. From the first pedal stroke, I fell madly in love with the raw torque of a fixed gear. The bike came alive, forcing my feet to spin faster and faster. If I tried to coast, the pedals launched my knees violently into my chest. The all-or-nothingness of the fixed gear drew me into its devoted tribe.

Drafting off my Dad's back wheel, I marveled at how easy he made pedaling a fixie look. Every one of his pedal strokes had a purpose. Like a boxer throwing jabs, hooks, and uppercuts, he pedaled combinations of force to move methodically. He read the traffic, calling out cars that were about to stop or turn into our lanes before their signals blinked. His hands pointed out potholes, sand, glass, and other tire-popping perils. I had always assumed he was reckless on his bike, but here I witnessed just how much control he had.

I came to appreciate the invigorating allure of bicycling through city traffic, which delivered the same adrenaline rush I imagine people get running with the bulls. Your focus needed to be cranked to the max as you anticipated drivers' erratic behavior, swerving around fenders, blocking out car horns, and darting past pedestrians. When shooting through the tight gap between a city bus and a dump truck to catch a traffic light that was flicking yellow to red, it was hard not to feel like something of a superhero.

All your senses, your instincts, your brute physicality were firing off in unison for the sole purpose of keeping you alive—and *Holy shit, did you feel alive!* Of course, just as with running with the bulls, even if you did everything perfectly, you could still get gored. My father had tangled with those chrome horns of city traffic more times than he'd like to admit.

AFTER SUCKING DOWN ENOUGH free coffee to stop the heart of a baby rhino, Dad and I pocketed a handful of pastries, packed up our tiny backpacks, and checked out of the hostel after two days. Wearing our cycling kits beneath our street clothes, we set out to find the bike shop. After much debate, we'd decided the best option was to simply rent bikes in Florence, as opposed to shipping our own overseas. A cycling guide had suggested we rent from Florence by Bike, a hole-in-the-wall shop on the outskirts of the historic city. From what I could see on their website, their road bikes appeared high-end and not the cumbersome cruisers I feared would be our only option.

Entering the shop, I had one main concern. "Whatever you do," I said under my breath, "don't tell them where we're going."

"Why not?"

"Honestly I didn't read the rental agreement," I said. "I have no idea if we can even take these bikes out of the city."

"Oh, I'm sure it's fine."

"Yeah, but mum's the word." This was one of my errant tendencies. If something fell outside the plan I had in mind, or didn't fit the story I was telling myself, I simply denied its very existence. Rather than quickly checking to see whether we could take the rental bikes outside of the city, I preferred to avoid the possibility of bad news. As it was throughout my life, when I feared the truth, I instinctively opted for ignorance. It was a trait I inherited from my father.

One of the mechanics peered at us suspiciously from his closet-sized workshop where he tinkered with the gears on a road bike. He wore surgical gloves so as not to get grease on his fingers as he worked the gears. As Dad and I waited for one of the other mechanics to set us up with our rental bikes, we pretended to peruse the various jerseys for sale. The mechanic stared.

I often forget what a curious sight my father and I make together. I looked like a replica of him, if you subtracted thirty years and added sixty pounds, seven inches of height, and a few more layers of hair. Our shaggy blond mops fall to our shoulders in a surfer-dude style that I fear make us impossible to take seriously. The hair was definitely what got people. After high school, I decided to grow my hair out a bit while studying abroad in Europe. Dad loved the idea. He'd been rocking a golden mane since the 1970s and was more than encouraging to see me break out of my "boy's regular" routine. When I returned to the States and went into his shop for a haircut, he refused to give me anything more than a trim. "It looks dynamite," he'd say. "Why do you want to look like everyone else?" I'd concede, with my hair looking longer than when I arrived. A decade later, I was still negotiating with him to cut it back whenever I landed in his chair, but he always succeeded in talking me out of it.

The hair made us look more Scandinavian or Australian than American. We certainly didn't look Italian. "Yeah, my family is from Southeast Italy," I'd often explain. "Which I guess has a lot of blond people." Of course, that was a bunch of bull. Up until booking our plane tickets to Florence, I had absolutely no idea where exactly my great-grandfather was from, let alone what its residents' physical characteristics were. That's why we were here.

"Alo," a man called out, waving us to the back.

"Yo . . . Dad," I said, nodding.

We followed the mechanic through a beaded door and into the back of the shop where rows of bikes hung like slabs of beef in a meat locker. He eyed us from the waist down, mentally sizing us to a bike, then disappeared into the sea of wheels and frames. The man emerged a minute later with two shining red beauties.

"Provalo," he said, motioning for me to get on.

I threw my leg over the bike. The mechanic took hold of the front wheel and gestured for me to sit and clip into the pedals. All the components gleamed like polished pearls. The wires to the brakes and gear shifters on the handlebars slipped into portals along the glossy red frame and out of sight. The handlebar tape was plush as an old leather pocketbook. The man gestured for me to pedal backward. The chain purred as it passed silkily over the big ring, through the derailleur, and into the small cassette. It was beautiful. "Can't believe they rent these bikes out," I said to Dad.

He nodded approvingly, watching the mechanic fine-tune the components and fit the frame to me like a classic Italian tailor. My father was a sucker for a good bike mechanic. Back home he'd probably put his local bike mechanic's kid through college with all the business he'd given him over the years. He dreamed of someday having a shop of his own. "With coffee," he'd add.

With my rental dialed in, the mechanic motioned for my father to step onto his bike. The two bicycles looked nearly identical, except for one minor detail that my father was quick to point out. "This thing has a granny gear," he said.

"A what?" I said. The bike mechanic looked up quizzically.

"A granny gear . . . look at the front cassette. That small gear ring—that's for old ladies."

I laughed, but he was serious. "Who cares," I shrugged. "Just don't use it, if you don't want." But I knew it wasn't that easy. For a pure-bred fixie-rider like my father, a granny gear was the equivalent of strapping on a pair of training wheels. We might as well add a pair of streamers to the handlebars and a baseball card in between the spokes while we were at it. For a guy who wanted his tombstone's epitaph to read "Lived Life in the Big Ring," looking down to a granny gear between his legs was akin to being neutered.

"Yeah, that's exactly what I'm going to do," Dad said defiantly. "I'm not using it."

The average person might not see the logic in my father's thinking. Why not just use the small gear and make the ride easier? After all, this wasn't a competition. No one was watching us or keeping our times. Pedaling nearly a hundred miles a day was a feat no matter what gear you were in. This ride was entirely about survival.

But when it came to physical tests, my father never wanted to have an unfair advantage. If anything, he looked for ways to make them more challenging. A few years ago, he had his bike mechanic increase the size of the big gear on his fixie. This made climbing hills, coming to a stop, and even just getting started significantly more difficult. The bigger ring made pedaling the equivalent of climbing up fifty flights of stairs, bounding two at a time, while wearing eight-pound ankle weights. For the first two months with the bigger gear, Dad was forced to walk his bike up the hill leading to his house. He'd get about a quarter of the way up, grinding down on the pedals with every bit of strength in his sixty-plus-year-old legs, until he just couldn't turn them anymore. But still he refused to downsize the gear. Instead, the big ring forced him to get stronger, until he could grit his way all the way to the top.

We wheeled the bikes up to the front desk to check out. "Do you need a map?" the woman at the desk asked.

"No, I think we're just—"

"Yeah, let's take a map," Dad said.

We're about to pedal halfway down the boot of Italy, I thought. *What good was a map of Florence going to do us?* I plucked one from the desk and handed it back to him.

"If something happens to the bikes," the shop clerk continued, "you must contact us immediately." I nodded emphatically. "Immediately," she repeated, staring at me over her glasses.

"I got it," I said.

WE SLIPPED OFF OUR street clothes in the bathroom and stuffed them into our backpacks. I attached the twenty-pound saddle bag to the seat post, cinched on my backpack, and wheeled outside. Dad rolled out behind me and did a long, lazy circle down the street. I always appreciated how perfectly he fit on a bike. At 5'6", 140 pounds, his svelte body draped effortlessly on the frame. He had that light, compact physique of legendary climbers such as Alberto Contador and Marco Pantani. He rode with his hands almost exclusively in the lower part of the handlebars—what were known as "the drops"—like a throwback to the classic days when cyclists carried spare tires across their chests.

Meanwhile, I was an awkward sight on a bike. My stubby legs and long torso made me look clumsy and unathletic, which at this moment I was. I threw my leg over the frame and caught a reflection of myself in the window of a parked car. Several extra pounds of winter weight hung from my gut, making me look like an overstuffed tube of toothpaste in my cycling kit.

"Alright, Dad, let's get out of eyeshot of the bike shop and get our bearings."

"Sounds good," he said cheerfully. He was happy to be back on a bike. The familiarity of gliding on two wheels again brought his foreign surroundings into terms he could handle.

We rolled down the narrow street until it culminated in a roundabout. I checked oncoming traffic and pedaled across to the center of the circle. The chaos of morning traffic was ramping up. Cars, motor bikes, and trucks swarmed around us in a cloud of fumes. Now was the moment of truth: time to lead. I pulled out my iPhone and connected it to my handlebars using a plastic mount I'd bought back in the States. Activating the Strava navigation app, I punched in the route for Siena, our first stop on this five-hundred-mile adventure.

The Strava route from Florence to Rome was given to me by Andy Levine, the founder of Duvine Cycling and Adventure Company. Based in Boston, Andy's guide service led high-end cycling tours in Africa, Asia, Europe, and South America. When I told him that I was looking for a Florence-to-Rome route, Andy tried to talk me out of it. "That's a hell of a lot of climbing," he said. "Sure you guys are up for that? I mean, how old is your dad?" After I waved off offers for routes through Sicily and Capri, Andy kindly connected me with his lead guide in Tuscany, who shared a four-day route for Dad and me to follow on my phone.

Part of me hated the fact that I was relying on my cell phone to navigate from place to place. It felt like cheating. We should have been unfurling a map on the cobblestones and stitching a route together with compass in hand. I desperately wanted to use this trip as an excuse to rip myself from my addiction to the glowing screen, but I feared that with all the potential pitfalls of this journey, relying on my nonexistent map skills was foolhardy. If left to my own sense of direction, we'd undoubtedly end up wildly off-trail. Back home, I'd become completely reliant on GPS to get just about anywhere. Even when driving to places I knew by heart, I developed a pathetic habit of punching the address into my map app to see if there was a quicker way. I'd cling to those automated directions like they were the instructions in a ransom note.

During a road trip through Colorado, for instance, my GPS rerouted me from what was supposed to be an eighty-five-mile route to a five-mile route. I should have realized something was amiss when the GPS indicated that covering those five miles would take two and a half hours. Only after fording two rivers and sputtering halfway up a steep logging road did I realize the GPS had routed me directly over the Rocky Mountains. I made a twenty-seven-point turn on a narrow cliff band and backtracked—all the while my phone screaming: "Rerouting! Rerouting!"

I had no clue how the Strava app was supposed to work. I foolishly hadn't taken the time to try it out before this trip and was hoping it would magically start calling out directions *Knight Rider*-style as we pedaled. "Alright, ready?" I asked Dad, zooming into the route.

"You know where we're going?"

"Think so. Just follow me." I sensed that he was itching to break out that map he'd pocketed at the bike shop to get his bearings. He'd never relied on GPS to get anywhere. Like ATMs and smartphones, GPS was a futuristic quagmire he refused to wade into.

"So that thing is going to get us to Sienna?" he asked.

"Should," I said.

He fastened the strap of his helmet and clipped into his right pedal. In addition to his suspicion of technology, Dad was completely unaccustomed to following anyone else's lead. There was a reason why he never joined a big cycling group back home. As in life, my father beat his own path on a bike. He wanted full control over where he went, but now I took that away from him.

"Lead the way, Magellan," he said.

I clipped my right foot into the pedal, made one big stroke, and rolled onto the shoulder of traffic. Vespas swarmed around us like angry hornets. I stared down at my phone, waiting to see what the Strava app would do. No directions were being called out. I pressed the volume on my phone, but it didn't make a peep. Instead, there was just a blinking dot—*me!*—and a glowing blue line laid over the map to follow. I clipped in my left foot and pedaled gingerly, watching how the blue dot ate the glowing line like Pac-Man. *Keep the dot on the line is the name of the game.*

"I think I got it," I said, peeking back over my shoulder.

"Keep your eyes on the road," Dad yelled.

We pedaled a few blocks until we reached the Arno River, then hung a left along the four-lane Lungarno della Zecca Vecchia. *As long as I keep the blinking blue dot over the glowing white line, we should be fine*, I reasoned in my head. Crossing the Ponte San Niccolò, we picked our way through a congested intersection and began climbing the Viale Michelangiolo. The residential boulevard was draped in trees. Sunlight scattered along the pavement as leaves rustled overhead. My eyes continually darted from the route, to the road, to Dad, and back again. With so many moving parts, I struggled to breathe with any cadence. The hill steepened and began to wind up big, long circles. I clicked into an easier gear. They switched one to the next with snappy, mechanical precision. Sweat beaded under my helmet, sticking my hair to my forehead. I reached desperately for my water bottle.

Up and up we climbed until the boulevard culminated in the Piazzale Michelangelo, a sprawling parking lot of sorts that offered a sweeping view of the city below. I knew it would irk my father to pull over, since we'd only just started riding, but we needed to take in this view of Florence. I led us past T-shirt stands and plein air painters, by yet another replica of Michelangelo's *David*, bronze this time, and out to the railing overlooking the Arno, which meandered between the red stucco rooftops, church spires, and domes.

"Dad, you remember this from the book?" I asked.

"Which book?"

"The Gino Bartali book," I said. "This is where he would ride with his friends when they were kids." According to *Road to Valor*, Bartali would blow by them up the hill we had just ascended. He'd stop here to catch his breath and wait for his friends.

"Oh, that's right."

"Pretty cool, huh?" I said, grabbing my water bottle again. It was enchanting to think that this was the same view Gino Bartali gazed upon all those years ago.

"Yep." My father still had one foot clipped into the pedal. He lifted the front end of his bike and spun his wheel, then ran his hand over the tire to remove any gravel or shards of glass. With all the stopping and starting, Dad just wanted to get on with it. He didn't share in my enthusiasm for this site of living history. I placed my water bottle back into its cage. "Alright, let's do it."

We passed around the vendors, through the tourists, and by the parked tour busses, then returned to the main street. I checked for cars, turned right out of the Piazzale Michelangelo, and began pedaling slightly uphill. I clicked into an easier gear. The air felt cool and refreshing whipping across my face as I gathered speed, the wheels purring as they spun along the smooth pavement beneath my legs. This was definitely the nicest bike I'd ever ridden. Every component, from the brakes to the gears, was tuned like a concert piano. Rustling trees canopied the road, creating a tunnel of green punctuated by ancient stone buildings that blurred in my periphery. *We were off!*

I turned my head back to find my father zipping right behind me. "Pretty awesome, huh?"

"Keep your eyes on the road," he yelled.

"Yeah, yeah. I got it."

I gazed gleefully down the road. *This is unreal,* I thought. *Here we are. Cycling in Italy. Just Dad and me. Surrounded by history. Tracking our roots. Two guys off the grid. On a mission to find our village. Papa's village! Here we are. Here. We. Are.*

Where are we exactly? I looked down to the GPS, where—*shit!*—the glowing white line had disappeared. *Where was the line?* The blue dot tumbled into digital oblivion. I thumbed the map, zooming out to get my bearings. *CRACK!* My front wheel hit a pothole.

"Holy hell," I called out, throwing my free hand back to the handlebar to save myself from crashing.

"What's up?" Dad said, catching up.

"I think we're . . . " I eased on the brake. "I think we're off track."

"Already? This looks right to me," he said. "I'm sure it leads out to where we're supposed to go."

"Yeah, hold on." I zoomed out, trying to locate the glowing line that was our course. *How pathetic was this?* I thought. Standing on the side of the road, only a few miles from where we started, already off track. How far we'd strayed from navigating by the stars. "Found it," I said. "Yeah, we missed a turn just back there."

"You sure?"

"That's what it says."

Dad looked back up from where we'd just come and down the hill again. The steep pavement was begging to be coasted down. "Really?"

"Yeah, unfortunately."

He repositioned his bike, picking up the frame next to his seat. "Well, if that's what it says."

"Yeah, that's what it says. Just up there." I checked for traffic, made one pedal stroke across the street, and turned back uphill. I struggled to get my other cleat back in the pedal. *C'mon. C'mon, you bastard. Get in there. There, it's in.* I pushed down on the pedal, but the cleat popped out, sending my groin directly into the cross bar. Pain shot up into my stomach. I sucked down two deep breaths as cramps seized my gut. *This is going to be a long day.*

We grinded a quarter mile back uphill until the blinking dot was reunited with the glowing blue line on my phone, to my deep satisfaction. "Here we go, Dad. This is it—Torre del Gallo." We turned up what looked to be a one-way side road. A wall of meticulous stone slate was to our left, while the right side was dense trees swaying in the light breeze. I clicked into an easier gear. After a mile or so, the narrow street gave way to the countryside. Red stucco villas emerged on the rolling horizon, their distance marked by lines of cypress trees. Billowing white clouds gave scale to the cornflower blue sky. The scene looked peeled off the side of a jar of tomato sauce. Dad drew close behind me.

If Papa could only see us now, I thought. *Dad and I plotting our course through the back roads of Florence.* When my grandfather visited here, he was stuck in the confines of a tour bus, at the mercy of a guide and his fellow passengers. He would have loved the freedom Dad and I now felt as we glided down streets too narrow for a bus. How different our realities were in this moment. I pictured Papa at home stuck in his chair, watching golf, wishing he had the strength to clear the snow off the front porch. Meanwhile, Dad and I felt strong, moving fast through a foreign world.

The thought filled me with guilt. *Should we even be doing this? Shouldn't we be back home with him? Keeping him company and filling whatever time we had left together with meaningful memories?* Yet here we were on some vacation dressed up as a mission to find meaning in our family history. *Wasn't that meaning found at home with him?* I looked out upon the dreamy landscape, where there wasn't an answer to be found. I looked back down at my GPS, where . . . we were lost again.

CHAPTER 8

The world is a book and those who do not travel read only one page.

—Saint Augustine

"There. Route 22 takes us right into Siena," Dad said, running his sweaty finger down the map that he pocketed thirty-five miles earlier at the bike shop. "It's a straight shot." Somewhere during the last climb, I'd taken us off course—again. In my growing fatigue, I had stopped looking at the route on my phone again and now we were lost again. But by God, I wasn't about to admit that to my father *again*.

"I see that," I said, "but let me just . . . " I frantically thumbed the map on my phone trying to find the glowing line again. "Let me just see if I can . . . figure out . . . where exactly . . . the . . . "

Dad laid his bike down and took a seat on the curb. We were on the side of a country road on the outskirts of a no-name village forty miles outside of Florence. Both our water bottles were just about dry. Heat radiated off the pavement. My pulse surged in my skull in thick, anxious waves. We'd just slogged up a thirty-five-minute climb—the fourth big hill of the day. *Please tell me we don't have to backtrack*, I prayed, scanning the map. *Please, please tell me we don't need to backtrack. Anything but that. Where in the hell is that goddamn glowing line?*

"Look," Dad repeated. "Route 22. Straight into Siena."

"Yeah, I see *that*, Dad, but Route 22 could be a highway. Did you come all the way here to ride on a highway for thirty miles?"

"I want to get where we're going," he shot back. We were beaten down. Our jerseys were soaked in sweat. The backs of my legs had been scorched red by the sun. A festering stew of frustration boiled in my brain.

"Dad, obviously I do too. But my route has us going 408 and connecting with 22 right before Siena."

He scanned his map. "That's going to add . . . like . . . another twenty miles to the day," he said. "What are you taking us on . . . the scenic route?"

"That's exactly what I'm doing," I muttered. *Wasn't that the whole point of this?* I thought. *To take the scenic route? To seek out the places that we couldn't find on a postcard? To understand where our ancestors came from, where Papa came from, where we came from? To see it all from a bike seat. Wasn't that the whole point?* Dad was clinging to his commuting mentality. He wanted to get from A to B in the fastest way possible. But this trip wasn't about the final destination. It was about seeing as much as we possibly could before we got there. *Didn't he get that, goddamnit?*

I wanted nothing more than to get off this godforsaken bike. Andy Levine was right: the climbing was brutal. These hills weren't like the hills back home. They went on and on, switchbacking tightly around jackknife turns. Over the course of the day, I peeked over my shoulder a few times to find my father's face contorted in excruciating pain. *He's not drinking enough water*, I thought, *and I haven't seen him eat a bite of food.* Here he was: sixty-four years old, four stents in his heart, screw in his ankle—not to mention countless screws loose elsewhere. Any one of these ascents could kill him—*literally* kill him. I pictured his old heart like a leathered coin purse stuffed with pennies until it burst at the seams. *How would I get his body back to the States?* I thought morbidly as we climbed. *How much does an urn cost in Italy, anyway? Would they take a credit card?*

And I was right there with him—teetering on what felt like the brink of death. This sucked. Maybe it was the jet lag—*please be the jet lag*—but we weren't prepared for this ride at all. Not. At. All. I sure as shit wasn't. This wasn't even fun. My head was on a constant swivel from my phone, to the road, to my father, and back again. Over and over. Apart from a few sights at Piazzale Michelangelo earlier in the day, I couldn't recall seeing anything but the pavement beneath my legs. Frustration growing, the steady drumbeat beat of anxiety was mounting. Dad took the last drag out of his water bottle and jammed it back into its cage.

He's about to freak out, I thought. *I just know it.* On day one of the ride, not even halfway through it, we were going to have our first blowout. I waited, counting the seconds for Dad to snap. *Come on blue line, where the hell are you?*

I INSTINCTIVELY FEARED MY father's hair-trigger temper. The fear stemmed back to my childhood. The slightest misstep or transgression would ignite a disproportionate amount of fury. His outbursts were completely illogical and outrageous, marked by screaming, swearing, and occasionally hysterical crying. We all walked on eggshells whenever he was around. Outside of the privacy of our home, his anger made him something of a liability. Even at an indoor climbing gym.

Dad introduced me to rock climbing as a young kid, and before I entered high school, we went to the indoor climbing gym together a few days a week. Most of the time, I cherished being climbing partners and spending that much father-son time together. But being on the other end of his rope wasn't always fun. After falling on a climb, he'd unleash his frustration at the wall while I held him suspended in the air. Everyone in the gym would stop and stare at this 140-pound Tasmanian devil kicking, spitting, and screaming at a slab of plywood.

The sad irony was that the source of my father's most suffocating tantrums stemmed from how much he loved us. He worried about our family constantly, but not in a cute, doting way. His worry brewed unhealthy, irrational fears that viscerally consumed his thoughts. If my mother was late after grocery shopping, he assumed that she had been in a car wreck and was bleeding out in the street. He'd pace the house in a growing storm of despair. When she walked in the door, his anguish gave way to screaming.

So it was for my brother, Mark, and me. We were given strict curfews. Even when I was a senior in high school, Dad expected me home at 9 p.m. on the dot. If I came home fifteen minutes late, he was at the door waiting. Thirty minutes late, he was standing in the front yard. If I was an hour late, he came out looking for me. One summer night, I was hanging out with friends down the street. I didn't think anything of being past my curfew because my house was well within eyeshot. Suddenly my father screeched up in his beat-up junker, broke into the crowd, and screamed at me in front of my friends. I ran home, absolutely mortified.

Years later my brother pointed out just how absurd it was that Dad should get so riled up over our safety. After all, we weren't the ones routinely getting hit by cars like he was. We weren't limping in with our skin torn to ribbons. We weren't calling him for a ride from the hospital after getting a CT scan because we landed on our heads in traffic. And yet to question any of his choices would only provoke his anger.

Long stretches of my childhood were painted with a brush of anxiety. I remember my mother huddling around my brother and me after one of my father's particularly nerve-wracking fits. Whether he was wrong or right, my mother always played the role of peacekeeper. "Remember, you've inherited this temper—it's *in* you," she'd tell me over and over. "Don't let it control you. You can choose not to be angry like him."

This idea of inheriting my father's temper existed in my mind like a benign tumor. I thought I had to keep it in check, keep monitoring it, or else it might fester and rot and turn malignant. I didn't want rage to consume me. I didn't want to live with that lack of control or wield that level of anxiety over others. But I overcompensated and suppressed my anger until it exploded from me uncontrollably. My fits of rage, although exceedingly rare, were blinding, escalating to a point where I'd bark guttural expletives that made me feel ashamed of myself once I calmed down. In those quiet moments of reflection, I saw that despite my best efforts, my father's anger had found its way into me. I had more work to do. I eventually started seeing a therapist who helped me manage my emotions and weather recurring bouts of depression. I didn't attribute my depression to my father's temper—I didn't know what the cause was—but I wondered whether I'd inherited it, on a biological level, from him.

Going off to college was a turning point. When I returned home for winter break my freshman year, I observed with fresh eyes just how bizarre my father's behavior was. I couldn't understand why he was so pissed off all the time. On one occasion, he was in a huff because the vacuum cleaner had a sock stuck in its tube. I couldn't take it anymore. "Jesus Christ, would you give it a rest already?" I said.

He shot me a look, slightly taken aback. "Forget it, I'm out of here," he snapped before shoving the vacuum cleaner to the floor. "I'm done with this. I don't fucking need this." He slammed the closet door and stormed out of the kitchen. I couldn't remember a time before that when I stood up to him. Right then and there I decided to not let him get away with terrorizing us anymore.

Life went on while I was away for college. Dad took it upon himself to work on his anger management. He gave up swearing, started meditating, and made a concerted effort to control himself. Days went by without a blowout and then weeks. Like a giant freighter changes course through a million undetectable pivots, Dad slowly emerged as a completely different person than the man I'd known when I was younger. By the time I graduated, he'd become Zen-like and contemplative. His idiosyncrasies—the tattoos, sleeping on the floor, getting hit by cars—didn't ratchet down at all, but his rage was mostly in check. He was no longer a slave to it.

The change dramatically improved the climate in our household. When new people entered my life, like my girlfriend, Jenny, they couldn't believe the stories I had told them about my father. How could this super mellow guy be capable of rip-roaring rage? The two versions of him were completely incompatible. Yet for me and Mark, the memories of those early years were never too far from our minds.

EVEN NOW, AT THE age of thirty-one, a grown man in my own right, sitting on a curb, lost in the Italian countryside, I still feared my father's wrath. Sensing his frustration transported me back to my childhood. I no longer felt like a strong, independent adult. I became an anxious adolescent doing everything I could not to make my dad mad. *He's about to explode*, I thought, trying to hide behind my phone. *Any second now . . . I just know it.*

"Alright, well, we should get going, don't you think?" Dad said finally. He stood up from the curb and calmly folded up the map and slipped it into the back pocket of his jersey. "It's going to get dark soon."

I looked up from my phone, genuinely surprised. He wasn't going to freak. He had walked himself back and made a choice to be calm. My pulsing anxiety settled.

"How beautiful is this?" he said, taking in the quaint village. "Absolutely incredible. So where to?"

I gathered myself, calming my nerves. "Yeah, so I think if we just cruise back down this hill, we'll reconnect with the route. It shouldn't add too much to the day."

"Cool, sounds great," he said. "Lead the way." He threw his leg over his bike and flashed me a smile that completely cleared the air. He was loosening the grip on control he'd tried to maintain over my entire life. He was letting go. Embracing the adventure. And putting his entire faith in me—no matter how lost we got along the way.

CHAPTER 9

The human body has limitations. The human spirit is limitless.

—Dean Karnazes

Nobody could suffer quite like my father. He took perverse pride in his capacity to find his physical limits and live there for hours on end. "It's like fasting," he once told me. "There's the physical challenge, but it's really a mental challenge. The body would love to just sit and do nothing, but the mind keeps you going." Every summer, he set out on a 130-mile ride by himself in ungodly hot temperatures. Last year, he slogged through the whole ride in horizontal rain. As if to raise the bar, he'd endured the ten-hour gauntlet subsisting only on a couple of bananas and two bottles of water.

Dad was notoriously bad at bike nutrition. No matter the distance, he rarely ate on a ride. Maybe he was afraid of upsetting his stomach, but he would burn through thousands of calories without ever replenishing them. Same went for water. He seemed to drink only when his mouth went dry. There was never a strategy to fueling his body to perform and endure. Instead, he was a master of suffering. He seemed to possess a mutant physiology that could burn through more calories than he consumed, all while powering him forward mile after mile. At the end of each long ride, he'd drag himself into the house as dehydrated and emaciated as a tumbleweed—but euphorically happy. Of all the physical tests I'd witnessed my father submit himself to over the years, I'd never seen him crack—until this moment.

"Yo! Hold up! Hold up!" he yelled to me.

I whipped my head back to find him on the side of the road. He was limping around a ditch of tall grass, leaning his bike up against a stone wall. I looped back around and rolled downhill toward him. "What's up?" I asked. "Your stomach?"

"No . . . stomach is fine," he said, catching his breath. "I've never been so hungry in my life."

According to my GPS, we were forty-three miles and some five thousand vertical feet into our first day of the ride. After getting us lost for an hour or so, I had put us back on track, but the route had been grueling. The hills ascended for miles—two, four, sometimes more than five miles seemingly *straight up*. Pain pulsed from the pads of my feet to the palms of my hands and everywhere in between. As much as they were a physical test, the climbs were mentally exhausting. It took every shred of will that I had not to unclip and get off the bike. We still had another six miles until we reached Siena, where we'd be spending the night. My father knew that we only had six miles left, and yet he chose to stop and get off his bike. This worried me.

"I'm starving," he gasped, reaching into his jersey's back pocket and pulling out an energy gel.

"This is our last hill," I said. "Then it's all flats to Siena."

He nodded and desperately tore open the packet with his teeth and squeezed the paste into his mouth. He chewed through his exhaustion with his eyes closed. His face was ghostly white and he looked afraid. He didn't have the energy to talk. He was broken. I'd never witnessed him so defeated. Even when he was laid up in that hospital bed waiting to get his shattered ankle drilled back together, he possessed an air of indestructibility. He raised a perpetual middle finger to anyone who claimed he was too old to be testing his body day in and day out. But now he looked like a meek old man who was second-guessing himself for the first time.

"Have you been drinking water?" I asked.

He glanced down to his water bottles. One of them was half full. The other was bone dry.

"Take a second, Dad. There's no rush. We're in the home stretch here. Sun's not going down for a few more hours."

"No, I'm good. Let's just get this done." He hobbled back on his bike and winced. He closed his eyes and nodded up the hill: "Let's go."

He didn't say much for the rest of the ride. I could tell that he was deep inside his pain cave. He didn't want to exert even the slightest bit of energy to talk. Instead, he hung over his handlebars like a wet towel. I clicked to an easier gear and set a slow methodical pace, checking on him every few minutes.

It was cold and dark when we arrived in Siena. Just as I feared, I instantly got us lost when we entered the confines of the city. Siena was constructed like a beehive, with narrow stone streets intertwined and meandering in mind-numbing complexity—especially in my fatigue. I frantically searched for the hotel on my phone. "Alright, I think I got it this time," I said, before leading us down a series of rights and lefts that delivered us back to the same exact spot where we started. I looked up at my father, anxious that he was going to erupt, but he was too shell-shocked to be angry. He had a distant look in his eyes. He was running on instinct.

When we finally found the hotel on Villa Piccola, I quickly checked us in. I forced the door open to our room, which was dimly lit and painted lime green, and Dad collapsed onto the bed—wearing everything except his helmet. He threw his arms over his head. The pattern on the chintzy duvet swirled around him. He kept his eyes closed for a few minutes. "That was . . . that was brutal," he finally said.

"Yeah," I said, sliding down the wall into a heap on the floor. "I'm freaking worked . . . and starving." Dad lay in silence. He was never one to admit defeat or back down from challenge, but he was bewildered.

"Robbie," he said solemnly, "that was . . . probably . . . the most physically challenging day of my life." He didn't dole out statements like that regularly. After all, he had a resume of athletic suffering unlike anyone I'd ever known. More than twenty marathons. Thousands of miles riding in scorching heat and soul-crushing cold. But I could tell by the weariness in his voice that he meant it. "Fifty-four miles taking us over six hours . . . you know, that's . . . that's a grind," he said. "What's tomorrow look like?"

"More of the same," I said. "Just a little longer and a few more hills." The reality was that today was one of the easier days of the trip. From here the hills only got steeper, the mileage longer. But I didn't want to freak him out. He'd learn the truth soon enough. "I'm going to hop into the shower," I said. "Then we'll grab some grub."

I entered the tiny bathroom and peeled off my cycling kit like it was a layer of sunburned skin. I put my hands on the side of the sink and looked into the mirror. My face was caked in dried sweat and sunblock. *Well, you're in it now, kid.*

When I came out of the shower a few minutes later, Dad was sitting at the edge of his bed still fully zipped up in his cycling clothes. He was watching a television program about deep sea fishing, all in Italian. "What's up?" I asked. "We eating?"

"Yeah," he said, pulling himself out of his daze. "I'm going to rinse real quick. Why don't you figure out a place for us to go?"

I walked out of the hotel, and the crisp evening air cooled my wet hair. My legs felt rubbery, and my feet, lower back, and tailbone ached. But the pain felt good. I had *fully* exerted myself today, expended every bit of energy—how rare that was. I took a seat on a bench and pulled out my phone to call Jenny. Siena was slathered in warm yellow from the street-lights. There was a pizzeria connected to the hotel. *Pizza will work fine for dinner*, I thought, as I listened to the phone ring.

"Hello?" Jenny answered.

"Hey, it's me."

"Oh, hey! I had no idea who this was. Phone number was like seventeen numbers." I was calling through Skype. "How's everything going? What time is it there?"

I looked down at my watch, but there was just a band of white skin on my wrist surrounded by a sunburn. "Not sure. I took my watch off in the shower. It's dark here."

"How are you guys doing? How's your dad?"

I sighed. "Umm, I mean, it's a lot," I said. "A lot."

"What do you mean?" she asked.

"It's harder than I thought it was going to be. Lots of hills. Lots of climbing. Dad crashed pretty hard today."

"He fell?"

"Oh no, he just bonked out, like he lost his energy. We were almost done with the day and he just started falling apart." Frankly, I was worried about the rest of the trip. Jenny asked how we were getting along. "Good for the most part. We had a few tense moments this afternoon. I got us lost a couple times. But we kept it together."

"And how are you doing?"

"I feel alright," I said. I was definitely not in the best shape to do this, I told her, but I figured I'd get stronger as the trip went on. The hardest aspect would be keeping track of everything. Looking down to the route, then back at my Dad, making sure he hadn't been hit by a car. "It's just a lot," I said. "I need to make sure he's drinking enough water and eating. You know, a lot."

"Well, that's what you were looking for right?" she teased. "A full-on adventure?"

"Guess so." Dad came limping out of the hotel wearing his only outfit and his ninja shoes. "Oh, babe, my dad's here. We're going to grab some food."

"Sounds good," she said. "Be careful, okay? And tell him I said hi."

"I will." It was comforting to hear her voice. I relayed Jenny's greeting to my father.

"You called her long distance?" he gasped. "Isn't it like fifteen dollars a minute?"

"I actually called her using this service online. So it was free." He was surprised to hear that—he loved *free*—and asked if we could ring my mother at some point.

"Yes, of course. We can call after dinner if you want. Shower felt good, huh?"

Our stomachs groaned audibly as we entered the restaurant, which was completely empty. A waitress with thick, meaty arms was sweeping around the bar. "Ciao . . . Non apriamo per dieci minuti," she said, pointing to the clock. It was ten minutes to six.

I nodded toward one of the tables in the back and asked if we could sit and wait. She leaned her broom against the bar, tucked two menus under her arm, and waved for us to follow her.

"Could I have a coffee?" my father asked the woman when she returned to fill our water glasses.

"Un caffé americano?" I translated. That much Italian I knew. She nodded. My father could drink coffee at any hour, day or night. He pulled out his readers and studied the menu. We scanned for dishes that we could identify, although we knew that we'd end up ordering pizza. The waitress returned with Dad's coffee. It was a dainty shot of espresso.

"Oh, not what I was expecting, but I'll drink it," he said gamely.

We closed our menus. It felt good to sit and just stare off into space. With my eyes fixed on a series of black-and-white photos of farmers riding an ox-drawn carriage, I asked my father how he was feeling about the day to come.

He took a slow sip of his espresso. "We'll see," he said. "Just have to take it piece by piece."

"How's the bike riding?"

"Rides like a dream—nicer than any of my bikes at home."

"And you have that extra gear too."

He put down his coffee. "Yeah, I haven't touched that gear . . . " I shot him an exasperated glare. "I told you I wasn't going to use it," he continued. "I'm not using that granny gear."

A few hours ago, my father was a walking corpse on the side of the road, yet still his pride was preventing him from using the one tool he had available to make things easier. "You gotta be kidding me!" I said. "Who gives a shit if you're riding in the granny gear? No one's watching. What do you have to prove?" He chuckled to himself and reopened the menu, hoping to snuff out the topic.

"Honestly, Dad, why do you always want to make things more challenging for yourself?"

"I don't want you to suffer any more than me," he said. "I want to suffer as much as you."

"Dad, this isn't about suffering—this is about *surviving*," I said. "Jesus, just use the extra gear. We need to get out of here alive."

He tried changing the subject to the extra bag I was hauling off my seat post, which I knew he thought was another imbalance in our suffering scale, but I doubled down on my plea. "Really, we've got to be on the same page here, Dad. There's no reason to make this ride any harder than it already is."

He knocked back the rest of his coffee. "I know . . . I just have this voice in my head. And you have it too, this voice that never wants to take a shortcut."

I chose not to remind him that six hours earlier he was pushing for us to take a shortcut, but I knew what he meant. I asked him where he got that mentality, as it was clearly a trait I'd inherited.

"It's just part of my DNA, you know?" He pondered the question. "I've always had that in me. You're just determined to push on. I always want to be able to get the absolute most out of myself. I never want to settle or take the easier of two paths." He explained that his inner voice was constantly challenging him, pushing him harder and faster. "I argue with it all the time," he said. "It's that voice that says, 'Don't be such a wimp. Push yourself.'"

I told him that using the extra gear wouldn't make him a wimp; it made him sane.

He laughed and shared an anecdote to illustrate the point. Years ago, during the dead of winter, when the temperature dropped below zero and Mass Ave. turned to ice, my mother pleaded with him to simply drive to work. She didn't understand why he felt compelled to bike through such god-awful conditions.

"I guess the reason is," he concluded, "if I don't ride my bike, I'll just be like everybody else."

CHAPTER 10

It is by riding a bicycle that you learn the contours of a country best, since you have to sweat up the hills and coast down them.

—Ernest Hemingway

We rolled tentatively through the narrow streets of Siena. The stark morning sun cast slabs of light into stone alleyways. The brick buildings and medieval churches towered overhead. Little old ladies popped open shutters to hang laundry on the line suspended across their window sills, while hunched old men walked the streets below. I pulled out my camera. I'd taken a total of seven photos during yesterday's sufferfest from Florence, and I realized that if I didn't force myself to take more photos, we'd have no meaningful evidence of being in Italy.

"Dad, just pedal down about thirty feet into the light," I said, taking the lens cap off my camera. He appeased me and rolled unenthusiastically down the street with one foot dragging along the cobbles. Not exactly the model material I was hoping for. He came to a stop and scowled back at me like a wet cat. I waved him further down the street.

Dad wanted nothing to do with photos. We hadn't talked much during coffee this morning. Zipping his damp cycling kit, he was palpably nervous and admitted, "I'm feeling like I do before a marathon . . . a nervous energy. Mixture of excitement and a feeling like I won't make it."

Peering at him through the viewfinder reminded me just how surreal this all was: Dad and I cycling through Italy. I couldn't believe we were actually here. Years of talk finally culminating into action. Pride rose up in my chest, but it was short-lived. Zooming in on him, I could make out my father cussing at the street. I was pushing my luck. I packed away my camera and pedaled to him.

"Ready to go, Ansel?" he asked.

"Yeah, yeah, let's go." We made our way through Siena. Around every corner was another charming vignette that begged for my camera, but I stuck to navigating us out of the ancient city. Legend had it that Siena was founded by the son of Remus. According to Roman mythology, Remus had founded Rome with his twin brother, Romulus, centuries before Christ. We passed the Piazza del Campo, where twice each summer, tens of thousands of people gather for the Palio di Siena—a bareback horse race started around the fourteenth century in which riders from the surrounding neighborhoods compete. The city was built on a slope, sending us down steep, winding streets until we were spit back out into modern Italy with smooth blacktop and morning traffic.

"How you feeling?" I asked Dad, after we pulled on to the shoulder of a highway.

"Little stiff, but I should be fine after we warm up a bit."

I'd studied the route that morning over coffee. "It looks like we're on this highway for just a couple miles and then we'll break back into the side roads."

An eighteen-wheeler hauled past us, scattering dusty debris in the air. Two cars careened by, followed by another big rig. "I can see what you were saying about riding on a highway," Dad yelled. "I definitely wouldn't want to do this all day."

I, on the other hand, wasn't exactly sure I wanted to ride my bike at all today. My body was a wreck. I felt like the Tin Man in desperate need of an oil can. Unlike the day before, when pain pulsed everywhere, from fingers to toes, the aches were now localized on my neck, lower back, tailbone, and right knee. My knee worried me the most. *I can power through everything else*, I thought, *but if my knee locks up, I'm screwed.*

I deduced that the acute soreness in my knee stemmed from hauling the bag off my seat post. Whenever I stood up out of my seat to climb, the twenty-pound bag caused the bike to rock wildly from side to side and almost tip over. Just keeping the frame upright required more energy than actually pedaling, so I eventually decided to click into the easiest gears and pedal the hills from the seated position. However, this maximized the torque on my joints, especially my right knee. Soon my knee began ticking audibly with each stroke of the pedal, shooting dull pain into my lower quadriceps that pooled back down around my knee cap. The ticking thwarted any attempt to zone out.

"Here we go, Dad," I said. "We're taking this left."

"Alright, you got an opening here," he said, scoping the traffic. "Ease into the lane."

I pulled into the one-lane highway along the double lines and stretched my neck to see if any cars were coming. "We're good."

We turned onto a country road shaded in trees. Quiet returned. The road steepened and I clicked into an easier gear and mounted the hill sitting in the saddle. *Tick! Tick! Tick!* went my knee. Meanwhile, Dad stood and danced up the incline with ease. He looked strong. My God, did he look strong. His sinewy legs drove the pedals like two well-oiled pistons, never breaking cadence.

Cresting the top of the hill, he sat back down, returned his hands to the drops, and spread his torso evenly over the frame with his elbows tucked directly under his shoulders. Every one of his movements was balanced, made for efficiency. Most striking of all, his face was calm and serene. There was no more anguish in his eyes. If he was suffering, it was deep within, undetectable on the surface. He flashed me a grin. *Asshole*, I thought. *How can that old bastard feel so good and fancy-free while I'm stuck here in the pit of misery?*

THE COUNTRY ROAD EVENTUALLY opened up to lush green hills that undulated out to the hazy blue horizon. The patchwork of grass swayed in psychedelic waves. "Wow, that's trippy," Dad said.

"Yeah, no question about it, this is Tuscany."

The road spooled out before us like a strip of ribbon. "Let's crank this," Dad called. He lined up on my back wheel, lowered into the drops, tucked his knees in, and hid from the wind. We found our rhythm. Our chains hummed together in a methodical *hmm hmm hmm hmm.* We zipped down each hill with enough momentum to deliver us to the top of the next hill with little effort. A rollercoaster effect took hold. But we didn't coast. We kept feeding the fire, clicking into bigger and bigger gears that sounded like handsaws being ripped through supple wood. Faster and faster. Faster and faster. *Hmm hmm hmm.*

We . . . are . . . hauling . . . ass! I thought, before peering over my shoulder to catch a glimpse of my father. He was grinning like a lunatic. I glanced down at my GPS: we were going twenty-seven miles per hour on the flats; thirty-five down the hills.

"Mooooving!" I yelled. "Freaking . . . moving!" My pain was gone. My body felt light and strong and undeniably powerful. I clicked into a bigger gear and heard my father do the same. Time, thought, noise—everything fell away. We were two wild stallions galloping through an impressionist painting. Down one hill and up the next, over and over. *Hmm hmm hmm.*

I broke from my trance and looked down at the GPS again. Twenty miles had passed by without us noticing. I didn't want to stop, but I also didn't want this joy ride to end too quickly. I didn't want to gobble all this up too fast. I slapped my rear end to signal that I was going to ease on the brake. "Let's stop up here," I yelled back.

I ceased pedaling and stood. The wind enveloped me. I glided along until I came to a stop and popped my cleat out of the pedal. Dad pulled up alongside me. We stood there for a few quiet moments. Endorphins exploded in my brain. Goosebumps bristled under my jersey. The Tuscan sun blanketed us. Dad finally broke the silence.

"I've never felt so close to God," he said, with such sincerity it was as if he were saying it to himself. Maybe he was. His eyes remained fixed on the landscape as he straddled his bike.

Dad wasn't much for religious talk. He was a spiritual guy, who no doubt had a number of his own private rituals and practices, but when it came to discussing the divine, I couldn't recall him ever sharing a sentiment so direct. The words were perfect for the moment, standing on this picturesque patch of the globe, awash in euphoria. In that moment, after so many years away from my faith, and so few conversations with the Almighty, I too felt close to God again.

FAITH PLAYED A PIVOTAL role in my upbringing. My mother was a deeply devout Catholic. My earliest memories were of her standing at my bedside leading my little brother and me in nightly prayers. Every Sunday she dragged us out of bed to attend mass. I became heavily involved in the church, serving as an altar boy, a lector, and even a soloist in the children's choir. The latter of those three acts of devotion was painfully ill advised.

News of the Catholic Church clergy sex scandal broke in the Archdiocese of Boston while I was a senior attending a private Catholic high school. At the time, I was attending mass every morning before class in the small chapel on campus. In the wake of the horrific reports published by the *Boston Globe*, the offices of which just so happened to be directly across from my high school, I did my best to remain committed to my faith. I even formed an afterschool student group to embolden Catholics my age, as attendance at churches began to plummet.

But the scandal started hitting too close to home. First a priest in my high school was removed for abusing a student, then another from my home parish—the same priest I had served under as an altar boy. I went on to enroll in a Catholic college, but my faith was badly shaken. I started to drift from the church. I stopped attending mass, stopped praying at night. I couldn't get over the hypocrisy of the institution. Who was the church to come down as the moral authority on issues like gay marriage in the face of its own terrible transgressions?

Meanwhile, my mother doubled down on her devotion to our local Catholic church. Our parish sponsored her to get her master's in ministry at Saint John's Seminary. I was deeply proud of her for returning to school. When she graduated, she wanted to give back to the church and took a job as the pastoral associate of our parish, essentially organizing all the moving parts of the church's day-to-day operations. If they would have let her become a priest, she would have. She modeled herself after Dorothy Day, a progressive Catholic devoted to helping the needy. She was unafraid to question the tenets of the church that didn't align with her moral compass.

Nevertheless, it pained my mother that I drifted from the church. She petitioned me to return to mass. "Do it for me," she said. But I just couldn't bring myself back. When my Catholic guilt weighed especially heavily on me for not attending mass, I thought back to the wisdom of a Jesuit priest from my high school who once told me that above all, we must follow our own conscience—even if that meant going against the church. Our conscience, he said, is the word of God.

Meanwhile, my father remained committed. He attended mass every Sunday. He knew how important it was to my mother, and his devotion to the church was a reflection of his devotion for her. Seeing him in the pew was the greatest gift he could give her, and a clear sign of their commitment to one another.

Outside of my immediate family, Jenny and I wrestled with the topic of religion as we discussed marriage. She is Jewish and it was important to her that she raise her family in the Jewish tradition. Given my estrangement from the Catholic Church, initially the idea of raising my children Jewish didn't faze me in the least. I'd come to appreciate the Jewish traditions, sitting shiva when Jenny's grandmother died or participating in the Passover meal with her extended family. The sense of hospitality I found in the Jewish traditions was familiar to me, reminding me of the many dinners we had around Papa's table.

But as we continued to discuss the implications of having a Jewish family, certain discrepancies began to rub me the wrong way. We fiercely debated having a Christmas tree in the house, for instance, which for me was hardly a religious symbol but a cherished family tradition. Jenny insisted that a Christmas tree would confuse our Jewish children. Yet in my mind, if we were going to raise open, tolerant kids, wouldn't it be smart to start with teaching acceptance under our own roof? "This is a Christmas tree," we'd tell them. "This represents Daddy's religion," and so on.

These kind of debates continued. Jenny and I knew we wouldn't have a traditional religious wedding. But would we incorporate pieces of the Catholic and Jewish faiths in the readings and vows? If we had children and raised them Jewish, would I attend temple with the family? And if not, would I feel left out and resentful? On and on these debates raged, until the dichotomy of our faith traditions seemed completely insurmountable.

In the back of my mind, I desperately wanted to find some common thread between our faiths, a storyline that would unite our fledgling family. But even here in Italy, all I found were more sources of division.

ON A SEPARATE TRIP to Florence years earlier, I visited the Great Synagogue (formally known as Tempio Maggiore). A fifteen-minute walk from the Duomo, the temple was in a quieter section of the historic city, surrounded by residential buildings and Jewish cafes. Heavily armed guards shuffled in place around the synagogue as I made my way to the entrance. A sign reading NO CAMERAS. NO RECORDING DEVICES. NO SHORT SKIRTS. was posted by the ticket window. I paid and passed through a sophisticated metal detector, which closed around me, scanned me, and released me to the synagogue's grounds.

I walked into the manicured courtyard that led toward the pink stone synagogue with its towering copper domes that over time had grown green. Unlike at other historical sites I'd visited in Florence, there were only a handful of people touring the grounds that afternoon, most of them wearing yarmulkes. To the left of the synagogue entrance were two large stone tablets carved with the names of hundreds of Jews killed during World War II. As I read the names, I was surprised that they weren't more Jewish sounding, whatever I thought that was. Instead, they had Italian last names like mine. I was painfully ignorant of the fact that Italy had the oldest Jewish population in Europe—my knowledge of that history was dreadfully inadequate.

I made my way inside the synagogue. The walls and high vaulted ceilings were spectacularly ornate, with mind-numbing detail. With my head cocked back, I studied the vast mosaic of colors until the lines blurred together and my eyes tired. A pulpit loomed to the left, while rows of what I would call pews faced one another. As I explored this foreign place, it occurred to me that this was the first time I'd ever stepped inside a synagogue. That wasn't an intentional omission in my life. Perhaps it was a consequence of my surroundings. I was raised within a Christian community, and growing up, I knew of only two Jews in my school. Then I went off to Catholic high school and Catholic college. The homogeneousness of my peer group continued essentially until I met Jenny after I graduated. Though I often shrugged off the differences that came up because of our religious backgrounds, I really didn't know much about the Jewish faith beyond studying the Old Testament in high school.

After touring the main temple, I climbed five flights of stairs, where I found a small museum of Florence's Jewish history. At the entrance there was a placard providing a timeline beginning in 1304, when the first signs of Jews in Florence were dated. The timeline stopped at 1943, the year Florentine Jews were deported during the Nazi occupation. Studying the timeline more carefully, I noticed a trend. The 639 years between 1304 and 1943 detailed a gut-wrenching history of struggle. One century the Jews were granted rights in Florence and the next they were harshly revoked, leaving them worse off than before. According to the timeline, in 1437 they were allowed to open banks. But a little over a hundred years later, this autonomy was snatched away and they were forced to live in ghettos. Some two hundred years after that, Napoleon freed them from the ghettos when he took control of Italy. But fewer than twenty years later, they were forced back into ghettos. In 1848 they were liberated once and for all from the ghetto, but their freedom wouldn't last. Less than a hundred years later, Mussolini implemented his racial laws and the Jews were sent to intern-ment camps. And then the Nazis arrived.

I entered a small side room where a machine projected a film onto one of the walls. Sitting in a plastic chair, I watched the film, which described life in the Jewish ghettos. In 1540 Florentine Jews lived in a fenced-in area where the Piazza della Repubblica now stood. *How tragically ironic,* I thought, *that the playful merry-go-round that kids rode today was once the site of human suffering and debasement.* The film gave greater gravity to the timeline I'd read at the entrance. It described how Jews were often cast as witches and targeted as scapegoats. Eras of progress and tolerance were often followed by extreme repression, depending on who was in power.

When the ghetto was finally destroyed in 1848 and the Jews were rein-tegrated into Italian culture, they made a deliberate effort to assimilate, many of them going as far as to change their last names to sound more Italian. This explained the names I'd read on the stone tablets outside the synagogue. This impulse to embrace everything it was to be Italian continued through the rise of Fascism and World War II. Many Italian Jews joined Mussolini's Fascist party and remained devoted to Il Duce even after he handed down his anti-Semitic law of the land. In fact, ten thousand Jews counted themselves members of the Fascist party the year Mussolini took Hitler on his grand tour of Italy and hung swastikas throughout Rome and Florence.

I made my way back out to the courtyard. The afternoon sun glared overhead, and a pack of Hebrew school students played around the grounds. I walked by the wall of names again and considered them in light of the history I'd just absorbed. Up to this point, I considered the onus of the Holocaust to fall squarely on the shoulders of the Nazis. Italy's role as a Nazi ally was convoluted in my mind. I understood now that the subjugation of Jews wasn't introduced to Italy by Hitler, or Mussolini for that matter. Rather, that history stretched back to Roman times when Italy's Jews numbered in the tens of thousands.

The deeper I dug, the more divided I felt from Jenny and her Jewish faith. I needed a new narrative. *We* needed a new narrative. Otherwise I feared that the differences in our faith traditions might render our marriage impossible.

CHAPTER 11

What lies behind us and what lies before us are tiny compared to what lies within us.

—Ralph Waldo Emerson

An old woman stood bent at the waist on a leafy hillock, plucking vegetables from her garden in the outskirts of Tuscany. She was surrounded by six or seven scrappy goats that grazed freely. With a kerchief covering her head and tied snugly under her chin, she looked transported from the past. Hearing our chatter on the side of the road, the woman stood up, gave us a brief once-over, and returned to her task without much more than a blink.

These glimpses into the old world were the real reward of exploring Italy by bike. We swung through one dusty old village to the next, pulling over to fill our water bottles at the market and maybe slurp down a coffee at a roadside cafe. Two or three old men were usually sitting at the counter, watching soccer, drinking beers, and smoking cigarettes. Just as the woman in the field, they'd cast us a glance and then return to the game.

Though there was an intimacy in the way that we were experiencing Italy, we felt removed from each scene, as if we were watching from behind a thick pane of glass. The language barrier deepened the divide. My father seemed especially reluctant to try speaking Italian, and I cringed every time he responded with a wooden "thank you very much" instead of a *grazie mille*, which I tossed around with bravado. Just two days into our ride, we were still in the immersion period of travel. The comforts and conveniences of home lingered in recent memory. We were watching Italy from the sidelines, waiting to get called into the game.

In the distance, behind the old woman, I could make out a castle perched on a hilltop, surrounded by smaller stone spires. "That must be it right there," I told Dad. "San Casciano dei Bagni."

"That's where we're stopping?"

"Yeah, apparently this place is world renowned for its hot springs." The night before, I'd read that "dei Bagni" literally means "of the baths." Legend had it that during the beginning of the Roman Empire, Augustus himself soaked in one of the forty-two thermal pools surrounding this Tuscan village. From then on, the rich and powerful in Italy made the pilgrimage for a royal tub.

"As long as they have a place to eat, that's all I care about," Dad said.

"I'm sure they will."

After four or five miles, we coasted into the village, which was built around a medieval castle. I had booked us at a bed-and-breakfast in the heart of San Casciano dei Bagni the night before. The young innkeeper came out and greeted us as we arrived. "Welcome," he called out.

"Hi there," I said, dismounting my bike, grateful that the man spoke English. "We have a reservation."

"I know," the man said. "Cocuzzo—you're the only reservation we have. Where did you come from?"

"From Siena, but we started in Florence a couple days ago."

"Siena?" he gasped. "On a bike?"

"Yep, on a bike," I said.

Nodding to my father, he asked, "Your brother?"

Dad chuckled. He never tired of that question. "No, he's my father," I told him.

After stowing our bikes, the innkeeper led us to our room. "You should visit the hot springs," he said, jiggling the keys into the lock. "Just down the hill. Ten-minute walk."

Once again, Dad and I would be sharing a bed for the night, but after more than a hundred miles sweating, grunting, and spitting inches away from one another, that no longer registered as an inconvenience. He flopped his little backpack on the bed and pulled out a mass of wrinkles that was his only outfit.

"We should check out the hot springs," I said. Dad smiled. "I'm serious. Probably do us some good."

"I don't have a bathing suit or anything."

That wouldn't stop me. "Just wear your underwear. Who cares?" But he wouldn't have it, hobbling over to the television and turning it on. "You don't want to try them out?"

"No, I'm good," he said. "You go."

"So you're just going to watch TV, in Italian?"

Slumping onto the couch and studying the remote control, he didn't respond. I couldn't understand his lack of interest. Chances were that we'd never return to this remote village. Didn't he want to see this place's historic claim to fame? Didn't he want to soak in the waters of kings and emperors? But I wasn't about to push the issue. He was already *way* outside his comfort zone. He'd pedaled nearly seventy miles and seven thousand vertical feet through the most mind-blowing scenery he'd ever set eyes on. *No mystical bubble bath is going to change that*, I thought.

I LIMPED MY WAY through the village and onto the dirt path that the innkeeper told me led to the public baths. My body ached, especially my feet, lower back, rear end, and, worst of all, my right knee, which was now plump and swollen. Wearing my only pair of boxer briefs, I picked my way down gravel and allowed my imagination to wander. *Was I about to roll up on three buxom Italian beauties wading in a sapphire pool?* I wondered. *Through the steam, their black curls bouncing on their sun-kissed bronze shoulders.*

But there were no sexy ladies at the hot springs—or anybody for that matter. In fact, if I didn't know any better, I'd say this was the village's water treatment center. Ducks quacked around the pool, paddling by dried leaves and lily pads. The main hot spring had a wrought-iron fence around it that was chained shut, leaving me with only the smaller pool to explore. It looked like a glorified dog bowl. There was some viscous sludge crusted on the surface. *Gross*, I thought. *Thank God I didn't drag Dad down here.* But I wasn't leaving without a fight. I slipped my right leg into the hot water, submerging it to my swollen knee cap. *Jeez, I hope there are no snakes in here . . .*

"How was it?" Dad asked when I returned to the room.

"Yeah, awesome," I lied. "You want to eat?"

"Yeah, man," he said. "I'm *starving.*"

Outside, we entered Ristorante Daniela, a cavernous restaurant that looked chiseled into a mountainside. Candlelight danced across the rough-hewn stone ceiling and walls. Dad threaded his hands together over the table and studied the dining room. "This place is incredible," he said.

"They got ravioli," I said, scanning the menu for words I recognized.

"Yeah, I'm going to go with the tagliatelli," he said. "And hopefully they bring over some bread for this oil."

My stomach was tight as a raisin. According to my Strava app, we were burning more than four thousand calories a day, so when it came to dinner, anything we wanted, we ate with abandon. Heaping plates of hand-cut pasta. Crusty bread and oil. Cheesy pizzas. Powdered sugar–dusted cannoli and warm biscotti. Plowing through plate after plate over the past three nights, I had monitored my father's bites. Overeating was one of the triggers to his gastrointestinal attacks. On two consecutive Thanksgivings, we had to take him to the emergency room after he gorged on too many cookies and pieces of pie. I'll never forget the sight of him crawling across the kitchen floor on all fours, begging me to call an ambulance. The memory came to my mind as I watched him eying the menu rabidly.

"Allora," the waitress said, returning to our table.

I raised my menu and pointed to the ravioli. She nodded and smiled, then turned to my father.

"May I have the tagliatelli? Does it have any meat?" he asked.

"Come?"

"Meat," Dad repeated. "I don't eat any meat."

"Carne?" I offered, hoping the word for "meat" in Spanish was the same in Italian.

"Carne?" she asked.

"Sì, no carne," I confirmed.

"Oh, sì, no carne," she responded with a smile. "E vino?"

We both knew what that meant. "No, no wine."

"But can we get some bread?" Dad asked.

"Pane?" I said, taking another stab at Italian.

"Sì." The waitress left and came back with a basket of crusty bread. We drizzled golden olive oil onto our plates and inky black vinegar that oozed out slow and thick.

"Oh my God, this bread is fantastic!" Dad said, inhaling a piece. Within two minutes the entire basket was reduced to crumbs that my father pecked at with his finger. "Think we could get some more?" he asked.

"Definitely." I picked up the basket and motioned to the waitress. Another basket of piping hot bread appeared and then disappeared. I saw in my father's eyes that he wanted a third basket and was waiting for me to suggest it. "You want—"

"Yeah, man!"

Moderation was never our strong suit. It's a mental mode that neither of us possessed. We couldn't eat just one cookie or three cookies; we needed to eat the whole box. Jenny rolled her eyes whenever I talked about my inability to exercise moderation. "That's a story you keep telling yourself," she'd say. "You're making it your reality." I'd nod in agreement, but in my head I thought, *You don't get it.*

For my father and me, making choices along extremes was much more manageable than being wishy-washy somewhere in the middle. We either did something or we didn't. Once we made that decision, a flip was switched in our minds and we'd give ourselves over to it entirely. There was no turning back. Perhaps not surprisingly, alcohol fell under the category of indulgences we weren't very good at moderating. My father quit drinking before I was born. He didn't go to AA meetings or have a sponsor. One morning, he just woke up and decided to stop. When I turned twenty-one, I tried to get him to break his sober streak. I asked him to have a beer to celebrate, but he adamantly refused. At the time I didn't understand why. "What's the big deal?" I crowed. "One beer isn't going to turn you into a full-blown booze bag."

What I came to understand was that even the tiniest, seemingly insignificant decision could drive a crack in the levee of my father's mind that would get bigger and bigger until a deluge exploded through the wall. Because that's exactly how my mind worked. My drinking wasn't a problem in the ways people might expect. I was never a slurring embarrassment in public. Never climbed behind the wheel after one too many. My hangovers weren't even that bad. But before I met Jenny, I could go stretches of months drinking a bottle of wine every single night, all by myself. It just became part of my nightly routine. Have a glass while I cut up the veggies. Another glass while dinner simmered. One more for the meal. And then there was that last glass in the bottle—I couldn't just leave it sitting there.

Although I didn't recognize it at the time, the cumulative effect of this bottle-per-night routine exacerbated the bouts of crushing depression and anxiety that I'd been dealing with since I was eighteen. Even when I was curled up in the fetal position in the shower, hiding from my reality, I failed to recognize the truth that alcohol dragged me deeper into a depression. Instead, I'd drink more to try to drown out the crummy way I felt. My parents had no idea about the months I lived with a personal apocalypse raging within me. I didn't make the connection between my depression and my drinking until I decided to stop.

Working on my first book, I pledged to get up at 5 a.m., to write before having to report to my magazine job. No matter what, when my alarm went off, I shot out of bed and got in front of my computer. Drinking wasn't conducive to this early morning routine, so I added sobriety to the recipe. Within two weeks my depression and anxiety subsided. Neither was gone entirely, but the lows weren't as abysmal and the darkness not as consuming.

After nine months I finished the book, and Jenny and I celebrated with a pricey bottle of Italian wine, a Gaja Barbaresco. With the very first sip, the moment the juice hit my gullet, a switch flipped in my mind. I did the bottle math: *If Jenny and I have one glass each now, there will be two glasses left in the bottle, then I could probably order a night cap here and then maybe we'll grab another drink with friends.* Within ten days I was back to my old routine of a bottle of wine per night, followed by my mornings curled up in the tub. It took me four months to break the habit. I went back on the wagon and had stayed for what was now going on two years. So while the oenophile in me desperately wanted to try Tuscany's fabled wines, the extremist knew where one sip could lead. Instead, I raised the basket again over my head and motioned for more bread.

"Do you ever wonder why you like giving things up?" I asked my father.

"What do you mean?"

"You know, like not eating meat, not swearing, not drinking. You seem to love to give shit up."

"There's something about abstinence that really appeals to me," Dad said after a couple seconds of thought. "I remember, years ago, when I first gave up meat, a friend said to me, 'Life's too short . . . you shouldn't deny yourself of this or that. You'll be missing out.' But I feel that through abstinence, you're actually gaining something. I believe I'm stronger for it."

"Physically stronger?"

"Yeah, I mean, it's the whole mind-body connection, where less is more." He grabbed for another piece of bread. "I remember painting with my childhood friend Sergio. He's a fine-art painter. He taught me to limit your colors when you're doing a painting. The fewer colors you use, the stronger the painting will be, he told me. I think that's true in life. It's like they say, 'Creativity thrives under constraints.'"

"What about when you decided to stop drinking?" I asked. "What was that process like?"

"Well, it was an evolution," he said. "It started at the beginning of the summer. Every night after work, I'd go down to this field where I grew up in Brighton, and there would always be softball games and a bunch of people I knew. I'd have a few beers, smoke a few joints, and in the back of my mind, I'd think, *I'm really enjoying this a little too much.* But it wasn't until Mom and I went on vacation down the Cape. This was before you were born. We were away with six couples, and I was getting up and having a few beers in the morning, and then I would go for a thirteen-, fourteen-, fifteen-mile run."

That sounded crazy to me, polishing off three beers in the morning and then running a half-marathon.

"I was running all these miles," he continued, "so I thought there's no way I could have a drinking problem." Dad poured more oil into the dish and sopped it up with the last of the bread. "I'd get back from these runs and then *really* start drinking, getting into the tequila. Anyway, I blacked out one night and woke up at midnight. Everybody was gone but your mother, and I could tell she was pissed at me." He stared off past my right shoulder, recalling the scene. "I said to her, 'I think I have a problem.'" He shot his eyes back to me. "As soon as I said that, as soon as I heard myself say that, that was it. I never touched another drink. That was more than thirty years ago now."

"So just like that? You stopped cold turkey?"

"Yeah. I realized there's always going to be an excuse to drink. You have to make a stand. There's always going to be an excuse to say, 'Oh, I can start tomorrow.' You don't pick a date to quit. If you make up your mind to quit drinking, it has to be right now." The waitress returned and put a spoon down by Dad's plate, for his pasta. "Everything I've done, I've hoped that it would make me a better person," he continued. "I was looking for any way in my life to quell my anger, my anxiety, my stress."

This was the first time I could recall him volunteering thoughts about his anger. Apart from that one time when I challenged him, I'd never directly asked him about it. "When you were younger, you recognized that you had a temper?"

"Yeah. I feel guilty thinking that you guys had to listen to me growing up."

"Where do you think you got it?" I asked. "Did Papa have a temper?"

"No, Papa had a really good temperament," he said. "There was only one time where he ever really lost it with me. Well, that was the only time he ever hit me. I was out playing football with a brand-new shirt on and it literally got torn to shreds. I came in the house, walked up the stairs, and Papa had just come in from work behind me. He worked hard; he was a laborer. He busted his chops for us, and he saw my brand-new shirt ripped apart. He wacked me on the leg. He hit me pretty hard. But he was sick over it afterward."

I found it impossible to picture my grandfather—the definition of a gentle giant—raising his hand to anyone, let alone his firstborn. Papa would pull over his truck to ferry a bunch of ducklings across the road. But I guess everyone has their limits.

"It was like the time I slapped you," Dad said. "I'll never get over that. It was a knee-jerk reaction . . . It's one of the few things in my life that I totally regret."

The memory shot to the surface of my mind. I hadn't thought about the episode in decades. My little brother and I were roughhousing and I threw him to the ground. When he started sobbing, my father burst into our room and smacked me across the side of the head. I remember that the smack itself didn't hurt. The real pain was knowing that Dad had crossed the line. Like a lot of other painful memories, I had brushed the episode under the rug and forgotten about it—but he hadn't.

"You have a handle on it now," I said. "Your temper?"

He nodded. "Maybe it's because I'm older now," he said, "but I stop and think more. You know, it's funny. They say, 'Stop and count to ten.' That really works."

"What about when you get really worked up and worried?" I asked. "Like when Mom comes home late or something, and you think she's dead on the side of the road? Where do you think that comes from?"

"Now that—I get that from Papa," he said. "Papa worried so much about everybody. If there was something I inherited, I definitely got that from him."

"Has it gotten any better?" I asked. "Like have you been able to control it better?"

"That's a good question. I don't think it's something I can ever get over," he said. "As much as I'll take a risk here and there, I always feel that I'll be fine. But when it comes to you, your brother, and your mother—I just worry so much. There's so much madness out there in the world. It's irrational. It's total fear. It's terrible, but I think that's always going to be there."

The waitress returned to our table with my father's pasta and my ravioli, stacked on my plate like four fluffy pillows. Dad's pasta was spun into a neat nest, drizzled in hearty red sauce. We retreated into our minds (and our mouths), intent on getting the most satisfaction out of each bite. Slicing a ravioli with the side of my fork and revealing the gooey ricotta inside, I pondered our conversation. *What behaviors had I inherited from him? Were they genetically a part of me, or had I learned them through observation? And of those traits I didn't admire, what control did I have to exorcise them from my future self?*

CHAPTER 12

Cycling is suffering.

—Fausto Coppi

This was bad. This was *really* bad. My knee looked deformed. The swelling started from the top of my tibia and ended at the base of my quadriceps. I clenched my teeth pulling on my spandex cycling shorts and hobbled to the bathroom. Every other step unleashed a wave of pain that exploded from my knee and assaulted the rest of my body. I leaned onto the sink pedestal, taking the weight off my leg, and stared into the mirror. "You're fucked."

Dad had our bikes lined up outside the B&B when I finally dragged myself out of our room. He'd polished off three cups of coffee at breakfast and was bouncing around like a golden retriever. His enthusiasm only magnified how little I wanted to be on a bike today. And what a day we had ahead: eighty-two miles, with nearly seven thousand feet of climbing—all of which would come in the afternoon. We'd essentially be cycling uphill for forty straight miles. Just the thought of it made me sick.

"How you feelin'?" Dad asked.

"I'm fine," I said, gingerly guiding my right leg over the frame. I drew a deep breath and oriented myself with the upcoming turns on the GPS.

"That right?" he asked.

"Yeah, yeah," I said. "Knee is a little sore, but I'm sure it will loosen up when we get going."

If I told him how bad I actually felt, that's all he'd be thinking about for the next eighty-two miles. I didn't want him to worry. He had plenty on his plate already. We did a little loop in the medieval courtyard of San Casciano dei Bagni. Birds chirped. Dew-covered stone walls glistened in the morning sun. Had I not been strapped to this torture device, I might have commented on how beautiful the morning was. Instead, I clicked into an easier gear and got on with it.

Right off the bat, my knee screamed out in agony. The pain was all-consuming. I clenched my teeth till my jaw hurt. My mind pictured the joint as having no cartilage left—just the bones mashing together, swelling and filling with blood, and crying out: *Stop! Oh please, just stop!*

We hit a long descent. I ceased pedaling, stood up, straightened out my leg, and coasted down the hill. *There's no way I can deal with this for eighty-two miles,* I thought. *No freaking way.* The road leveled out and I begrudgingly began to pedal again. *Bang!* Withering pain rushed back worse than before. Stopping and starting only made it worse. *I need to keep pedaling, but this is brutal.* My mind raced to come up with solutions. *Pedal with your left leg,* I thought. *Just let your right leg get pulled around.* But no matter what I did, every *single* pedal stroke made my eyeballs spin in their sockets. I clicked to yet an easier gear.

In a profound oversight, I'd forgotten to pack any Advil or Tylenol. I needed something to dull the pain. Ibuprofen. Icy Hot. Booze. Something—something to take the edge off. I searched ahead in the GPS to see when the next town was. *Ten miles away. Alright, I can do ten miles.*

Mounting the next small hill, I caught a glimpse of my father. He looked even stronger than the day before, with his head up, looking around, taking in the scenery, breathing through his nose. He shifted easily through the gears, keeping the high cadence of his pedaling. *Goddamn, he's a machine*, I thought. I clicked to an easier gear.

"Yo, Dad, I gotta stop up here," I said when a pharmacy finally came into view.

"What's up? You out of water?"

"No, I need to grab some Advil."

I limped into the pharmacy and frantically scanned the shelves for any-thing resembling pain relief but came up empty. "Advil?" I asked. The pharmacist stared back at me blankly. "Ibuprofen?" I asked desperately.

That he understood. He pulled two boxes off the shelves: 60 mg and 90 mg of something called Brofen. I reached for the 90 mg, dropped a sweaty twenty euro note on the counter, and tore open the box with my teeth. *I must look like a drug addict,* I thought, tapping my way out of the pharmacy with my helmet still on. I popped five of the big painkillers and swallowed hard.

"Hurting, huh?" Dad asked.

"Yeah, I should have iced it or something last night. I'm an idiot."

"At least you hit the hot tub."

I chuckled grimly, picturing the putrid dog bowl. "These ibuprofens should help."

But they didn't. I knocked back two more an hour later, but the pain only got worse. Around the thirty-mile mark the agony gave way to doubt. I began to question whether I was physically capable of finishing the day—or worse, finishing the trip at all. The pills did absolutely nothing to ease my misery. Every single pedal stroke was more tormenting than the one before it. Magnifying my pain was the crushing thought of having to stop. *At some point, I might be physically incapable of going any further*, I worried. *My knee might just seize up and that will be it.*

It was a quandary. If we stopped now, only four days in, and pulled the plug on this trip, we'd never come back. Life would get in the way, as it had for so many decades. I had dragged my father across the Atlantic Ocean, shaken him out his comfort zone, and now I was going to let him down. He was riding his best right now, while I was falling apart. I kept pedaling, pedaling, pedaling—but the voice of doubt only got louder and louder. I played out the scene of having to stop, of pulling over and telling him I couldn't go any further. The voice haunted me. I clicked to an easier gear, gasping for each breath.

You got this buddy, you got this, I told myself. *You got this buddy, you got this.*

TRAVEL IS ALL ABOUT uncertainty. It's a gamble. That's why you go: to embrace the unknown, no matter how sick and twisted it might become.

The only sure thing is that at some point you're going to be faced with a mind-bending set of circumstances that requires tapping into a deeper part of yourself.

I've been violently sick with giardiasis in a remote Indian reservation in South America. I've been bitten by a bat while camping in Moab. I've been stricken with skull-crushing altitude sickness in the Himalayas. I've been lost, sunburned, food poisoned, and robbed of everything. The fact is that there's no adventure without misadventure. The key is to be mentally prepared for it and know it's coming one way or another. As I clenched my teeth through the torture, I decided that my banged-up knee was definitely the challenge of this trip—but I was wrong.

Fifteen miles from the last village, the road trailed off into an industrial wasteland. The broken pavement passed defunct chain-link fences with rusty barbed wire hanging down like poison ivy. Mechanical debris—lug nuts and worn-away brake pads—was strewn on the side of the road. Despite these signs of civilization, however, there wasn't another person in sight. No signs of life at all. Instead, this long, lonely stretch of road felt abandoned and forgotten, and as it always tended to do, it began to steepen.

Here we go again, I said to myself. I clicked to an easier gear—but then *bink!* the gear shifter went loose in my hand. I tried to click to an easier gear again, but nothing happened. I looked between my legs. The chain was still intact. I tried the shifter again, but still nothing. "Hold up, Dad," I called out. "Hold up. Something's wrong with my gears."

Throughout the ride I'd played out the various scenarios we might face with our bikes. Flat tires would be inevitable, so we carried several spares. If the chain got mangled somehow, we had a chain-breaker to fix it. We had extra pedals, brake pads, a pump, patch kits, and wrenches. To the best of my knowledge, we were equipped for any eventuality with the bike. But I was wrong again.

"Shit," Dad and I said in unison.

The cable to my back derailleur, which shifted the gears, had snapped and been sucked into the frame like a severed tendon. Dad pulled back the rubber on the horn of my handlebars to find where the wire should have been attached to the shifter—he found it completely frayed. I'd clicked through those gears thousands of times over the past three days, and just like my knee, the cable finally gave up. Without it, not only was I not going to be able to shift gears, but my bike was now stuck fixed in the biggest, hardest gear.

Dad dropped to his knees and walked his hands over the bike, searching for a solution. "The problem is we can't get to that cable," he said. "It's inside the frame. It's stuck in there."

I scanned our surroundings. Never had the description "middle of nowhere" been so fitting. We were at least fifteen miles away from the closest town and hundreds of miles from the bike shop in Florence. We hadn't seen a car in at least an hour.

"You're not going to be able to change gears," Dad said, stating the obvious.

We stood on the side of the road for a long time in silence, studying the frayed cable from every angle. My knee was an absolute mess. I looked at my GPS. We were forty miles in on the day's route, with another forty-two to go. Worst of all, we had nearly seven thousand vertical feet of climbing ahead of us, and (I repeat) my bike was stuck in the biggest gear. Even if I had a perfectly healthy knee, climbing those hills in this gear would be near impossible. *So this is where it ends*, I thought. *Here in the middle of nowhere. My leg is broken. My bike is broken. We're not finishing today. We're not ever finishing. We're not getting to San Donato. This is where the road ends.*

WHEN I WAS A senior in college, Dad moved me into my house off campus on a frigid fall morning. We strapped a mattress to the roof of his car and set off on the hour-long ride. About halfway through the trip, a loud thud echoed through the car. One of the ties had come free, and the mattress flapped in the wind. Instead of pulling over and refastening the ties as reasonable people would, Dad and I just rolled down our windows and held the mattress by hand for the next thirty minutes in the biting cold. I learned a defining lesson that morning. For better or for worse, for my father and me, if the solution came down to a matter of suffering, nothing was impossible.

Now, staring down at my bike in this desolate state of affairs, he perked up. "I got an idea," he said. "If we can get it into the easiest gear, you can climb the hills and coast the rest."

"So basically make it a single speed?"

"Exactly," he said, flipping the bike upside down and pulling a hex wrench from his jersey's back pocket. "If I can just pop this spring off the derailleur, that should free it up and we can shift the gear manually." He stuck the wrench into the spring and worked it free, then took hold of the derailleur. "Spin that," he said. I cranked the pedal by hand while he manually shifted the gears until it was in the easiest ring. "There," he said triumphantly.

I flipped the bike upright and reassessed the situation. I now had one gear, one good leg, and one long-ass day ahead of me. I looked over at my Dad. He wiped the grease from his hands onto his jersey. He lifted his bike off the ground and pulled his water bottle from the cage. There was no question about it: he flat-out refused to admit defeat. It had been the refrain of his life: *Tell me it's impossible and then watch me do it, asshole.*

Pride throbbed in my chest. I was beat up, tired, and mentally tapped, but I felt that same defiance rising within me. This was my inheritance: one part fiendishness, one part raw will. Dad and I were holding the mattress again, and we weren't letting go no matter how cold it got. I threw my aching leg over the bike, squeezed a long blast of water into my mouth, and shot him a crazed grin. Herein lay another truth about traveling. If you can endure and overcome catastrophe, you'll unlock new depths of capacity within yourself. Breaking through walls turned tough times into touchstones for when things got tough again down the line. Dad reminded me of this.

WE DIDN'T TALK MUCH during the ensuing climbs. Instead, the air was filled with the sounds of suffering. Heavy, methodical breathing. The quick squirt of a water bottle. Spit hitting the hot pavement. The buzz of our chains. I entered my mental pain cave. I visualized a little gremlin inside my skull who was looking out the windows of my eyes and casually pulling levers to prompt my body to move. I pictured myself as that little creature—fully in control of my body but free of all the pain associated with its movements. I tried to mentally disconnect from my body and make myself a mere passenger on this grueling slog.

The merciless hills came fast and steep. The gremlin in me reached to click to an easier gear, forgetting that there were no gears to click. Instead, I sat up with my hands on the horns and my toes pointing to the sky, driving through the pedals with the strongest part of my legs. For three miles the route switchbacked like a taut spring up a thousand vertical feet. Some sections were so steep, between 5 and 9 percent grade, that we needed to zig and zag up them or else we'd flip off our bikes.

"That was brutal," Dad gasped when we finally crested the top of the first climb. "Even my eyebrows hurt."

We rolled along the flat before dropping off the back side of the hill. I lowered into my drops, flattened out my spine, and tucked my knees into the frame. My wheels purred over the pavement, spinning faster and faster, as trees, guardrails, and the old stone walls whistled by my ear. At the turns I eased on the back brake slightly, pointed out one knee, and let my body flow with the bike around the bend. Deep cement gutters lined the right side of the road. I tried not to picture the bloody carnage that would result if I duffed my front tire into one of them at high speed. The thought prompted me to turn my head and check on my father. He had a shit-eating grin plastered on his face. For seven miles we didn't pedal once. The road plummeted in a screaming whirlwind. When it finally flattened out, Dad pulled up alongside me.

"Whooo!" he screeched. "What a rush!"

"Yeah, baby!"

"Listen," he said, "I don't want you checking on me. Stop looking back. I don't want you going down."

"Yeah, but if you stop or if something happens, I don't want to go too far down the line."

"I'll yell up to you."

For the next five miles, the slope rose gradually, until the hill pitched again steeply. We clawed up more than 1500 feet, feeling every single inch. With each switchback I hoped the turn ahead would reveal a break in the misery, but it only got worse. Forty-five minutes later, we topped out. Dad clipped out of his pedals and limped off his bike to go pee. My cycling kit was drenched in cold sweat. Everything in my body hurt now almost as bad as my knee. We'd been on our bikes for eight and a half hours, and the sun was beginning to fall behind the trees.

When Dad returned, I sensed that his resiliency was beginning to fade. His mouth was frozen in a grimace. He had black grease on the creases of his nose. He wheeled his bike over to me begrudgingly. He was near his breaking point. "How much further?" he asked, pulling out his last granola bar.

I looked down at my odometer, which read 59.1. About twenty miles to go. "But it looks like that was the last big climb. The rest is mostly flats until the end."

His expression was desperate. "I don't want to have to sleep outside." I laughed uneasily. "I'm serious," he said.

"We're going to be fine. I have our bed booked already."

"Yeah, but we have to get there first. And it's getting dark."

And cold, I thought. Dad was coming undone. It was my turn to rally the troops. "Let's go," I said. "We have a nice long descent here. Worst case scenario, we stop in one of the towns before Trevignano Romano." But in my head, I wasn't going to allow us to stop early. Like a climber with the summit in his sights, I was going to get us to the top if it ruined us.

The cold cut deeper into my bones on the descent, forcing me to squeeze my body over my bike frame. The hill spilled us into a national park and along the banks of Lago di Vico. Through beech trees and across the lake, I could make out a handsome waterfront town.

"Is that us?" Dad yelled through the wind. I shook my head. When the road flattened out, he repeated his concern. "We need to find a place to stay."

"We got ten miles left."

"Robbie . . . " He was getting anxious, calling me by my childhood name.

"We're good, Dad. Just a little longer." After curling around half the lake, the road pointed due south through the town of Ronciglione and then on to Sutri. Whenever I spotted an inn or a hotel, I pedaled away from my father so I couldn't hear him calling for me to stop. *We're in the home stretch*, I thought. *Just a little bit longer.*

Entering the center of Sutri, the road narrowed into a web of busy streets. Cars zipped back into the mix. Hazards swarmed us. I zoomed into the GPS to navigate the tight turns. We were speeding through an intersection. Almost missing a turn, I peeled hard left and then I heard a scream. I snapped my head around just in time to see my father hit the pavement. He rolled into the center of the intersection. Two cars screeched to a stop around him. *Oh God, had he been hit?*

"Jesus, are you alright?" Dad quickly peeled himself off the pavement and tried to hop back on his bike, but he couldn't manage to get his cleat into the pedal. He barked something into the air, got off his bike, and marched angrily over to me. I waited for him to explode, but he was too exhausted. "You alright?" I asked. "Did you get hit?"

"No . . . my gears locked up on me and I went down." He looked at his elbows and knees. "I think I'm fine," he said with a sigh. "I might have scraped my back though." He reached behind and pulled out a handful of white mush. "No, I'm good—it was just a banana."

My father gawked at me, exasperated. We were pushing way beyond the pale, and now things were getting sloppy. "You're going to get us killed," he huffed.

"We're almost there."

"How far?"

I zoomed in on the map. Ten miles. "Just five to go," I lied. "It's like commuting to work—easy." He squeezed his water bottle to his mouth but only dust came out. Dusk was setting quickly. We had a couple of hours of light left and then we'd need to break out our headlamps. *Wait, did we pack headlamps?* I wondered.

"There was a hotel about a mile back there."

"Yes, we could definitely stay there . . . no problem," I said. "But Dad, I promise you, you'll be glad we pushed to the finish." He looked at me and threw the squashed banana into the bushes.

IT WAS IMPOSSIBLY DARK when we finally reached Trevignano Romano. According to the map, the town overlooked a giant lake, but we couldn't pick it out in the darkness.

"Alright, you hang here with the bikes," I said. "I'll find our room." Dad nodded, having long since stopped talking to me.

My body was wrecked from the nine and a half hours on the bike. Back, legs, neck, knees, and toes—totally mangled. I wobbled around in the dark, trying to orient myself with the map on my phone. There were no street signs. I was looking for a cheap B&B, where I'd booked us a room, but every alleyway brought me back to where I began. I knew my father was stewing with every minute that passed. My own desperation was beginning to brim.

Forget it, I said to myself. I entered the first hotel I saw. "I'll take whatever bed you got."

CHAPTER 13

These mountains that you are carrying, you were only supposed to climb.

—Najwa Zebian

I t was on top of me from the moment my eyes peeled open—that cold, suffocating sense of dread I'd been running from off and on for most of my adult life. The pressure squeezed my chest, making each breath labored and short. Even if I could breathe, I found it impossible to sleep. A funny thing happens when you exercise all day. You fall asleep the moment your head hits the pillow, only to be ripped awake a few short hours later by all the endorphins surging through your body. My eyes were pegged to the ceiling at 3:30 a.m.—my heart pounding and my chest fighting crashing waves of anxiety.

By 5 a.m., I gave up trying to sleep and slithered out of bed, hoping not to wake my father. Ice packs slipped off my leg and splatted on the floor. Our room was palatial. The honeymoon suite. I pushed open the balcony door and sat at a little table overlooking a lake as large as an ocean. The sun was just beginning to rise over the water. Birds were singing. A fisherman cut silkily across the lake in a long, skinny outboard skiff. Dad eventually joined me on the balcony.

"I didn't sleep at all," he said, sniffling.

"Well, you look rested."

"Yeah, right. I look like I should be *arrested*." He had that rough-and-tumble appearance of a late-night Hollywood mug shot. His hair was matted and possessed a bird's nest quality. We sat out in the warm morning sun, sipping coffee and devouring pastries that I'd picked up from a nearby cafe. "How much did this place run us?" Dad asked, looking back through the bay doors at the luxurious king bed.

"You don't want to know." In my haste to find a place for us to sleep, I'd thrown down my credit card on what appeared to be the nicest room in town. With our cycling gear scattered in piles on the marble floor, I felt like a squatter. We certainly looked the part.

"Yeah, when I woke up and saw the chandelier staring down at me, I figured it must have cost us a pretty penny."

I sighed.

"So it's on to Rome today, huh?"

"Uh-huh," I said. "Should be a breeze compared to yesterday. Only forty miles and a couple hills."

"How's the knee?"

"Better," I said. "Ice helped." But my knee wasn't what was bothering me this morning. It was my mood. Something had shifted within me overnight. When we mounted our bikes an hour later, I worried what that might mean for me for the rest of the day.

Pedaling into the outskirts of Rome, I found my father's mere presence more and more annoying. For no apparent reason, he was pissing me off. He wasn't doing anything differently from the past four days. He wasn't talking any more or less, wasn't pedaling any slower or faster. The mental burden of setting the route, managing our food and water, and worrying about his well-being every waking moment was taxing. Being connected at the hip was beginning to wear on me. I just wanted to be alone, especially today.

After twenty miles the route led us onto a smoothly paved bike path that snaked alongside the Fiume Tevere (the Tiber River). I pedaled harder and harder, tapping into a power reserve I hadn't yet unleashed on the trip. I wanted to break away from my father. I got out of the saddle and sprinted down the track. He clung to my back wheel for a few seconds. I caught a glimpse of him standing up in his pedals and then I just dropped him. I knew he was doing everything he could to try and catch me, but that only made me accelerate more.

I pedaled harder and harder, whizzing around other cyclists and runners. I still only had one gear, but I was spinning it fast enough to make the world melt away. My lungs and legs burned, but I welcomed the pain. I pedaled harder and harder—hard enough that I couldn't think about anything except physical agony. Finally I broke and coasted for a long time. Guilt flickered in me. *Why did I just do that? Why was I running from him?*

MY FATHER EVENTUALLY CAUGHT up to me. He didn't say a word, but resumed his spot behind my wheel. I wasn't running from him, I decided. I was running from myself. Running from something within me that had been chasing me my whole life. And for some reason, today it was on me like a shadow. A side of myself that my father knew nothing about—or at least I'd never told him about it. I never really told anyone for that matter, except for Jenny and eventually my mother, who pried it out of me. Today the shadow flared up again. I felt it creeping over my mind this morning.

"Only about five more miles ago," I said. "Almost there."

"Great," Dad said, still catching his breath.

Rome reached out and pulled us into its jarring embrace. After the tranquility of Tuscany, the city assaulted our senses. The *wang! wang! wang!* of ambulances. The collective buzzing of Vespas. Horns and exhaust and traffic and chaos. We crossed the river over a bridge, passed the National Gallery of Modern Art, and entered Villa Borghese. With rolling green grass, walking paths, and trees that shook in the warm breeze, Villa Borghese was Rome's version of Central Park. We rode along the path for a bit, passing people walking dogs and eating gelato.

"You want to chill under a tree for a few?" I asked. "And we can figure out where we're going to stay?"

"Yeah, let's do it."

We leaned our bikes up against a tree and flopped down in the shade. I pulled out my phone to see where the closest hostel was, while Dad laid back on his elbows with his legs crossed. "Looks like there's a place for thirty euros not far from here," I said, scrolling through the options on my phone.

"Hey," Dad said. "How you doing?"

"I'm good . . . just tired, you know?"

"Yeah, but *how you doing*?" he asked again.

I placed my phone in my lap. He sensed something was obviously amiss. *Do I brush it under the rug like I've been doing for most of my life?* I thought. *Just bury it back under the surface. Smile and pretend?* I drew in a deep breath and let it out slowly. "Has Mom ever told you that . . . that I deal with depression? Like, I have depression and anxiety?"

I could see in his face that the question came out of left field. "Yeah," he said. "Yeah . . . but . . . you know . . . you and everybody else." It wasn't the response I expected. "This is the thing you have to understand," he said. "We all have anxiety. You just have to . . . you have to remember what you're going through will pass. Nobody is going to die from it."

This wasn't exactly my father's field of expertise. In trying to minimize the stress in his life, he warded off the negative realities of the world. He didn't watch the news or read the newspaper, he didn't sit through sad movies, and he shied away from difficult topics around the dinner table. This was one of those topics we never discussed.

"You especially, who have accomplished so much," he said. "You know, you get these highs, these highs that most people don't get. So it's difficult. You must ask yourself, 'What do I do next to equal this?' You know what helps?" I nodded. "Thinking about your accomplishments. Think of your mental toughness. You always have to keep that in mind."

Sharing this part of myself with my father was totally uncharted territory. For whatever reason—maybe the societal stigma or the weakness depression and anxiety unfairly seemed to imply—talking about my struggles with mental illness with my father felt like I was coming out. I wanted to explain it. "The challenge with depression and anxiety is that it doesn't really matter," I said. "Like you could have the greatest accomplishment in your life in front of you, but it doesn't really counterbalance the way that you feel. You're basically wearing clothes that you have to wear and no matter what you do, you're still wearing those clothes. Make sense?"

"Right . . . " he said, running his hand through his scruff.

"Have you ever had any experiences with that?" I asked.

My father paused. "Umm, well, yeah, I mean . . . " Trailing off, he didn't offer an example.

"I guess I'm asking, and talking about this with you, because I'm wondering if it's . . . hereditary." There, I said it. "I don't know if you've ever had any experiences like this, have you?"

Dad took a few seconds to examine the question. "Well, I'm finding that the older I get, the things that I thought were so important, or things that I thought caused anxiety, when I was your age—well, they were really nothing in the grand scheme," he said. "But it's hard to get this through to someone that's much younger than me, like you. If I could just project this perspective onto you, your life would be so much easier. But you're in the thick of it. Anyone who doesn't have any stress or anxiety is some sort of sociopath."

He was conflating stress and anxiety, which are from the same family but the result of different causes. Stress is caused by external circumstances, while anxiety brews from within. I redirected the question. "What about depression?" I asked.

There was a long pause. "What do you mean?"

"Have you ever been depressed before?"

My father fell silent for what felt like forever. He tried to say something but stopped and thought some more. He clearly had never experienced depression like I had. For those who have, there's no ambiguity about whether or not you've been depressed. And for those who haven't, it's virtually impossible to understand why someone can't just will themselves out of feeling unhappy.

"I mean, does it happen often to you?" he asked.

"Probably every three months."

"Yeah?" he said. "How long does it last?"

"Could last a month, could last a week."

"Is it basically having to do with meeting a deadline, or something like that?" he asked.

"No, it really doesn't have to do with anything related to work or responsibilities," I said. "It's a foreboding sense of dread." I laughed softly, trying to bring some levity to the conversation. "It's basically . . . it's basically beyond my control."

"Do you talk to anyone about it? Do you see anybody? Like a therapist or something?"

"Yeah."

"Alright," he said. "And how's that going?"

"I mean, yeah, it's good," I said. "I think I have a handle on it . . . "

"Well, that's it right there!" he exclaimed. "I think you *do* have a handle on it." He perked up, happy to have landed on a logical explanation. "Because I don't think there's a single soul on earth that's so secure that they never suffer from anxiety . . . that's the way we're all designed. No one escapes it completely. I hate to think that you're going through this, but I know there are many, many more people who have far worse anxiety than you do, but you seem to have more control over it."

Though I was relieved to have finally shared this part of myself with my father, I felt disappointed in our conversation. We look to our parents for answers, yet for this problem my father seemed ill-equipped to offer a meaningful solution, let alone show a basic understanding of what I experienced. That was no fault of his own. I'd never given him the opportunity to contemplate the topic before, and now I had just sprung it on him. Perhaps my disappointment was in realizing that of all his traits I'd inherited, my on-and-off struggle with mental illness wasn't one of them. Had it been, I hoped he could have shown me a better way to outrun the shadow.

THE BOOKING WEBSITE SAID the hotel was five minutes from the Villa Borghese, but it took us twenty. We found ourselves in the foyer of an apartment complex where apparently our "hotel" was located on the fifth floor.

"Why don't you wait here with the bikes, and I'll go up and get us situated," I told Dad. The service elevator wasn't working, so I clicked and clacked my way up the marble flights of stairs in my cycling cleats. Maybe it was my imagination, but it seemed that whenever I reached the landing after each flight of stairs, I'd hear the swift turn of a lock.

Number 507, this is it. I pressed the doorbell and waited. Nothing. I pressed it again, holding the button down a little longer. Still nothing. There was a piece of paper to the right of the door with something written in Italian. I knocked and waited. Finally, I heard the shuffling of feet inside.

Three locks clicked open and a little old woman with curlers in her hair peeked out.

"Is this . . . " I looked down at my phone. "Art Domus Reale?"

She looked at me for a long two seconds, clearly not expecting a scruffy, long-haired American in a helmet and tights to come knocking at her door today. "Oh, sì sì sì, come," she said. "Come. Come." Pulling open the door, she waved me in. I tapped inside. "Siediti, siediti," she said, pointing to a chair by the door. The room was dimly lit. Posters of Renaissance paintings hung crookedly in gilded frames without glass. The furniture looked pulled together from a thrift store. A door down the hall was slightly ajar, and I could just make out a teenager sprawled on a bed playing video games. Evidently, this was the woman's apartment.

She mosied back and closed the teenager's door on her way: "Come, come." I followed her down the narrow hallway, past her kitchen and another closed door until we reached the room. Two rubber mattresses slumped on metal frames. The air smelled like cigarettes. The space was as welcoming as a minimum-security prison cell. *The old man is going to love this*, I thought.

"What the hell is this place?" Dad said, after closing the bedroom door behind him.

"This is twenty-five bucks a night," I said, flopping onto the mattress. "That's what it is."

"We're, like, in this old lady's apartment," he said. Dad has a high threshold for zany sleeping arrangements, but sharing space with strangers was not exactly in his wheelhouse. He dropped his bag and poked his head into the bathroom. "I'm going to take a shower."

I lay on the bare mattress, still in my cycling kit. The sound of the rushing water drifted me off to sleep. When I'm depressed, sleep is my only refuge. The click of the bathroom door reopening a few minutes later woke me from my catnap. Dad came out with a towel wrapped around his waist, carrying two pairs of dripping-wet underwear and socks.

"You know what's the best thing about getting old?" he asked. He didn't wait for me to answer. "You don't care how crazy you get!" He broke out in a villainous cackle. "I did a wash in the sink."

"Why don't you just use the lady's washing machine?" I asked. "I saw it on the way in."

"I don't trust that woman," he said, reaching into the closet and pulling out a couple of clothes hangers.

"Why? Think she would steal your tighty whities?"

"That's not the point," he said, neglecting to tell me what the point actually was. He emerged from the closet still wrapped in a towel, with his undies and socks hanging from the clothes hanger. "This will work out great," he said and laughed. His arms, neck, and face were bronzed chestnut brown by the sun, while his bare chest and biceps were milky white. This extreme farmer's tan only accentuated the many tattoos that covered his upper body like patches on a NASCAR driver's jumpsuit. He started getting these tattoos at fifty-five. He designed the first one himself: a stick figure riding a bicycle. In the beginning, my mother was surprisingly amenable to his midlife-crisis body art. She bought a secondhand convertible, so he got a tattoo.

But just like everything in my father's life, it didn't take long for him to start taking tattooing to the extreme. First he got my name and my brother's name on one arm. Then he put his own name on both arms. Next was my mother's birthday and her astrological sign. His tattoos didn't discriminate. Quite the opposite: they dotted the globe. He got a Chinese symbol in the center of his chest, a Celtic knot on his back, a Latin proverb on his shoulder, and the crescent moon and star of the Turkish flag on his arm. All the while, my sweet, churchgoing mother smiled and shook her head, probably hoping that his ink lust would eventually run out and give way to a new obsession.

One day Dad took his tattoos one needle prick too far. He returned home with a huge tattoo stretching down the length of his left arm. The sheer size of it was certainly a point of concern, but that's not what caused my mother to faint at the sight of it. Without consulting her, he had a voluptuous mermaid tattooed from his upper shoulder to the top of his elbow. But the mermaid wasn't enough. Oh no, Dad decided to go full pirate. Wrapped around the mermaid's shoulders was a serpent with its jaws open, about to clamp down on her breast. My brother and I were sure that would be it. From then on, we thought we'd see our father on the weekends, probably under court-ordered supervision.

But when my mother finally came to and the shock wore off, she took a few deep breaths and moved on. She taught me a defining lesson about marriage during that episode. For sicker or poorer, tattooed or pierced—my mother was in it for the long haul. She took her wedding vows as gospel. Although my father may have overlooked the balance required in a healthy marriage in that moment, he would have her name tattooed on his forehead if she asked. Suffice it to say, the mermaid was my father's last tattoo—at least so far.

"YOU REALLY DON'T CARE what people think, do you?" I asked him.

"Not at all," he said. "Never have."

It was a genuine fascination of mine. Most people who claim to not care about what people think actually care very deeply. But he truly didn't seem to give a hoot. "Is that an intentional decision?" I asked him.

Sitting on the corner of his bed and pulling on his ninja shoes, he said, "I felt like that since I was a little kid. I've always felt different. I don't mean better or superior—just different. I felt like I had a little different step than everyone else. I didn't really identify myself with any particular group growing up."

"So you felt like you were an outsider?"

"Yeah, exactly," he said. "And as you get older, you feel like you don't have to fit in as much. You know? If people don't like it, well, so what? That's their problem. The only people I care about are your mother and you and your brother. I care what you guys think of me—that's big for me. Because I'd never want to disappoint you guys. But as far as the public and anybody else—they just don't know me."

Something about that sentiment shot an arrow into my heart. I thought the world of my father, but maybe I hadn't told him that enough. Instead, I only harped on his idiosyncrasies. The tattoos and the car crashes. *Oh yeah, my father is out there*, was a common refrain. But before I could interject this realization, he was on to the next thought.

"The other thing that's most important to me is my health," he said. "As long as you have your health, it doesn't matter how old you are."

"Yeah, but you take a lot of risks that threaten your health."

"Yeah," he said with a sigh. "I know . . . but that . . . well, that's true. But that's something you really can't be thinking about when you're doing it."

"What do you mean?"

"When I get home, I do thank God for a safe ride, but when I'm out there in the streets, the confidence I have to zigzag through traffic is high. I know my abilities. Every once in a while I do something where I say to myself, 'What were you thinking?' But that doesn't happen too often."

"Well, what goes through your head after you get hit by a car?" I asked.

"That's something I really haven't figured out yet," he said. "For some reason, once I pick myself up, I never think about not riding again. I don't know what it is. I can't put my finger on that one. Never once have I thought, 'Maybe I should just drive to work.' I don't want to kill myself, that's for sure, but I always think, 'You may get hurt, but you're not going to die.' You just always have to be cautious. With age comes caution."

"Yeah, but even after all these years, even after getting hit by all these cars, you're still riding a fixed gear with no brakes," I said. "It's not exactly like you're getting more cautious."

"So much of it is confidence and ability," he said. "I can handle a bicycle really, really well. If you *think* you're going to get hurt, you're *going* to get hurt. You can't think about getting hurt."

I knew what he meant from my experiences skiing. When skiing incredibly high-consequence terrain—where if you fall, you die—confidence is almost as important as ability. Once you lose confidence, ability quickly follows, and accidents happen. "What's the worst crash you think you've had?" I asked. "With a car, I mean."

"The one that I still can't believe I walked away from was on Mass Ave.," he said. According to Dad, he was pedaling as the light was changing to yellow, pushing as hard as he could. A car coming in the opposite direction, with no blinker, took a left right in front of him. "I was looking at this car head on," he said, "and I hit it so hard that I broke her headlight, bounced off her hood, and landed in the street." In midair he remembered thinking, *I can't believe I have to buy another bicycle.*

We broke out in laughter. I flopped back on the bed. "You're out of your mind!" I said.

"I swear to God that's what I was thinking." He chuckled a bit more and then got serious. "I've been lucky. I feel like there's someone watching over me. I've felt this my whole life, like I have this guardian angel—and I don't abuse it. I just feel like there's a reason why I'm still here. I'm trying to figure out what that is exactly, what I'm here for—and it may be nothing. But I feel like there's a reason . . . and you should feel that way too."

CHAPTER 14

How is it possible to say an unkind or irreverential word of Rome?
The city of all time, and of all the world!

—Nathaniel Hawthorne

Dad was fighting the impulse to naysay the city—and I couldn't blame him. After pedaling through the tranquility of Tuscany over the last week, Rome grabbed us by the collars and screamed in our faces with spit flying. Cars were intent on mowing us down as we walked the streets. Throngs of people impatiently mobbed the sidewalks. And as much as I felt obligated to seek out the requisite archaeological sites of this historic city, I didn't want to spend another minute in Rome. We yearned to get back on the road where the villages, the people, the very air we breathed were museum quality. Those scenes were so rare, as if we found them hidden behind a canvas. The Italy on the road wasn't in the guidebook. You couldn't pay five euros to see it. You needed to earn it, one pedal stroke at a time. We were desperate to get back into that rhythm, but first we needed to get my bike fixed.

The bike shop in the heart of Rome wasn't at all what we hoped. It was simply too clean. There was no greasy tune station. No wall of tools. The air smelled like aftershave. A handsome, immaculately dressed man greeted us in English. "Gentlemen, welcome to my shop," he said. "What do we have here?"

"We're having some problems with the derailleur," I explained. "The cable snapped and now I can't shift gears."

"Oh, I see," the shop owner said. He barely glanced at the bike before calling into the back room: "Andrea!" A bespectacled Andrea emerged through the curtains, wearing a scarf and white chinos. He lowered to a knee, careful not to actually touch the ground, and assessed the situation.

"It's in there," Dad said, pointing to the spot on the frame where the cable had disappeared. "It snapped up at the handlebar and now we can't get at it."

Andrea eyed the bike, before waving off my father and muttering to the other man in Italian. "He says he's got it," the owner translated. "Come back in an hour."

Dad took another long look at the bike and then back at Andrea. He shook his head and left the shop. "That guy has absolutely no idea what he is doing," he said. "I mean, he's wearing a scarf! What bike mechanic wears a scarf?"

We sat for cappuccinos at an open-air cafe in a nearby piazza. Attentive waiters in black ties floated from table to table. We ordered a couple of biscotti and watched pigeons fly in formation from one shady perch to another. I closed my eyes and basked in the sun. Then my phone buzzed in my pocket—a text message from my mother: *Call me.* I dialed her up.

"Hey, Ma, how's it going?"

"Where are you guys now?" she asked.

"We're in Rome. Waiting for my bike to get fixed."

"Is Dad with you?"

"Yeah, he's right here. Having coffee. Why, what's up?"

"No, nothing . . . Papa is not doing well." I mouthed the news to Dad. He looked off.

Mom continued, "He hasn't eaten anything in days. I'm taking the week off to go down there and help him." Since we'd left the States, hospice care had brought in a hospital bed for Papa that was now set up in my grandparents' living room. Papa hated it. He hated having nurses poke and prod him. He hated that he no longer had control over his own life.

"So what are you thinking?" I asked.

"We're going to move Papa in with us," she said. "He's taken a couple falls, and because your grandmother doesn't have the strength to pick him up off the floor, she's been calling the fire department for help. Hospice thinks he's becoming a liability."

"What should we do?" I asked. "Should we come home?"

"You guys need to decide that for yourselves," she said. "I mean, he could hang on like this for weeks or months." I looked over to Dad. "We neither know the time nor the hour," my mother said, quoting scripture. "Why don't you give Papa a call?"

"Okay, we will," I said. "But what are *you* thinking?"

"Well, when you and Dad get home, I think you guys should drive down the Cape and transport him to our house. Otherwise we're going to need to get an ambulance." My mother worried that Papa would think he was moving out of his house for good. She suggested we present it to him like it was only temporary, until he got his strength back, then we could return him home. I agreed with this general plan.

I handed the phone over to Dad so they could talk, and I mulled the news. *We could easily hop on a plane here in Rome and get back*, I thought. *But then what? We sit at his bedside and wait for him to die? Papa wouldn't want that.* I watched my father as he heard the news for himself. He'd been handling grief in his own way, which is to say, not outwardly handling it at all. Before we left for Italy, when conversations about my grandfather's final wishes were broached, Dad grew uneasy. While he never said as much, I thought that my father struggled to accept Papa's mortality in part because it would force Dad to acknowledge his own. Dad depended on control for his sanity, and control over the end of life was beyond his reach.

"He's going to hate this," Dad said, after saying goodbye to Mom. "He's not going to want to live with us."

We didn't talk much on the walk back to the bike shop. When we entered, we found a much different scene than before. Andrea was sitting on a piece of cardboard, his scarf wrinkled and undone. Little wrenches were scattered around him, and beads of sweat had collected on his bald head. The lenses of his glasses were fogged. The shop owner was yelling into the phone. "This isn't going to be done for a week," he snarled at us, pressing the phone to his shoulder. "We don't have the parts to fix this. We need to order them."

Dad and I looked down at the bike. Wires were splayed out in every direction. This once sleek, clean machine now looked like shrapnel from an exploded piano. It was in worse shape than when we left it an hour earlier. "What do you mean, you need to order parts?" Dad asked. "It's just one wire." The shopkeeper turned his back on my father and continued to yell into the phone. Andrea stared down between his legs in defeat. Dad lowered himself to the carcass that was my bike. "Jeez," he muttered.

The shop owner returned from the back room. "Is this bike yours?" he asked.

"No, we rented them in Florence."

"Florence? Well, I suggest you return it to Florence. We can't get the part for at least a week."

"Forget it," I huffed. "Grazie, grazie. Let's get out of here, Dad." I snatched the bike and wheeled it out into the street, feeling totally defeated. "We're not going back to Florence. I'll pedal the rest of the way with one gear if I have to, but I'm not turning back now." I kicked every rock I saw on the long walk back to the old woman's apartment.

Dad tried to buoy my spirits. "Let's go back and grab a coffee," he said. "We'll figure it out."

"What's there to figure out?" I snapped. "This bike is a fucking piece of shit."

"Robbie, it's a bike . . . the simplest machine in the world. We'll find someone who can fix it. C'mon, let's get someone to take a picture of us for Mom . . . I think that's the Vatican." He was laying the resiliency butter thick on my burnt toast. We enlisted a tourist to take a photo of us standing with the domes of Rome in the background. He handed the camera back to me after taking the shot. I studied the image and was shocked at what I saw. Dad and I were both emaciated. Our shirts hung loosely off our shoulders and our pants appeared comically baggy.

When we got back to the apartment, I bit the bullet and emailed the bike shop back in Florence for advice. I didn't want to waste any more time with scarf-wearing mechanics. They suggested a mechanic on the outskirts of Rome: Cicli Rossi.

"Place is twenty miles away," I said, complaining to Dad.

He sprawled out on the bed beside me and pulled on his readers to look at the map. "That's cool," he said. "At least we'll get a ride in."

THE NOW FAMILIAR RITUAL of donning my cycling kit soothed some of my frustrations. We set off into the heat of afternoon traffic, the route leading us around busy roundabouts, along three-lane thoroughfares, and through congested intersections. Dad and I had mastered the forms of bike sign language, pointing out glass in the street, potholes, and sewer drains. I slapped my hip to indicate cars pulling out and clenched my fist when I was coming to stop. For an hour and a half, we flowed through traffic like two trained assassins.

"I think that's it right there, Dad," I hollered back.

"Can't be."

"Yeah, Cicli Rossi—that's it. See the sign?"

"What's a bike shop doing out here?" The shop was located in a strip mall in what felt like the hairy, sweaty armpit of Rome. The kind of place you'd expect to find the overflow lot of a used car dealership or a cheap nail salon.

"This should be interesting," I said. A bell clinked against the door as we walked in. A late-middle-aged woman was on the phone at the front desk, her olive-black hair wrapped up in a tornado held together with a pencil. "Un momento," she said, tapping her long red fingernails on the counter.

We smiled and proceeded to click and clack around the bike shop in our cycling cleats. Classic steel frames hung from the rafters. The walls were covered in framed cycling jerseys, dated photos, and yellowed newspaper clippings. WD-40 wafted in the air. In the back corner of the shop, an old man sat hunched over a wheel. Surrounded by tools and tires and tubes hung on pegs, he made a few adjustments to the spokes and raised the wheel to his eye. The bike was an antique clunker, something a grandmother might ride to go fetch bread for dinner, and yet the wizened mechanic was giving it his full attention. He didn't even notice us walk in.

I turned back to the photos and news clippings on the wall. They radiated the delightful nostalgia of the golden era of Italian cycling. No helmets. Simple frames. Cyclists smoking cigarettes. Spare tires across their chests. There were photos of all the greats: Eddy Merckx. Fausto Coppi. It was like a bicycling hall of fame, a museum, a tribute to the legends of yore. My father's man cave on steroids. Among all the photos and news clippings, there was one man, one face, who kept appearing.

"Alo," a young man called over. He wore sweatpants and a frumpy green sweatshirt. He extended his meaty hand for me to shake. "Marco—how can I help?"

I walked the bike over to him. "The cable to my back derailleur snapped," I said. "And we can't—"

He waved me back to his workshop. "No problem," he said.

I looked back to find the older man still transfixed with the wheel and then followed my new friend Marco. He was probably in his early thirties, with a bulky build that was hard to picture balancing on a bike—but *man* did he know his way around one. He lifted my bike up on a workstand and swiftly peeled off the tape left behind by the scarfed wonder. Marco deftly fished out the severed cable and tossed it in a bin. Pivoting back to his workbench, he reached for a spool of cable, eyed the length, and snipped it with a pair of pliers. He fed the wire into the frame, pinching it at the other end, and drawing it out. Marco was a vision of efficiency and expertise, a cross between a concert pianist and an Indy car pit crew.

"Tulio Rossi," Dad said, excitedly. "The guy who owns this place is Tulio Rossi."

"Who is Tulio Rossi?" I whispered.

"A legend. I've been reading some of the articles on these walls. Or trying to read them anyway—most are in Italian. It looks like he rode in the Tour de France and the Giro d'Italia. He even won a stage in the Giro!"

"Really?"

"Yeah, go check out the photos."

I left Marco with my bike and reexamined the clippings on the walls. "Secondo Successo Italiano al Giro per merito di un Certo Signor Rossi" read one clip. "Second Italian success in the Giro thanks to a certain Mr. Rossi." From what I could gather, Tulio Rossi was born in Rome and had a celebrated cycling career as a *domestique*. Like worker bees, *domestiques* did all the heavy lifting for a cycling team. They shuttled water bottles and food from the team car to the front of the pack. They were set out on grueling missions to catch breakaways and reel them back in. They suffered for the sake of the team, doing everything they could to try and get their leader into the yellow jersey. At the end of his career, Rossi rode for Bianchi, the legendary Italian cycling team of Fausto Coppi. Continuing to scan the clippings, I came across the crown jewel of Rossi's career. He won a stage of the 1973 Giro d'Italia. For a *domestique*, winning a stage in the Giro was like coming off the bench and throwing a no-hitter in the World Series. He'd never have to buy another drink in his life.

"That's him," Dad said. "Tulio—that's him over there." He gestured to the old man working on the clunker.

"*That's* him?"

"Yeah, look at the photos."

I studied the old man and then looked back at the photos on the walls. Same crooked nose. Same bushy black eyebrows. "You're right, that is him."

"Here you go," Marco said, wheeling my bike back into the main part of the shop. "You're all set." The wheels clicked smoothly and the bike gleamed good as new.

"Amazing. You fixed it," I said. "Dad, check it out." My father peered into the back room where the cycling legend continued to work away. I'd never seen him so starstruck. "Dad?"

He looked over. "Marco," he said. "Can we . . . can we get a picture with him?"

"Il mio papà?"

"That's your father?" he asked.

"Sì."

"Wow, well, yeah. Can we take a photo with your father?"

"Sì," Marco said, clearly accustomed to this request, and walked back to his father's end of the shop. "Papa." The old man finally looked up from the wheel and back out to Dad and me. We shifted around awkwardly like a couple of fanboys. He waved to Marco, stood up, and walked toward us, grabbing a rag to clean his hands. His back was permanently hunched from spending most of his life crouched in the drops. "Ciao," he said, extending a bony hand to my Dad, who took it and shook excitedly.

"Sorry to bother you," Dad said, "but can we take a photo with you?"

Tulio looked blankly to his son for a translation. "Vogliano fare una foto," Marco said. The legend smirked coyly. He reached over to the wall and pulled down one of the framed photos. He handed it to my father with a mischievous grin.

"Allora," he said. "Una foto."

"No, no . . . a photo *with you*!" Dad laughed. He was kidlike in his excitement.

The old champion chuckled and pulled us under his arms, smiling while Marco snapped the photo. My father beamed ear to ear and even had some tears in his eyes. "Can you believe this?" he gushed out loud. As we stood there mugging for the camera with this cycling legend, I glanced down at the photo in Tulio's hand. He looked familiar. Narrowing my gaze, I immediately recognized the cyclist in the photo: Gino Bartali.

CHAPTER 15

Real heroes are others, those who have suffered in their soul, in their heart, in their spirit, in their mind, for their loved ones. Those are the real heroes. I'm just a cyclist.

—Gino Bartali

Ever since landing in Florence a week earlier, the scenes of Gino Bartali's life were never far from my mind. I kept picturing the McConnons' descriptions in *Road to Valor* of the brute-faced Bartali muscling his way up the climbs that were laying waste to my father and me. We pedaled along some of the same dusty stretches where the Florentine champion had trained. On these timeless roads, it wasn't hard to imagine Bartali zipping by in goggles and a silk jersey, spare tires across his chest and his wavy black hair hidden beneath a BARTALI cap.

But beyond the bike, I was most intrigued by who Gino Bartali became during World War II. In the prime of his cycling career, he was forced into military service along with hundreds of thousands of Italians in the 1930s. Already fighting a war of expansion in North Africa, Mussolini signed the Pact of Steel with Hitler in May of 1939, aligning with the Nazis and dragging Italian soldiers into battles around the world. Italian forces fought by air in the Battle of Britain, by land on the Eastern Front, and by sea in the Atlantic, the Mediterranean, the Indian Ocean, and the Red and Black Seas—all on the wrong side of history.

Fortunately for Bartali, he was assigned as a military messenger in Italy and convinced his superiors to allow him to deliver his missives from place to place on his bicycle, instead of on a motorcycle. He even competed in occasional races held in Italy during the war's early years, but he soon realized that Mussolini was only holding the competitions as propaganda to distract Italians from Fascism's impending collapse.

Many Italians came to hate Mussolini and Fascism. He'd dragged them into a war that killed tens of thousands of their countrymen and strangled their economy. So when the Allied Forces invaded Sicily in July 1943, Italians rejoiced and greeted the British and American soldiers as liberators. Mussolini was removed from power and taken prisoner in a ski resort in the Apennine Mountains. Italian soldiers deserted their posts. Among them was Bartali, who returned to his wife in Florence, where he planned on waiting out the rest of the war.

But the Nazis weren't giving up on Mussolini so quickly. In September of 1943, Nazi paratroopers freed Il Duce from his makeshift prison and returned him to Berlin. Hitler invaded Italy from the north and halted the Allied advance just below Rome in Monte Cassino. Occupying everything to the north, the Nazis rounded up thousands of Jews in Italy and shipped them off to concentration and extermination camps in Central and Eastern Europe. Mussolini was returned to power as a puppet of Nazi Germany, and Italian troops were ordered back into service.

Bartali refused to return. Instead, he and his wife fled to the countryside, where he heeded a different call of service. Around the time the Nazis began rounding up Jews in Italy, Bartali was approached by an old friend, Cardinal Elia Dalla Costa. Widely thought to be next in line for the papacy, Dalla Costa had presided over Bartali's wedding during the war and had a long history of resisting the Nazis. During Hitler's first grand tour of Florence in the 1930s, Dalla Costa denied Hitler access to his churches and refused to hang swastikas from his steeples. When the Nazis occupied Italy in 1943, his resistance became legendary—and Gino Bartali became one of his chief coconspirators.

Cardinal Dalla Costa collaborated with the Delegation for the Assistance of Jewish Emigrants (DELASEM). When the Nazis seized control of Italy, DELASEM became like the Underground Railroad for sheltering Jews and sneaking them out of Italy. Florence became the epicenter of the Jewish rescue effort. Jews had been living in Florence for more than six hundred years, making it one of the oldest Jewish communities in Italy. But those hiding in Florence weren't only Italian Jews. Jewish refugees had flooded into Italy from Germany, France, Yugoslavia, and elsewhere in Europe as the Holocaust raged. For a time, Jews were smuggled into Switzerland or out to sea by way of the Port of Genoa, but when the Nazis occupied the country, Jews in Italy were trapped. Many went into hiding and received aid from Catholic leaders like Cardinal Dalla Costa, as well as a number of other courageous Italians.

Critical for their survival were fake identifications. If Jews were caught by the Gestapo, papers identifying them as non-Jews were the last line of defense to prevent them from being shipped to Auschwitz. To aid the Jews, Cardinal Dalla Costa hatched a plan with a Franciscan priest from Assisi to start counterfeiting identifications. The IDs would be transported back to the Jews hiding in Florence by none other than Gino Bartali.

Without telling a soul, Bartali smuggled false IDs in the frame of his bicycle in 1943. In Florence he rolled up photos and information of Jews needing false identifications and slid them into the tube of his bike frame under his seat. He set off on the 110-mile ride to Assisi. Relying on his international fame, Bartali slipped through Nazi and Fascist checkpoints by claiming that he was on a training ride. Because he wasn't carrying any-thing but a water bottle, the soldiers didn't stop him—other than asking for an autograph. Seventy miles south of Florence on these smuggling rides, Bartali always made a pit stop at the train station in Terontola, where he bellied up to the bar in the cafe and ordered a sandwich and espresso. Word that the world-famous cyclist was in the station drew flocks of cycling fans, passengers, and soldiers to the cafe. Bartali played to the crowd, signing autographs and telling tales about his past victories. The whole scene was a strategic ruse. Bartali was creating a diversion to distract Nazi and Fascist soldiers while fleeing Jews switched trains. When the trains left the station, so did Bartali, continuing on to Assisi.

In Assisi, Bartali met with the priest who had convinced a local printer and his son to assume the extremely dangerous business of forg-ing identifications for Jews. To create the IDs, the printers used names and birthdates of non-Jews living in the parts of Italy under Allied control. Although not subjected to the same pressure as in Florence, Assisi was occupied by the Nazis, and the father and son had to be vigilant in their secrecy. When their resolve was tested, the duo was emboldened by the knowledge that they worked alongside the great Gino Bartali in this covert mission to save lives.

After collecting the fake identifications, Bartali turned around and pedaled back to Florence, where Jews awaited these lifesaving pieces of paper. Occasionally he would hand-deliver the IDs to their grateful recipients. Even after his work was done and he stowed his bike, Bartali couldn't breathe a sigh of relief. His efforts to save Jews went beyond the road and into his own home.

WHILE WORKING AT THE bike shop in Florence as a young boy, Bartali became friends with a man named Giacomo Goldenberg. Sixteen years older than Bartali, Goldenberg immigrated to Italy from the Russian empire. He had lifted himself by his bootstraps, quickly mastering Italian and emerging as a successful businessman. There was just one problem: Goldenberg was Jewish. When Mussolini implemented his Leggi Razziali, Goldenberg and his family suffered under its restrictions. Goldenberg was stripped of his business, his son was kicked out of school, and he was eventually arrested and sent to an internment camp where he remained until Mussolini was removed from power.

When the Nazis occupied Italy, a much more lethal threat seized Goldenberg and his family. The Nazis and their Fascist collaborators ramped up their hunt for Jews of all ages, descending upon schools and retirement homes alike. The Goldenbergs could no longer simply keep their heads down and avoid the Fascists—they needed to be hidden. That was when Goldenberg's old friend Gino Bartali came to the rescue. For the remainder of the war, Bartali hid the Goldenberg family in his home outside of Florence. He scrounged together rations in the war-starved city to keep the Goldenbergs fed while hidden from sight. At the height of the Nazi occupation, the Goldenbergs lived in Bartali's cavernous, one-hundred-square-foot basement, where the family of four stayed twenty-four hours a day, sharing a double bed and trembling through Allied bombings and Nazi raids.

Life was no less precarious for Bartali, whose wife was expecting their second child at the time. He continued to keep his wartime missions secret from her, giving no explanation for where he was going days at a time on his bicycle. Along with smuggling false identifications and sheltering the Goldenbergs, Bartali performed reconnaissance missions on his bike, scouting Nazi checkpoints during each ride. He shared that information with the rescuers smuggling Jews across the border. Despite barely being able to feed his own family, Bartali sent food and supplies to the Vatican, where war refugees were being sheltered. Any or all of these actions could be punishable by death, if he was caught.

One day in 1944, Bartali was summoned to the Fascist offices of Major Mario Carità. Carità fashioned himself as Italy's version of Heinrich Himmler, a certified psychopath who orchestrated the Nazi's extermination camps. Carità and his band of collaborators were infamous for horrifically torturing anyone who resisted the Fascists or the Nazis. They ripped off people's body parts with pliers, whipped their skin until it turned to pulp, and attached them to electric shocks. As the McConnons described, at dinner these masochists often bound their captives in the corner of the room and tortured them simply for entertainment—while a pianist drowned out their screams by playing Napolitano tunes. Carità's office became known among Florentines as Villa Triste: the House of Sorrow.

These stories were well known to Bartali when he heeded Carità's call and entered the House of Sorrow, anxiously fearing that they'd discovered his ID smuggling or sheltering of the Goldenbergs. The Fascists brought Bartali into an interrogation room in the dungeons, where Carità was waiting. He had intercepted Bartali's mail, which included a letter from the Vatican thanking him for his help. Pointing to the letter, Carità accused Bartali of sending guns to the anti-Fascist resistance in Rome. The cyclist pleaded that he had only sent food and supplies, but Carità called him a liar and locked him in a cell for three days.

On the third day, Bartali was brought back into the interrogation room where he was submitted to the same line of questions, but he didn't budge. Carità was furious. Just as he was about to begin torturing the cyclist, another voice emerged in the room. As luck would have it, it was one of Bartali's former commanders from his time as an army messenger. The commander vouched for Bartali, insisting that he was telling the truth. Reluctantly, the bloodthirsty Carità let Bartali go.

Although he escaped with his life, Bartali suffered much loss during the war. He was addled with post-traumatic stress disorder from his covert bike missions and spent all of his savings trying to feed his family as well as the Goldenbergs. Bartali struggled to nourish his pregnant wife and keep her safe amid the air raids. As the bombing intensified, Bartali moved his young family out of Florence, planning to wait out the rest of his wife's pregnancy. But she went into labor too early and lost the baby. Heartbroken, Bartali buried his unborn son next to his younger brother. His heroism saved the lives of hundreds of Jews, but he could do little to protect those he loved most.

PERHAPS MOST REMARKABLE ABOUT Gino Bartali's story was that for most of his life, he never told a soul about his bravery during the war—not even his own son. "Good is something you do, not something you talk about," his son remembered Bartali saying. "Some medals are pinned to your soul, not to your jacket." It was only after stories about Cardinal Dalla Costa and the counterfeiting ring emerged in the 1970s that people learned about Bartali's heroism during the war. But even then, he refused to talk about it. In fact, when a group of filmmakers set out to shoot a documentary about his work with Dalla Costa and the forgers in Assisi, Bartali threatened to sue. As the McConnons explained in *Road to Valor*, Bartali didn't want his status as a cyclist to serve as fodder to exaggerate his role in the war. "I don't want to appear to be a hero," he said. "Heroes are those who died, who were injured, who spent many months in prison."

Pedaling through Italy with Gino Bartali on my mind made me wonder how many other untold stories of heroism were out there. Who else quietly wore pins of bravery on their souls while their lips were too modest to utter a word about their deeds? Bartali was a world-famous cyclist who captured the imagination and adoration of thousands. It was only a matter of time until his heroism would be known. But what about the average Italian who acted heroically during wartime? Would their stories ever see the light of day?

CHAPTER 16

Therefore keep watch, because you do not know the day or the hour.

—Matthew 25:13

My grandmother's voice sounded distant through the phone, tired and defeated. "Papa is hanging on for you guys," she said. "He keeps asking, 'Do you think I'll live long enough to see them again?'"

"Of course, he will," I said. "Of course, he will."

"I don't know—he's not doing good," she said. "It's so sad to see him like this. I don't know what to do. I just don't know what to . . . " Her voice trailed off. I looked over to my father sitting across from me at a cafe on the streets of Rome. He studied my face as I spoke with my grandmother.

"He's been asking about you guys every day," she said. "Asking about the village. Are you there now?"

"No, not yet. We're in Rome still. We'll start heading to the village tomorrow. Is he there?"

"Who?"

"Papa . . . can I talk to him?" I asked.

"Hold on." I heard her padding across the hardwood floor in her slippers. "Joe . . . Joe! *Here.* It's Robbie."

"Who?"

"*Robbie* . . . on the phone."

There was some rustling over the receiver and Papa finally spoke. "Robbie?" His voice was dry and meek as a whisper.

"Hey, Papa . . . how you doing?"

There were a few seconds of silence while he processed the question. "Getting there," he said flatly. "Getting there. Just trying to get stronger."

"Yeah?"

"Yeah, just got to get organized, know you? Get things organized."

I wasn't sure what to say. I certainly wasn't going to bring up the fact that we would be moving him to my parents' house when we got home.

"How's the trip going?" he asked.

"It's been incredible, Papa, absolutely incredible. We're in Rome. Been here for a couple days, but we're going to start heading to the village tomorrow. Headed to San Donato."

"Wonderful. I've been trying to imagine it," he said. "I wonder, I wonder if there's olive groves still there. I remember hearing about the olive groves and the olive oil."

"I'm sure there is, but we'll make sure to let you know when we find out."

There were a couple more seconds of silence and then he asked, "Are you taking care of your father?"

I looked over to Dad. "Yeah, Papa, we're taking care of each other." My voice caught in my throat. "Actually Papa, he's right here. He wants to talk to you." I handed the phone over to my father.

"Hi!" Dad said with an excited burst. "You should see it. It's been amazing. This place is absolutely incredible. Absolutely incredible." He flooded Papa with highlights. All the big meals. The hills. My bike breaking down. Meeting Tulio Rossi. On and on, my father gushed breathlessly like a kid who had just gotten home from summer camp. "And then, he took a photo with us! Can you believe it? Tulio Rossi, a tour champion in the middle of Rome, with us! Absolutely incredible."

My father paused, waiting for Papa's response. His gleeful face softened as he struggled to hear the weak voice on the other end of the line. His eyes lowered and studied the contents on the table. "Yes, well, it just takes time," my father said soberly. "You're going to get stronger. It just takes time." Dad's shoulders slumped slightly. The sad reality of Papa's situation broke through. "You will, you will," he said. "You just need to rest. We'll call you again when we get to the village." He paused, listening carefully. "Yes . . . yes. I'll tell him . . . Okay."

Dad looked up at me, then back to the table. "I love you, Dad," he said, his face breaking with emotion. "I'll see you again soon."

IT WAS HIGH TIME we got the hell out of Rome. Our minds and bodies were itching to be back on our bikes and back on the road. But before we could go anywhere, I needed to figure out where exactly we were going. Sitting on the edge of my bed, I pulled up the GPS on my phone and scanned the map. My great-grandfather's village of San Donato Val di Comino was about 115 miles southeast of Rome in the region of Lazio. We could probably get there in a couple of days, taking back roads through national parks and making a stop at the town of Colleferro before our final big push into San Donato. I zoomed in on the tiny village nestled deep in the foothills of the Apennines on the outskirts of Abruzzo National Park. *What would we find there?* I wondered. *Who would we find there?*

Dad methodically stuffed his tiny backpack, folding each item of clothing and vacuum-sealing it in special ziplock bags by squeezing the air out. He kicked off his ninja shoes and cinched them to the side of his backpack. He loved how light we were traveling, delighted in the simplicity of it all. Other than how hard it was to keep things clean, not having to think about what to wear was a luxury we both appreciated.

I pulled on my spandex bike shorts and strapped on my cleats. I reached blindly into the closet for my jersey and yanked it on. *Weird*, I thought, *this feels tighter than usual.* I zipped it up to my chin—and immediately gagged. The thick stench of foreign body odor rushed into my nostrils and grabbed me by the tonsils. I keeled over and dry-heaved like a cat choking on a hairball.

"What! What! What's up?" Dad yelled from the bathroom. I continued to yack, my eyes watering as I held back my breakfast. Dad hopped out of the bathroom. "Yo! What's going on? Are you sick?"

I ripped the jersey off and threw it at him. "That's yours!" I gasped. "*Ugh*. Disgusting. That smells awful!"

He broke into a hysterical cackle. "I'm, I'm sor . . . sorry," he said.

I fought off waves of nausea for a few minutes. It's one thing to smell your own body odor, but taking a giant whiff of my father's week-old sweat rag was like huffing smelling salts in a sulfur factory. "Guess that didn't make it into yesterday's wash, huh?" I asked.

"Didn't think it would dry in time."

The little old lady led us down to the basement of the apartment building where we had locked our bikes and bid us farewell. Dad still didn't trust her but thanked her for the hospitality all the same. The route I plotted through Rome took us past some of the city's historic sites. We had done little by way of sightseeing, skipping headliners like the Sistine Chapel and the Vatican, so I made sure our route out gave us at least a better sense of the city. Through Villa Borghese we rolled around the Piazzale Napoleone and into the cobblestoned Piazza del Popolo. Via del Corso led us to the Altare della Patria, built in honor of Victor Emmanuel II, the first king of a unified Italy, and then on to the Colosseum (formally known as the Flavian Amphitheater).

As we neared the ancient ruins, swarms of tourists forced us off our bikes. They looked like cattle being herded along in a line while a guide shouted fun facts into a microphone attached to their headsets. Even with the dramatic backdrop of the Colosseum, with its history so alive in the stone, the scene was repulsive. It had a tacky carnival feel that was so far removed from the Italy we had witnessed by bike.

"Let's get the hell out of here," Dad said.

I snapped a few photos of him walking by the Colosseum, and we slung our legs back over our bikes and pedaled happily out of the grips of Rome. We hadn't seen the Sistine Chapel ceiling, painted by Michelangelo. Hadn't received the Pope's blessing or even set foot in the Colosseum. But we were content with our time in Rome. My bike was spinning like a top, my knee felt bearable, and our ultimate objective lay on the road ahead.

Four miles outside of Rome, we returned to the hushed world we had so missed. The streets got smaller and smaller until we pedaled up narrow rock roads again. Despite the unrelenting bumping, we let our guards down and picked our heads up to take in the surroundings. The time off the bike had done wonders for my knee, which no longer ticked as I pedaled.

The cobblestones led us into the Parco della Caffarella, where we passed by archaeological sites with tombs, which, I read later, dated back to the second century.

The ruins reminded me, once again, just how ancient Italy is. Compared to Europe, the United States was still in diapers. Italians would probably think nothing of leveling a so-called historic house back home for kindling. When held alongside the long history of Europe, the United States was still a cultural experiment. This view of American history extended to my understanding of my own family history. I traced both sides of my family back to "the boat"—one branch from Italy and the other from Ireland. Any history predating my great-grandparents reaching Ellis Island was completely unknown to me. Passing these historical sites only reminded me that countless dominoes had delivered my great-grandparents to the United States—a history I hoped to discover.

FIFTEEN MILES SOUTHEAST OF Rome, we entered Parco Regionale dei Castelli Romani, a regional park where Italian families hiked, biked, and paddled around the emerald blue waters of Lake Albano. The smooth blacktop circled halfway around the lake and rose up long switchbacks for three miles, ascending more than a thousand vertical feet.

With hundreds of miles and thousands of vertical feet in our wakes, climbing had become our new normal. We no longer grimaced and huffed through each pedal stroke, but rather we settled in and got comfortable as we conquered each switchback. I had pedaled more than a hundred miles with only one gear, so having full access to all of them almost felt like cheating. Our bodies had also developed a capacity for unleashing power that we hadn't had before leaving the United States. I no longer felt like an overstuffed sausage in my cycling kit. I felt lean and strong. My body had been transformed into a calorie-burning machine. There was a streamlined connection between food and energy. Whatever I ate—pasta, pizza, cannoli—got tossed directly into the burning furnace, delivering an immediate jolt of energy.

The climb leveled out and we each bought a Coke at a little stand to wash down a banana. The real treat was the descent ahead. Ten miles of nothing but coasting. We each zippered into a light jacket, clicked in, and started to roll. Few experiences are more satisfying than soaking up the endorphins of finishing a climb by coasting downhill for miles at a time. That's when your mind wanders. The road sent us into the woods, where there were no cars, no houses, and no sign of civilization. We were out there.

When you're pedaling on far-off roads for hours at a time, you start seeing things. A growling stomach conjures a mirage of a pizzeria with a jolly, mustachioed man giving out free slices. A parched mouth pictures a roadside bar serving you ice-cold beers. Most of all, when you're tired and dragging, you dream of the day's final destination magically appearing right around the next bend. But on this hilly descent the hallucinations took a whole different form.

The first woman appeared halfway down the hill. Standing on the side of the road, she was talking on a cell phone and wearing a tiny lipstick-red miniskirt. She couldn't have looked more out of place. Behind her were twisted trees and a dense forest. We sped down the hill in the middle of nowhere, and yet as I neared on my bike, she stared blankly at me as if waiting for a bus. *What a weird spot to be waiting*, I thought.

No sooner had I stopped thinking about that woman than I spotted another woman down the hill ahead. She wore a black tank top and skin-tight, flesh-toned leggings. *What is going on here?* I thought. Flying down the hill toward her, I realized, *Holy shit, those aren't leggings!* The woman was naked from the waist down. She had her bulbous rear end facing the road, and as I passed in a flash, she began to shake it.

What was that? Before I could come to grips with what I had just seen, another woman appeared. And then another and another. This remote road, fifteen miles from the closest town, was lined with prostitutes, each with their pants pulled down below their dimpled bums. Some of the women shook and gyrated the goods, while others just stood there like they'd literally been caught with their pants down.

"Can you believe this?" Dad yelled from behind me. I shook my head. When the initial shock and hilarity wore off, a pang of sadness rose up in me for these women. They were so young, maybe in their late teens and early twenties, and looked to be of African descent. They stood next to dirty old mattresses among scattered heaps of trash that some degenerate had flung out his car window. *How discarded they must feel,* I thought. In the shadows behind them, I could make out men lurking in the trees.

When we reached our hotel an hour or so later in the town of Colleferro, I did some research on my phone into who these women might be. I discovered an article in *The Guardian* investigating the sex slave and human trafficking trade in Italy. Nigerians first started coming to work as laborers in Italy in the 1980s. By the 1990s the work ran out, and many of the women were forced to turn to prostitution. The article explained that the mafia and Nigerian drug-smuggling gangs saw how profitable this venture was and recruited Nigerian women.

When Nigerians took to sea aboard rafts in the 2000s, seeking asylum, mafia and Nigerian gangs gained a steady stream of women to prey upon. They'd snatch them from government-funded migrant camps and threaten to rape them if they refused to become prostitutes. Other women were recruited directly from Nigeria by so-called "sponsors" who would pay their way to Italy to work jobs in beauty parlors. When the women met their sponsor in Italy, it turned out to be a pimp or a madam. The women would spend the next five years paying off their debts by working as prostitutes. When the debt was finally paid off, many of the women didn't know any other way to survive and had little choice but to remain prostitutes.

The article explained how government corruption had been at the core of the sex slave trade. The mafia infiltrated Rome's municipal government and was leaching money earmarked for the migrant camps. In 2014 a police investigation exposed this despicable abuse. The police had wiretapped one of the mob bosses and recorded him boasting, "Do you have any idea how much I earn on immigrants? They're more profitable than drugs."

The whole story was deeply upsetting. This ugly reality stood in stark contrast to the idyllic view of Italy that beat in my heart throughout this journey. Rolling through charming stone towns, where the old men sat peacefully in the piazza while women hung the laundry out the windows overhead, it was easy to forget that dark history lurked in the corners of many of these areas.

CHAPTER 17

Not I, nor anyone else can travel that road for you. You must travel it by yourself.

It is not far. It is within reach. Perhaps you have been on it since you were born, and did not know. Perhaps it is everywhere—on water and land.

—Walt Whitman

The Apennine Mountains emerged through the afternoon haze, 485 miles south of Florence. Even in the heat of early spring, smatterings of snow clung to the highest reaches of these hulking peaks. This was the lower third of the range, which began up by the Gulf of Genoa and snaked nearly a thousand miles south to right above Sicily. In the foreground, terraced green foothills showed signs of civilization with their neatly plotted olive groves surrounding red-roofed buildings and crisp white churches at the very top. Somewhere beyond these foothills, nestled in the crook of the Apennines, was San Donato Val di Comino. Though my father and I were still miles away, this first glimpse of our final destination made one fact abundantly clear: we were descendants of mountain people.

That we were so naturally drawn to high-altitude adventures like skiing and rock climbing made sense. The mountains were in our blood. This tour had plugged us into our genetic hardwiring for climbing. From the early hills of Florence, we'd pedaled up almost enough vertical feet to reach the summit of Mount Everest—28,587 feet to be exact. Our initial suffering had gradually given way to strength. Now, as we mounted the foothills of San Donato, I couldn't think of a better way for us to arrive than by climbing.

"Oh man, look at that!" Dad shouted from behind. "That sign . . . look at that sign." Finally, we were almost there: SAN DONATO VAL DI COMINO—15 KILOMETERS.

Dad pulled over to the side of the road and hopped off his bike. "We should take a photo," he said, wading through the tall grass and reaching up toward the sign. "I can't believe it," he said, his eyes welling up with tears. "We're actually going to make it. I can't believe it."

We'd already slogged some sixty miles from Colleferro, but even as we approached the final hill to San Donato, I felt strong and energized. As did my father. In the distance above, I could barely make out stone buildings tucked into the green mountainside. Ominous clouds hung overhead, yet a beam of sunlight found its way through, illuminating the village in a way I could only think of as providential. *That must be it*, I thought. *Has to be.* The scene was too storybook to believe, but here I was, wide awake, sweat running down my legs, air expanding my lungs.

I allowed myself to feel excited. *We're actually going to make it,* I thought. *Lost, broken down, beaten up, and once defeated—we were going to make it!* Then the pessimist within me cleared his throat and piped up: *But what if the village is full of a bunch of assholes? What if this whole thing is a giant let-down? What if you learn something about your family that you wish you never knew?* I shook my head and reminded myself of the cliché: *It's about the journey, not the destination. Everything from here on is gravy.*

The road straightened for the final stretch into the village. Olive groves appeared to our right, made up of thick knotty trunks that were precisely aligned through the matted grass. *Papa was right. There are his olive gardens.* The village materialized ahead. San Donato was no longer a glowing dot on my phone, no longer a nondescript triangle of rooftops. The village now consisted of individual homes with shutters and doors with knockers. The first of these buildings reached out for us like a hand.

"Dad," I called back.

"Yo?"

"Take the lead. I want you to take us in." This was a homecoming for both of us, but in my heart I had wanted to do this whole trip for him. I had wanted to take him out of his comfort zone, bring him to Italy, and guide him to this place. We were nearing the straightaway, and it was his turn to lead.

"Absolutely not," he said. "You're leading us in. You got us here. You finish this."

I didn't argue. I nodded and continued uphill, through the open arms of the village and into its stony embrace. Two-story buildings came right up to the road, wedged tightly together to form a continuous wall of rock punctuated by heavy wooden doors. The road came over a hump, then opened up to a piazza dotted with cafe tables and four solemn trees rising up from the stone patio. I passed three old men hunched over playing cards at one of the tables. Another man in a fedora stood in the doorway of the cafe, smoking a cigarette.

Directly in the center of the piazza was a monument. An angel stood high atop a slab of granite, her head arched to the sky, one hand holding a shield and the other reaching out to the horizon. I rolled toward the monument, narrowing my eyes on the engraving at the angel's feet. My stomach dropped. *My God.* I eased on the brake, clicked my foot out from the pedal, and just stared. A lump lodged in my throat. My father pulled up alongside me.

"Look, look," I said. "Look at the name at the top of the monument."

Dad narrowed his eyes and his mouth slowly dropped open. "Oh my," his voice broke. COCUZZO was chiseled at the very top of the monument.

"Dad . . . we're home."

WE SAT AT ONE of the cafe tables, gazing at the monument and taking in our first sights and sounds of San Donato. Swallows were squeaking. The murmur of a soccer match drifted out from the cafe. A church bell tolled in the distance. A husband and wife sat on a stoop, smoking cigarettes and chatting, while their young daughter hopped around in front of them. An espresso machine screeched inside the cafe, followed by the clinking of spoons on saucers.

PREVIOUS: *Stephen descending the cobblestone streets outside Colleferro, Italy*
TOP: *Stephen at work in his hair salon*

TOP: *Papa in front of his pride and joy, before his father sold it* (Cocuzzo family photo)
RIGHT: *Three generations of Cocuzzo men* (Photo by Joshua Simpson)

TOP: *Stephen in Florence, enjoying the first of countless cups of coffee*
BOTTOM: *Stephen admiring the Arno River in Florence*

TOP: *Rob pretending not to be lost* **BOTTOM:** *View of the Tuscan hills just outside of San Casciano dei Bagni*

OPPOSITE: *Stephen cruising through the rolling hills of Tuscany on the second day*
ABOVE: *Rob preparing himself for more riding despite excruciating knee pain*

OPPOSITE: *Stephen approaching the Colosseum on their way out of Rome*
TOP: *Italian cycling legend Tulio Rossi poses with Stephen and Rob in his bike shop*
BOTTOM: *Rossi tinkering away in his shop on the outskirts of Rome*

TOP: *Entering San Donato for the first time* BOTTOM: *Stephen resting outside the B&B in San Donato*

TOP: *The rooftops of San Donato with the Apennines in the distance*
BOTTOM: *Some of the "San Donato sitcom" cast*

TOP: *Pasqualina Perrella saved the lives of a number of Jews during the Nazi occupation.*
BOTTOM: *The World War II monument in the heart of San Donato*

TOP: *Stephen fast asleep in the piazza of San Donato* BOTTOM: *Gaetano Cocuzzo explaining the Cocuzzo family tree*

Dal 1940 alla primavera del 1944 a San Donato fu internato dal regime fascista un gruppo di 28 ebrei stranieri che trovarono tra i cittadini accoglienza e condivisione.

Il 6 aprile 1944 sedici di essi vennero catturati dall'occupante nazista e dai collaboratori fascisti. Destinati al campo di sterminio di Auschwitz solo quattro fecero ritorno.

Sia ricordata tra le vittime la piccola Noemi Levi che non aveva compiuto i due anni.

6 aprile 2013

The monument in San Donato is dedicated to the Jewish people who lost their lives during the Nazi occupation, especially a young girl named Noemi Levi.

TOP: *Stephen speaking with Delia Roffo in the piazza* **BOTTOM:** *Via Orologio, the street where Rob's great-grandfather was born in San Donato* **NEXT PAGE:** *Rob and Stephen overlooking Florence from the Piazzale Michelangelo the day before returning to the United States*

"Coffee?" Dad asked.

"Absolutely." I started to get up, but he stopped me.

"I got it," he said. "Espresso?"

"Cappuccino," I said, sitting back down. "Thanks."

He reached into the back pocket of his jersey and pulled out a few sweat-soaked bills. "Be right back," he said.

As my father left the table, I was struck by the ease of his demeanor. He'd found the rhythm of the road, that pragmatic patience one develops while traveling abroad. He was no longer distressed by his inability to speak the language or navigate the unfamiliar cultural norms of Europe. He was no longer searching for creature comforts or routine, but rather seizing the foreign and the unknown. In a curious way I felt a deep sense of pride that I imagine may be reminiscent of what a father feels for a son.

At some point all children experience that moment when they realize their parents aren't perfect—they are flawed human beings like everybody else. This humanization of parents and their inevitable fall from grace is not a novel concept. But over these hundreds of miles with my father, I'd realized that another evolution takes place between children and parents. In caring for my father's well-being, I got a tiny glimpse into the stresses that must have weighed on him while raising me, leading me through a dangerous world while trying to prevent me from crashing.

This role reversal made me realize that just as a parent must accept a child for who they are, a child must accept a parent—warts and all. I had poked fun at so many of my father's idiosyncrasies over the years, yet when it came to my own quirks, he never questioned them. Not once. He never made me feel anything less than perfect. He was always there to throw more fuel onto my dreams and stoke my ambitions to a roaring blaze. As he neared the twilight of his life, it was my turn to affirm him for everything that he was and feed his fire for the rest of his days.

"Grazie mille," he called back into the cafe before returning to the table. "They're all very nice here."

The barista emerged shortly after him, balancing our coffees on saucers. She looked Eastern European, with pitch-black hair that was cropped just below her ears. She slid our coffees across the table and started speaking to my father in Italian. He looked up at her, nodding and smiling. "Okay, sounds good," he said. "Sounds good. Thank you. Grazie. Grazie."

"What was that all about?" I asked, after the woman left us. "You suddenly speak Italian?"

"I have no idea what she was saying, but while I was in there, I asked if she knew Delia Roffo. My friend Sergio's sister," he said. "I grew up with her in Brighton. She moved back here years ago."

"Oh yeah?"

"Yeah, so I was wondering if this woman knew her. Seems like she does. She kept repeating the name and pointing up the hill. Anyway, who knows? I haven't seen Delia in years, decades really. I don't even know what she looks like anymore."

We sat quietly sipping our coffee. Two finely dressed men stared suspiciously at us over their playing cards. *What a sight to see*, I thought. *Two scruffy, long-haired men in full-blown spandex. Perhaps a first for these parts.* Dad pulled his chair into a patch of sun. "I never thought I'd actually see this place," he said. "Never in my life." He crossed his fingers behind his head and leaned back. "That's it. From now on, I'm taking at least two weeks off a year and traveling."

"Is that right?" I said.

"Yeah, man. Your mother and me . . . we're going to be globetrotters."

"I love it."

"Maybe we'll come back here next year. Me, you, Jenny, and Mom."

"Sure, they can drive the support vehicle for when my bike breaks down." He laughed and took another sip of his coffee. "Seriously, Dad, that's what you guys should be doing. It's time to downshift."

"What do you mean?"

"I mean retirement."

He grimaced at the word. "I'll never retire. I'll be like Papa. Work till the day I die."

"That reminds me," I said, reaching into a secret pocket in my backpack. "We're going to need to find a place for this." I slid a 5 x 7 photo to him across the table. Dad picked it up and examined it: a photo of the three of us: Dad, Papa, and me. He didn't say anything, but wiped his eyes and nodded with a trembling smile.

Suddenly, a compact car screeched up to the curb. "Cocuzzo!" the driver called out. "Cocuzzo!" The woman pounced from her car and strode up to us in a flash. "Oh, the people, they're all talking!" she said. "Everybody's talking. They all know you're here!" She wrapped my father up in a hug. "Oh, Stephen, you haven't aged a day," she said, pushing him away and studying his face. "And this . . . this must be your son?"

I extended my hand, but she yanked me in for a hug. "So nice to meet you," she said. "I'm Delia." She pushed me out, sizing me up. "Oh, you look so much like your mother, doesn't he, Stephen? He does, doesn't he?"

Short and spunky, Delia Roffo had close-cropped hair and a mischievous smile. Her hands fluttered through the air as she spoke, energy radiating off every word. She had a Boston accent with Italian flare. "You guys must be starving," she said. "I'm bringing you home for some lunch. I live just up here. Come. Come."

"Delia!" the barista called out from the cafe.

"Oksana," Delia yelled back. "What the fah—" She broke off into Italian, then turned back to us. "Oksana called me. Said you guys were in town asking for me." The two went back and forth. Their animated banter was something to watch. There was so much action in their conversation. So much energy. Delia's hands waved through the air, her fingers pinched together. She talked so forcefully. If you didn't know any better, you might think she was arguing over a parking spot. "Cocuzzos," she said, pointing to my father and me.

"Fratelli?" the barista, Oksana, asked.

"She wants to know if you're brothers," Delia said, laughing. "No, padre e figlio."

"Oh," the woman nodded approvingly. "Bene bene." We waved back to her like two village idiots.

"But these guys haven't eaten," Delia said. "Not a bite. They must eat! I'm going to feed them. Oksana, addio addio." She turned to us. "Ready?"

"We have bicycles," my father said.

"That's what Oksana was saying. You came here on *bikes*? What the fuck? Take your bikes. Come, come."

We followed Delia up a steep and narrow walkway made up of countless sun-bleached stones. The intricate stonework of each home was bewildering, every piece fitting together seamlessly. San Donato appeared to be carved entirely out of rough-hewn rock that dated back thousands of years. The place felt biblically old.

"I'm just up ahead here," Delia said, charging up the incline. She looked to be in her mid-sixties, but she had a pep in her step that defied her years. She pushed open the wooden door to her home, revealing a tiny kitchen. "Come sit, sit," she said. "How 'bout some cheese and bread?"

"Really, you don't have to do anything," Dad said. "We're fine. We just had some coffee."

"No, no. You must eat. I insist. I only wish I knew you guys were coming. I would have had something ready for you. But you must come for dinner. I'm having you for dinner. That's it, forget it. We'll pick some wild asparagus. It grows just up there in the mountains. Oh, and we'll have some minestrone soup and some frittata. Do you eat rabbit? That's it, I'm cooking you some rabbit one of these nights. It will be wonderful." She sawed hunks of crusty bread with a knife, dealing slices onto plates. She pulled out a block of cheese. "You want some smoked salmon?"

"No, thank you. I don't eat fish," Dad said.

"No fish? You're like my little brother Sergio. No meat. No cheese. I mean, how do you live? How 'bout some wine?"

"I don't drink," he said.

"Jesus, Stephen, what are you, a saint? Robbie, wine?"

"No, thank you. I'm perfect with water," I said.

"You're like a couple of monks," Delia said, laughing easily. "Let's see what else I got here." She spun around her kitchen, pulling items out of the fridge and throwing a pan onto the stove. She dripped olive oil onto the pan and then a handful of greens.

"What's that?" I asked.

"Cicoria. Wild dandelion greens plucked from behind my house," she said. "You need to pick these right before they blossom or else they get too hard and they're no good." She stirred the *cicoria*. The hissing olive oil filled Delia's tiny apartment and softened the air. "Stephen, you must remember these from growing up."

"God, I haven't had it since I was a kid," Dad said. "My grandmother used to pick this in Brighton."

"You can't pick them back there anymore, unfortunately. The dogs pee on it. But here, you can still get it fresh."

Delia doled out the *cicoria* on our plates, along with a slab of veggie frittata that she pulled from the fridge. "The asparagus in the frittata is from up in the mountains," she said. "You can hike up there and pick it fresh. Wild asparagus. You need to be very careful up there, though, very careful. There's vipers in those mountains that can kill you." She returned the skillet to the stove and sat at the round table. She handed out some more bread. "Mangiate, mangiate," she said. "Eat, eat."

We devoured our dishes, savoring in the simple flavors. The kitchen offered just enough room for the table. The space was separate from her sleeping quarters, which she told us she accessed by walking outside and climbing a short flight of stone stairs. "Bought this apartment back in 1999 for five hundred dollars," she told us.

"Are you kidding me?" my father gasped.

"It's true, it's true," she said. "But I was born further up the mountainside. So where are you guys staying?" Delia asked between bites. "I'd say stay with me, but as you can see, I don't really have any space. I would love you to stay with me, but it's only a couch up there. Otherwise I would love it."

"Oh, no, that's totally okay," I said. "We really haven't figured out anything yet, but I know we passed a hotel down the street—"

"We can find something up here for you in the village. I mean, you want to be in the village, don't you? Down there you'd have to drive up, and you don't have a car. I mean, I guess you can bike up here, but I don't know . . . I don't know how you guys did that. How the hell did you bike here? From where?"

"From Florence," Dad said.

Delia nearly choked on her bread. "Florence? What are you, nuts?"

I looked at my father, still wearing his lime-green cycling kit, his hair exploding from the sides of his cycling cap. "Nuts?" I said. "Just look at us.

We're certifiable." We laughed, ecstatic to be here, eager for what lay ahead in this enchanting village.

Delia set her attention to finding us a place to stay. "Oh, let's go see your cousin Gaetano. He'll help us find something."

"Cousin?" I asked.

"Don't you know you have a cousin here? Gaetano Cocuzzo? He lives just down the way. He'll know something. Gaetano the carpenter. Good guy. They call him 'The King.' Loves Elvis."

We wolfed down the rest of our scrumptious lunch, and Delia led us back out into the village. The sun had dipped behind the mountains, and the air had turned crisp and cold. Everywhere I looked was stone, causing the temperature to drop a few more degrees in my mind. "Grab your bikes," Delia said. We headed to see Gaetano. "He speaks English."

We wheeled our bikes through another small piazza outside Delia's apartment and then down another tight alleyway lined by stone houses. "Gaetano lives just down here," she said, leading the way. "Do you mind if I call him?" I expected her to pull out her cell phone, but instead she just started yelling: "Gaetano! Gaetano!"

A woman popped her head out of a second-story window. "Delia, come va?"

"Gaetano?" Delia shouted back. "Where's Gaetano?" A heavy wooden door creaked open below and the King emerged wearing blue jeans.

"Allora, Delia," he said, wiping his hands on a rag. "Come va?"

"Gaetano, these are Cocuzzos," Delia said, pulling my father forward. "Your cousin, Stephen."

Gaetano sauntered up to us. He moved like Papa, slow and methodical and with a certain panache. Dad shook his hand and they studied each other's faces. Gaetano was most definitely a Cocuzzo. Not only did he move like my grandfather, he looked like a younger version of him—same ears, nose, eyes, and smile.

"Chi è quello?" the woman overhead asked. *Who is that?*

"Mio cugino," he said, turning back to my Dad. "This is my wife, Donata." The woman came down and hugged us both.

"They biked here from Florence," Delia said.

"Dio mio!"

Gaetano toured us through his dark and cavernous workshop, proudly showing us his tools. "The Cocuzzos have always been expert woodworkers," Delia said, after entering behind us. "They've carved most of the doors in San Donato. Gaetano has done a lot of them."

"You carved this?" Dad said incredulously, pointing to the doorway.

"No, just refurbished it," he said. "My father made that door." It was exquisite. He walked us into his dimly lit home and paused at an old black-and-white photo hanging on the wall. "That's my father, Carlo Cocuzzo," he said, pointing to a small boy in the far right of the frame. "He looks like my son. And that's my great-great-grandfather and that's his wife—she looks like an Indian. And that's my great-uncle; he was a priest. And this is Fulvio's grandfather—"

"Oh yeah, Fulvio Cocuzzo," Delia cut in. "That's another one of your cousins. He lives just down the way. You'll meet him, you'll see. He's brilliant. Knows everything about this place, your cousin Fulvio does."

There was so much to take in. By this time I had gathered that "cousin" was a loose term thrown around in these parts to describe relatives, no matter how distant. My father wasn't first cousins with Gaetano, nor this mysterious Fulvio character, but it was easier to call them "cousins" than to untangle the complex family trees that were so deeply rooted in San Donato.

"You must come for dinner," Gaetano said. "My wife, my wife will make you dinner." He peeled off and said something to her in Italian. She nodded empathically. "Where are you staying?" he asked.

"We're not sure," I said.

"Stay right here." He pointed out the window to the stone building directly across from his. "It's a B&B. The woman who owns it, a friend of my wife. She's away, but we have the keys." He turned to Donata and reiterated his thoughts in Italian. She lit up—*Sì, sì sì*—and turned into the house to fetch the keys.

GAETANO TOURED US AROUND the bed and breakfast. The home was spacious, with several bedrooms, but it had questionable decor. There was a clock in the shape of Australia on the mantel. A bow and arrow mounted to the wall. Photos of past Popes. A single deer antler. Two clocks side by side telling different times. Every surface had a miscellaneous item on it. A vial of holy water. A porcelain cat. A vase of fake sunflowers. Dolls, pottery, and an array of other knickknacks.

"We'll take it," my father said.

Gaetano informed us there was a two-tiered price system. "There's a price with heat, and a price without."

Dad laughed. "I saw some blankets in there . . . we'll take without."

Gaetano smirked approvingly. "Good."

We stowed our bikes in the front hallway of the B&B, then Delia proceeded to parade us back down into the piazza. "That's the wonderful thing," she said. "All the roads lead back to the piazza." Gaetano slipped on a jacket and tailed behind us. More people had gathered at the cafe since we'd left it earlier that afternoon. When they saw us coming, they shot out of their seats like we were a procession of royalty.

"I told you, everybody knows you're here," Delia said. "Everybody wants to meet you."

"How the hell?" Dad gasped.

"Word travels fast around here."

My father and I were passed around from person to person like newborn babies, meeting the town doctor, who was Delia's cousin, the cafe owners, one of whom was also Delia's cousin, the village's cultural arts director, a local gallery owner (also Delia's cousin), and even the mayor. People poured out of the cafe to see what all the commotion was about. We were given hugs, firm handshakes, and kisses on the cheeks. We received invitations for dinner and coffee. They showed us pictures of their kids and told us about other family members we had living in the village. All the while Delia translated for us as we smiled, shivering in our cycling tights.

Delia explained that when we first arrived, the villagers thought we were from a Nordic country. Or Australia. We didn't look like typical Italians— certainly not anyone you might see living around these parts. But once she told them our last name, we were treated as a cross between family and celebrities. Generations of families had left the village for the United

States, going back to the turn of the century. Some of them, like my great-grandfather, never returned. Thus the return to the village was celebrated as a great community homecoming.

Gazing back up at my last name carved in the village's stone monument, I felt this homecoming in an intimate and visceral way. Sure, I was the result of several genetic threads, connecting me to other faraway lands, but there was something about being in this village that blanketed me in a sense of belonging. My father and I were the first of our family to return since my great-grandfather shipped off in the early 1900s. When he emigrated, he left behind an entire history that hadn't been passed down. My father and I had returned to reclaim our historical inheritance. What was the story of this place, and where did my family fit in it? Perhaps the best place to start was figuring out what this monument was all about.

CHAPTER 18

We must take the adventure that comes to us.

—C. S. Lewis

I woke up to find plumes of my breath clouding in front of my face. The B&B was unbearably cold. Even wearing every article of clothing in my possession—cycling kit, shirt, pants, jacket, gloves, balaclava, all buried beneath thick blankets—my teeth still chattered. *What a ridiculous decision not to spring for the heat,* I thought. *Such a Dad move.* I dragged myself out of the twin bed and made my way down the stairs, past multiple crucifixes hanging on the walls, and entered the kitchen. Dad sat at the table wrapped up in a down comforter, paging through an oversized book and eating from a bag of cookies.

"Where'd you get those?" I asked.

"Found 'em."

Another Dad move. "You can't just be eating these people's food."

"They'll never know they're gone," he said. "Want an espresso? I found that too."

"Let's go get some real coffee," I said, reaching into the bag for a cookie, "down in the piazza."

We exited the stone B&B and entered the morning sun. Both of us stood still for a few seconds, eyes closed, letting the rays warm our trembling bones. "Jeez, it's warmer out here than it is in there," Dad said. Stray cats slinked out of the alleyway and ran across our legs. We lingered as we descended the cobblestone walkway, admiring each of the hand-carved doors, before passing under a stone arch and entering the piazza.

We took a seat at one of the cafe tables in the sun and ordered a couple of cappuccinos and some pastries. The village gradually came alive. Old men took their seats nearby and ordered coffee. Wearing fedoras and fine sport coats, they looked plucked straight from central casting. Their faces were wrinkled as crumpled pieces of paper. They stabbed cigarettes between their lips and sipped dainty cups of espresso. Meanwhile, their wives sauntered by in groups of three and four, kibitzing with one another in hushed voices. The cafe owner emerged and lingered at one of the tables, striking up a cigarette of his own. A street sweeper lurched by, brushing up bits of debris, while an accordion player took his post under a tree and squeezed out a melody.

There was no apparent sense of urgency from anyone to start the day. The lax pace felt so different from the life we left back in the United States. Everyone appeared so content, as if they were fully aware of their mortality, committed to stretching out each minute of every day as long as possible. *Perhaps living in a place this ancient helps reinforce life's ultimate impermanence,* I thought. Generations had congregated in the piazza, and now they were gone in the way of all things—so, really, what's the rush?

"I could easily live here," Dad said.

"I could actually picture you living here," I said. "This place is full of characters."

It was like a sitcom. We had been in San Donato for less than twenty-four hours, but we had already identified the usual suspects. Each villager was a curious caricature playing a role in a real-life comedy. There was the smooth-talking mayor. The sophisticated physician. The lovable town drunk. The convict. The scantily clad woman of a certain age. The shifty character who roamed the piazza with a possessed look in his eye. They each had a distinct quirkiness that reflected their mountainous isolation. For instance, there were a disproportionate number of albinos living in San Donato, which was rumored to be the product of incest generations earlier. With only so many families in town, it was bound to happen eventually.

At the center of it all was Delia Roffo, who at this very moment came strolling through the piazza like a dignitary, talking to one person after the next. Each exchange was a spectacle to witness. She spoke with the ferocity of a firehose, hands flailing in the air, her voice spiraling up into laughter. And just as quickly as the conversation began, it ended abruptly with "Ciao! Ciao! Ciao! Ciao!"

"Oh, there you guys are!" Delia shouted with arms raised. She pulled up a seat at the cafe table and ordered herself a cappuccino. "This is lovely, isn't it? I could sit here all day."

"I was just saying that!" Dad agreed.

"Really, it's true, I could. We even have music today," she said, gesturing to the accordion player. "Isn't this lovely? Clear sky. Look at that." She looked up to the green mountainside looming above the monument. The sun was climbing up its flanks. Returning her eyes to the piazza, she said, "I was gone for seventeen years, but when I came back, it was exactly the same. Even back in the forties and fifties—this was what it looked like. The men sitting there, scheming."

"What was it like growing up here?" I asked.

"I remember the beautiful air," she said. "The smell of it. How the spring air smelled different—like olives." She looked around again and smirked knowingly. "I remember playing soccer. Playing goddamn soccer at ten years old, and my mother hated it."

"Why'd she hate it?" Dad asked.

"Because I was a girl, and girls weren't supposed to play soccer," she said. "I was a tomboy in San Donato. Always pushing the limits of what little girls could do. I was curious and lively but, Stephen, they called me 'aggressive.' *Aggressive* . . . that's what they called me. I cursed a lot—which little girls weren't supposed to do. I still swear to this day to get my anger out. But it's been working for me for all this time, so—fuck!—why not?"

We all laughed. "When did you come to the United States?" I asked.

"When I was a little girl," she said. "We all had to go to the American Embassy in Naples to get our passports. We had to get a physical. I remember that. I think now about how strong my mother had to have been to just pick up and go."

"Where was your father?" I asked.

"He and my older brother Mario had already gone to the States a year earlier; they were already living in Brighton."

"What was the trip over like?" I asked.

"My experience on the boat was very emotional. I was vomiting for ten straight days. Totally seasick. They gave me something that made me feel a little better. We arrived at the Port of New York on May 26, 1961." Delia grew up down the street from my father. "Everybody knew me because I was a rebel there too," she said. "In high school we protested to change the dress code, so we could wear jeans. Shit. It was great. I loved it. It was bussing time, so it was tough. But let's not go there, or else I'll really get acid reflux."

After high school, Delia told me, she returned to Italy, where the education was free. She earned a master's degree in social work in Rome and moved back to San Donato. Living in this remote village, she saw that the needs of the elderly were not being met by the Italian government. Many of the elderly were shut-ins who could not access adequate health care. So Delia formed a cooperative with eight other people that petitioned the government for funding, with the aim of going into the homes of these elderly women and caring for them.

"I would sit with these old ladies and ask, 'What are your needs? How do you feel?'" Delia said. "They would go, 'Oh, this is so nice. During the war we didn't have anything like this.'" She motioned to the cafe owner for another cappuccino. "That's how I got to know the history of this place. It's a history you must know. It's your history too."

"Delia!" a man yelled out from across the piazza.

"Oh, Felipe, come va?" she shouted back, before launching out of her chair to embrace the man. We watched what was becoming a familiar scene of Delia gleefully mucking it up with some village local. People loved her around here. No one seemed to spark the same kind of enthusiasm as she did. After a few minutes of gabbing and gesticulating, Delia bid the man farewell—*ciao, ciao, ciao*—with a hug and kiss, and returned to our table.

"Why didn't you ever run for mayor?" Dad asked.

"There was a time that I thought about it," she said. "As far as the feedback I get from people, I probably would have won."

"Everyone seems to love you here," I said.

"Maybe I could have been the mayor of San Donato," she said. "I could have been on the town council. But it was so threatening to the men in the village. It was crazy. There's never been a woman mayor of San Donato. Never. No matter how emancipated this town is—and it is—they were never able to make the leap to have a woman mayor. I didn't want to be the first. I mean a *feminist* woman mayor . . . could you imagine? Oh my God. They would have died."

After she moved back to San Donato, Delia married a man in the village. "My husband was one of the biggest and smartest activists of the Italian communist party," she said. "I became a part of it too. We talked about Marxists and the working class. Beautiful, intellectual conversations of San Donato protesting the Italian government at that time. I loved that." But after several years of marriage, Delia and her husband drifted apart and eventually divorced. She later dated a woman in the village but remained deeply in the closet at that time.

When Delia's mother fell ill back in the United States, Delia returned to Boston to help her siblings care for their mother. "That's when I met my partner, Suzanne," Delia said. "We met at a party during Pride Week. We went out on a date and the first thing I told her was that I didn't want to get involved with anyone because I was going back to Italy. 'I'm only here for a little while,' I told her, 'maybe six months, and I just want to be clear that I don't want to get involved.' That was the last thing I said! That was eighteen years ago now." She giggled. "I couldn't believe Suzanne would actually want to date me," Delia said. "She was this very accomplished, brilliant opera singer who taught at the Episcopal Divinity School in Cambridge. She went to school in Iran and spoke five languages. And then here I was."

If you asked me, Delia could hold her own around anyone. She seemed so comfortable in her own skin. In a way, she carried herself with the same defiance as my father, as if to say: "This is who I am. Take it or leave it. I don't give a fuck."

"Where is she now?" Dad asked.

"Oh, she's back in Boston," Delia said. "She would love to be here right now, but she's teaching. She will be with me here once school gets out. We go back and forth. She loves it here." Thinking about Delia's old-world, Catholic background, I wondered how her family reacted to meeting Suzanne.

"I never told them about Suzanne until my mother died in 2001," Delia said. "Suzanne said, 'I'm coming to the funeral,' and I said, 'No! You can't. I don't want you to come. Everybody will find out!' But she did anyway. She came to the wake and the funeral. She actually sang 'Ave Maria' at the funeral. The whole place, all the Italians, were in tears. They fell in love with her soon after." Delia started coming back to the village after that, the first time with Suzanne in November of 2001. "If she was going to be my girlfriend, she had to know every little thing about me. For me, that meant knowing my village."

"How did the villagers react when you brought her to San Donato?" I asked.

"Oh, they loved her. And she loves it here."

"What's not to love?" my Dad interjected.

Just then a man came to our table with his arms full of books and folders. "Fulvio!" Delia shouted before hugging him. He was probably my father's age, and good looking, with soft round features, warm eyes, and a shock of salt-and-pepper hair.

"These guys, these guys are Cocuzzos," she said to him in Italian. Fulvio's face lit up. He unloaded his papers onto the table and excitedly embraced us. "This is Fulvio Cocuzzo," Delia said. "He's one of your cousins. Yes, these are the guys who biked here all the way from Florence," Delia translated for us. "I told you word gets around fast."

It turned out that Fulvio was a cyclist too. He spoke rapidly to Delia. He had a scarf wrapped dramatically around his neck, giving him an air of bravado as he spoke—of which not a word was in English. "He wants to take you guys on a bike ride tomorrow," Delia translated. "Can you?"

"Absolutely," Dad said, putting his hand on Fulvio's shoulder. "We'd love to . . . love to . . . grazie mille." My father's effortless acceptance of Fulvio's invitation struck me as out of character. He was normally reluctant to commit to spending time with others, even if they were long-lost cousins. But now he seemed far more open and game to new experiences. Referring to all the papers, my father asked, "What are you working on?"

Fulvio looked blankly at Dad and turned to Delia for a translation. She obliged, and Fulvio shot into action, opening one of his folders and spreading it out on the table. He turned to Delia, who translated. "Oh, this is for his Passion of the Christ performance. It's going to be performed up by my apartment. They're doing it all in fourteenth-century Italian dialect."

What a bold idea, I marveled. "Who is performing it?" I asked.

"The people from San Donato," Delia said. "Fulvio gets the villagers to act in his plays. He's a professor of early Italian literature."

How the hell is he going to wrangle the San Donato sitcom to perform a play, let alone the Passion of the Christ in fourteenth-century Italian? I pictured the town drunk up on the cross, slurring his lines while the woman of a certain age played Mary Magdalene, flaunting way too much cleavage for the children in the audience.

Fulvio spoke again, through Delia: "He asked if you can meet him outside the bakery tomorrow morning at nine for the bike ride. Does that work for you?"

"Perrrrrfect," my father said, patting Fulvio on the arm again. Shooting us a big grin, our long-lost cousin was off.

We sat down, resuming our posts and watching the morning unfold. "What do you think they think of us?" I asked Delia.

"Who?" she asked.

"The villagers."

"The whole town knows that you two guys are here," she said. "It's not just the people that you've met. The people that don't know you, *know* you. Because they're saying, 'Oh, the two Americans, oh, their origins are Sandonatese, their grandparents were born here.'" She explained that the people appreciate the sons and daughters of immigrants who come back to experience San Donato and learn about their history.

But it was us who could not be more appreciative. "We're so grateful for the hospitality," I said. "It's like out of a fairy tale."

"Well, you came in the right way," Delia said. "Sometimes people come back to the village and flaunt their wealth. They want to show off. People don't like that around here."

"Of course, and why would they?" Dad said.

"No one is super rich here, but they have the best life and that is really super rich," Delia said.

"Exactly. Exactly," Dad agreed.

"They're not economically rich, but they're emotionally, socially, and politically wealthy," she said. "And their history is incredibly rich."

"Speaking of which, what's the history of the monument?" I asked Delia.

"It's a World War II monument," she said. "It's for all those who were lost in the war."

My father asked for Delia to translate the inscription at the base, which she did: "'The sons of San Donato who have fallen in war. Some of them are soldiers who died and some of them are civilians who died during World War II." I wanted to know how the civilians died.

Delia looked into my eyes with such sincerity. "Oh, Robbie," she said, "you need to know the history of this place . . . the history of this village . . . it's your history too."

CHAPTER 19

I don't think of all the misery, but all the beauty that still remains.

—Anne Frank

"There's something I need to show you," Delia said. "Follow me." She led us out of the piazza, past a few small shops and a bakery, and back down the narrow road we had cycled up a day earlier. "That's the town council building to the left over there and that's the school," she said, pointing to two buildings that surrounded a small courtyard. Delia walked us under rustling trees up to a monument at the base of the stairs leading to the town council office. The simple stone slab looked vaguely like an oversized tombstone. It had the blue star of David painted at the top, and below was barbed wire carved through rough cement. In the upper-right corner of the stone was an inscription in Italian.

"Allora," Delia began. "It says, 'From 1940 to the spring of 1944, in San Donato, twenty-eight Jews were interned here by the Fascist regime. These Jews found welcome among the citizens.'" She read the next few lines quickly in Italian and continued translating. "'On the sixth of April 1944, sixteen of the Jews were captured by the Nazi occupiers and by the Fascist collaborators and sympathizers. They were destined for the concentration camps of Auschwitz. Only four managed to survive . . . Of all these victims, we remember a small child, her name was Noemi Levi.' She wasn't even two years old when she was killed."

Delia paused reverently for a few moments and turned toward us. "There's a history to this village that you wouldn't believe," she said. "A history that's never really been told, outside of this village." In 1940 when Italy entered the war, Delia explained, Mussolini began harshly implementing his racial laws, and Jews were arrested. Some were sent to one of the forty-eight internment camps that dotted Italy, while others were put under *confino libero*, essentially house arrest in remote towns throughout Italy. They were sent to one of 220 villages, where they were forced to check in with the Fascists every day. One of these towns was San Donato.

"It was totally isolated from the world, a place where the Fascists could keep an eye on them," Delia said. "Most of the Jews were business owners from Rome. In 1940, twenty-eight of them were exiled here. They were placed in homes and given strict curfews, and they were forbidden to work. They were allowed to walk around freely." She looked back up to the monument. "But that was in the beginning . . . everything changed when the Nazis came." After the Nazis invaded Italy from the north and reinstated Mussolini to power, they met the Allied advance south of Rome and occupied the *confino libero* outposts like San Donato. "They set up checkpoints on either end of the road," Delia said, pointing down the way. "They took over people's homes and the town council building." She paused. "And then they started hunting down the Jews."

An hour earlier, this village seemed eternally tranquil, and yet now as I scanned these quaint stone homes, it was not hard to picture helmeted Gestapo pounding on the heavy wooden doors. I could hear their boots marching on these cobblestones and the shutters creaking closed overhead. I could smell their trucks idling outside the homes, as they kicked down doors, rounded up the Jews, and bussed them past the checkpoint down the way that had closed on this village like a noose.

"But something unexpected happened," Delia said. "When the Nazis came for the Jews in San Donato, they couldn't find them."

"What do you mean?" I asked.

Delia's eyes flashed with unmistakable pride. "What the Fascists weren't counting on was the people of San Donato," she said. "The people had become friends with the Jews who were interned here. When the Nazis occupied the village, many of the villagers took it upon themselves to hide the Jews and protect them." She explained that the villagers hid them in their homes and in the mountains. When the Jews fled into the mountains, the villagers smuggled food up to them and took in their children as their own to protect.

The pride that illuminated Delia's face rose up in my chest. I looked at my father and saw the same pride rising in him. Unbeknownst to either of us, there was a story of heroism in our forefather's birthplace similar to that of Gino Bartali. In the darkest of times in Italy's history, a beacon of goodness shone from this tiny village hidden in the Apennines. There was a story of simple people risking their lives on the right side of history. I was desperate to learn more.

"How did you find out about all this?" I asked Delia.

"When I was a social worker taking care of the old ladies, they would tell me these stories from the war," she said. "See, most of the men were away fighting. Like my father, he went off to war and was captured and imprisoned. My mother thought he was dead. The women were back here fending for themselves, raising families—and leading resistance."

I wanted to meet one of these real-life heroes. While reading the story of Gino Bartali, I had grappled with the inevitable question of what I would have done in these dire circumstances. Would I have had the courage to risk my life for strangers? Where did that kind of bravery come from? Is it a conscious decision or a natural impulse? Gino Bartali couldn't answer my questions, but maybe there was somebody in this village who could.

"So, if the villagers hid the Jews," I asked Delia, "how did the Nazis ultimately find them?"

"Sympathizers," she sighed. "There were Fascist sympathizers living in the village who gave up the Jews. They collaborated with the Nazis and pointed out homes that were harboring and aiding Jews." She mentioned a relative of hers who was outed by a sympathizer for aiding the Allies; he was sent to the Nazi concentration camp in Dachau.

Sympathizers? I thought with dread. *What if my family were sympathizers?* In an instant my pride was subsumed by intense worry. *What if my family gave up Jews? What would that mean for my whole sense of identity? Jesus, what would that mean for my relationship with Jenny, my Jewish fiancée to be?* I wanted to ask Delia outright what role my family played in all this, but I was simply too scared of what the answer might be. Once again, I wondered whether it was better to be ignorant of an unfortunate truth.

LATER THAT AFTERNOON, Dad and I walked up the street leading out of San Donato and sat at a wooden bench overlooking the valley below. "Could you believe that story?" I asked him. "About the Jews?"

"No, I'd never heard that," he said. "Incredible."

For whatever reason—perhaps the life or death significance of Delia's story—the revelation had spurred a question that I'd been meaning to ask my father since we started our ride. "How did you know when you were ready to get married?"

He smiled, perhaps thinking of Mom. "You know, I really didn't know when. It was more your mother. She kinda just said, 'If we're going to be living together, we need to get married.' And that was that."

"So you didn't propose to her?"

"No, not really."

"Did you buy an engagement ring at least?"

"Nope. I didn't see the need for it. I mean, all that money on a ring? Your mother knew I loved her. She basically set up the whole wedding, paid for it. I just showed up." He looked at me. "Why, what are you thinking about? Jenny?"

"Yeah, I think it's time for me to take this next step with her. Just not sure what it all looks like."

"What do you mean? The wedding itself? Why, is she going to want a big wedding?" he asked.

It wasn't the size of the wedding that had me worried. "It's the style," I said. "I know we're probably not going to have a Catholic wedding service. I'm worried that's going to crush Mom."

"Oh, Robbie, you can't think like that," he said. "She'll be fine. She just wants you and Jenny to be happy. Who cares if it's in a church or not?"

"But what if it's in a temple?" I asked. "What if Jenny wants a Jewish ceremony?"

"That would be excellent. I'm sure I'd look great in a yarmulke!"

"No seriously, Dad."

"Seriously, it would be more than fine. Your mother just wants you to be happy. And just to have *some* religious element to the service—Catholic or Jewish—would be icing on the cake."

I was comforted by Dad's reasoning, but I also took it with a grain of salt. After all, this wisdom was coming from a man who didn't see the need for buying an engagement ring. He'd cast aside convention his entire life, and the topic of weddings certainly didn't fall outside of his twisted reasoning.

"Listen," he said. "You need to do what's good for you and your family. Your whole life people are going to try to make you fit in the box they set out for you. Forget about it. Take it from me: life is too damn short to care what other people think."

CHAPTER 20

Never go on any trips with anyone you do not love.

—Ernest Hemingway

Fulvio looked fresh out of the seventies with full-on Euro flare. He wore a flowy fluorescent-pink windbreaker that *whooshed* silkily as he moved. His black skin-tight spandex were tucked into his cycling cleats, and he wore a narrow white headband to keep his salt-and-pepper moptop out of his eyes, which were hidden behind big, chunky sunglasses. Of course, in true old-school cycling style, he wasn't wearing a helmet.

"Oh, man, Fulvio. Look at that bike," Dad said after we pedaled up. He bent down for a closer look. "Steel frame?" he asked. "Steeeeel?" Fulvio stared back at my father with an amused look. He wanted to communicate, but the language barrier stood between them. "The *frame*," Dad repeated a little louder and slower. "Is it steel?"

Fulvio smiled for a few more awkward seconds, then tentatively announced: "Hand . . . made."

"Oh, dynamite. Robbie, hear that? Handmade, check it out. What a beautiful bike."

"Really is," I said. "Total classic set of wheels right there. Love those polished chrome gear shifters down the frame." Fulvio stood silently as we talked and pointed toward his crotch.

"Allora," he said, grabbing our attention away from the bike. "Siete pronti?"

Dad and I grinned, lost as to what Fulvio said.

"Pronti?" He gestured up the mountain looming behind the village, then twirled his hand to mimic the winding road.

"Oh yeah, let's go," I said.

We shoved off, falling behind Fulvio as he led us back through the piazza. The old men at the cafe tables looked up momentarily from their card game, waving to Fulvio as he passed. He shouted something to them in a bellowing voice and hooted theatrically. Fulvio would surely have a starring role in the San Donato sitcom. Our long-lost cousin moved around town as if it were a stage, and although we couldn't make out a word of what he said, the tone of his voice was made for soliloquy.

We passed through the rest of the village and began climbing up the mountainside. Fulvio took us further up the main road beyond the village and into the mountains, where we hadn't yet ventured. I fell behind my father and Fulvio as they pedaled side by side. They tried to communicate, Dad listening intently as Fulvio spoke, struggling to interpret his hand gestures. "Capisci?" Fulvio asked.

"Ummm, no capisce," Dad said. After a while the two drew quiet, resigned to communicating in the universal language of the bicycle. Their legs found a rhythm together like two locomotive pistons, driving their pedals in unison.

The road turned up a steeper switchback, and Fulvio reached down to change to an easier gear, prompting my father to do the same. The steep road carried us into an alpine wilderness where gnarled trees towered overhead. *These must be the woods where the Jews fled when the Nazis came*, I thought. Delia had told me that hidden within this thick, twisted forest were ancient caves where the Jews hid for years on end. She said that there were wolves and bears and vipers in these mountains. And then there was the winter itself—cold, wet, and deadly. *How did those poor people manage to survive up here?*

As for our own survival, all the cycling up and down the hills of Tuscany over the past nine days had thrust me and my father into the greatest physical condition of our lives. Our bodies had been whittled down to efficient pedaling machines. Despite this, Fulvio was setting a grueling pace that had us both gasping for air. Even if I could speak Italian, I wouldn't have the oxygen to say a word to Fulvio. Instead, I watched the first bead of sweat drip off my nose and splat onto the frame of my bike. More followed. My world narrowed to the patch of pavement directly under my front wheel. I focused on my breath and tried to align it with the rhythm of my legs turning the pedals. *Right leg, left leg, inhale*, I meditated. *Right leg, left leg, exhale. Right leg . . .*

My breathing mantra was broken by *BOM-bom! BOM-bom!* As I tried to make out the low baritone drone, the sound became more pronounced. *BOM-bom. BOM-bom. Dooo bom bom!* Was Fulvio . . . singing? He broke out into a full-on ballad, throwing his head back and crooning at the top of his lungs: "Parle de storie vecchie, de ne tiempe ormai passate!" Dad and I remained hunched over our bikes as Fulvio serenaded the sky. "La neve del cinquantasei, le chenghe scapestrate . . . "

"How . . . the . . . hell . . . is . . . he . . . singing?" I managed to ask my father between breaths. He shook his head and laughed, then reached for his water bottle. We climbed higher into the mountains. The air cooled, making each breath as satisfying as a gulp of water. Hills undulated below, rising to high peaks where other villages were perched among the clouds. We passed an old man standing beneath a stone archway on the side of the road. He gazed toward the mountains across the valley and, as if seeing them for the first time, he raised his hand to his mouth in awe.

"Alvito," Fulvio said, breaking from his song and pointing to a castle high above us.

"Guess that's where we're headed," I said to Dad.

The road spiraled tightly up the final sections of the mountainside until we reached the castle ruins. Fulvio eased on his brakes and hopped off, leaning his bike against a well in the middle of a piazza. The castle had been reduced to stone walls that were open to the sky. I unzipped my jersey and reached for my water bottle. Fulvio pulled out a plump orange from his back pocket, peeled it, and handed me and my father each a section.

"Fulvio!" a voice called out. We turned to find a woman emerging from her car. She strode up to us and embraced Fulvio.

"Ecco i Cocuzzo," he said jovially. "Americani."

"Oh, you're from the United States?" she said.

"Yes," I said. "You speak English?" *Dumb question.*

"I do," she said. "Went to university in London." She became our impromptu translator, helping us communicate with Fulvio for the first time in four hours. He guided us into the castle ruins and, through our translator, explained its history. "Alvito Castle was built 1000 AD. That was the period when the rich people of the land were building their homes, their houses, their castles."

"Oh, wow, and they built this?" Another stupid question. I was just happy to be able to communicate.

"Yes," she said, not needing to translate.

Fulvio broke into another pronouncement. His voice had an operatic quality that boomed from his belly. He didn't so much speak as announce. The woman translated: "A few times a year, he says, he holds a big concert in here. All the people of San Donato and Opi and Alvito come, and he plays his guitar and sings."

"He plays?" I asked.

"Oh yes. I've attended these concerts. He's a talented musician. Lots of people come to listen."

"Must be incredible," Dad said.

"This guy's incredible," I said to Dad. "Freakin' Renaissance man."

We walked around the ruins. "What about San Donato?" I asked. "How old is the village? Was it around in, like, Roman times?" The woman translated the question to Fulvio, who launched seamlessly into an explanation, which she translated back to us. "In ancient Roman times, San Donato did not exist. It existed as a small village called Cominium that was owned by Sanniti people. The only village that existed in this area before Rome was Atina, but San Donato and Alvito and all the villages nearby didn't exist."

"So Cominium was the first village around here?" I asked. She explained that it was conquered by the Romans in 300 BC, and San Donato was born more or less around 1000 AD. By 700 AD, what existed in San Donato was just the church. "One small church that was dedicated to the saint Donato."

"So how did the village go from just a church to what it is today?" I asked.

Turning to Fulvio, she relayed my question. He seemed enthralled with this discussion. "The land became owned by the Monte Cassino monks," she translated. "These monks started to send some woodworkers for cutting and collecting the wood nearby the church in this land. From that point these men who were working on the land started to live there and build the first houses. So that's when the first part of the village was born, nearby the church."

"Fascinating," I said. "What does Fulvio think the history of San Donato means to the people who live in the village today? Do they celebrate it?"

"Really, no," the woman translated. "There's just a few people who are interested in the history. They research in the libraries and in the church to get ancient documents about the history of the village, but most people don't really care about the history, he says, and they don't know anything about it."

I wanted to know about the first Cocuzzos. "Does he know when they showed up in San Donato?"

The woman translated the question to Fulvio, who smirked approvingly. "He really doesn't know where they came from, but researching in the church registry he discovered that one Bernidino Cocuzzo was registered at the church in San Donato at about 1587."

The date was mind boggling. According to Fulvio, that date is known because the church started registering people in 1587. It's possible there were more Cocuzzos in San Donato before the registry began, he said, but they just don't know for sure.

It was astounding. The roots of our family tree stretched back more than four hundred years in San Donato. I struggled to grasp the gravity of that. For four hundred years my family had been living in this itty-bitty village in the mountains. Perhaps even more striking was that after four hundred years, my great-great-grandfather made the decision to leave. He turned away from four hundred years of what our family had known and jumped into a foreign world.

We exited the castle and returned to our bikes. "Thank you so much for translating for us," I said to the woman.

"No problem, happy to help," she said. "You can learn a lot about this place from Fulvio—he's our resident genius. Genio."

Fulvio threw his head back, chuckling. "No, no, no," he said, waving off the compliment like a showman. She shook our hands again, bid Fulvio farewell in Italian, and returned to her car. The three of us returned to our state of silence and makeshift sign language. There was so much I wanted to ask Fulvio. He had a wealth of knowledge beneath that shock of salt-and-pepper hair. I just didn't know how I was going to get to it.

WE SPED DOWN THE mountainside, the surroundings whipping by my peripheral vision as we wound around the switchbacks and hummed down the straightaways in between. Even with nothing but a headband protecting his skull from the pavement, Fulvio careened down the hill with brash confidence. Dad stuck to his back wheel like a shadow. *Please don't race him, Dad,* I thought. *Please just chill.* I pulled closer behind the two of them and caught a glimpse of my father's face. The grin said it all: he was having a ball.

We bombed down the mountainside for the better part of an hour until the road flattened out into the belly of the valley. Tall swaths of grass lined either side of us as we each clicked into a bigger gear and got to pedaling again. Up the road ahead of us, a small compact car buzzed toward us, beeping.

"Who the hell could this be?" I said. The car skidded to a stop on the gravel shoulder and the window rolled down.

"Delia!" Fulvio called out.

"Jesus Christ, wouldya look at you guys!" she said, poking her head full out the driver's-side window. "You Cocuzzos are crazy! I'd be dead by now. Where did you go?"

I pointed back up to the mountain. "Fuck," she said. I laughed. No one made the F-word sound as endearing as Delia. Fulvio launched into a flood of Italian with her. The two went back and forth, effectively screaming at one another, while Dad and I stood there, waiting for the translation.

"Oh, he wants you to come over for dinner," she said. "He really likes you guys." Fulvio said something else. "And he wants me to join you," she said. "I'm supposed to go see a friend, but I'll just go tomorrow. She's a pain in the ass anyway. So meet you in the piazza at seven?"

LATER THAT EVENING, MY father and I followed Delia through the village to Fulvio's house. Stemming off the main road that ran directly into the piazza and up into the mountains was a network of tiny side streets and walkways that tangled around the homes of San Donato. One of these quiet streets delivered us to Fulvio's doorway, which he opened promptly after our first knock. "Allora," he said. "Venite, venite." His hair was fluffy and styled slightly to the side. He was wearing a black mock turtleneck and blue jeans. He and Delia exchanged rapid-fire pleasantries as we followed them up a flight of mahogany stairs and into the kitchen where the air was warm and buttery. A woman was bent over the oven, wisps of her hair blowing from the waves of heat.

"This is Fulvio's wife, Maria," Delia said. Dark-featured and trim, Maria wiped her hands on her apron and pulled my father and me into a hug and a kiss. She said something in Italian and Delia translated: "Dinner will be ready soon. Make yourself at home. Grazie, Maria, grazie."

Fulvio toured us around his charming three-bedroom home. While the stone exterior was in keeping with the rest of San Donato, the inside was unlike any of the other spaces we'd toured so far, which had felt trapped in the 1500s. From floor to ceiling, every square inch of each room exuded fine craftsmanship. The rich wooden panels of the walls fit together seamlessly, framing the fireplace, the doorways, and the windows. The lines were clean and precise, coming together as neatly as origami and just as ornate. "This place is beautiful," Dad said, studying the beveled edges of the crown molding. "This woodwork is just, my God, it's *unbelievable.*"

"He did all this himself," Delia said.

"What?" Dad said. "He did?"

"Certo." Delia said. "Fulvio, you did all this?" Fulvio nodded nonchalantly and motioned for us to follow him. We tailed him down another set of stairs and into a workshop. The floor was painted a glossy white, and his tools were meticulously arranged on two separate tool benches. The workshop looked more like an operating room—there wasn't a speck of sawdust to be seen.

"What's this?" I asked, nodding to a tall cupboard on the back wall. Fulvio opened the door, revealing rows and rows of brightly painted marionettes all standing at attention. Each was hand carved with pronounced features and expressions, wearing little outfits and holding props. Fulvio threw an elbow onto one of the shelves of the cupboard and turned to us to explain the story behind the marionettes. "He carved these himself," Delia translated.

"Of course, he did," I snickered.

"I guess he started by making them out of papier-mâché, but they kept on getting damaged during his performances."

"Performances?" I asked.

"Oh yes, he puts on marionette performances in town, mostly for the kids."

"Jeez," Dad said.

"Anyway," Delia continued translating, "he ended up realizing that it was better to carve them out of wood and that's worked well for him."

Who the hell was this guy? Standing there proudly in front of his handmade marionettes, he looked like one of his own wooden creations—only larger than life. And that's how he seemed in the village: too big for this place. Here he was in a tiny town in the mountains, studying ancient Italian literature, playing concerts in castle ruins, putting on marionette shows, and directing theatrical performances in fourteenth-century Italian.

"How did he learn to do all these things?" I asked. "Like to play the guitar, to act, the marionettes . . . all that stuff?"

Delia translated the question. "Self-taught," he said.

"And the woodworking?"

"His father was a carpenter, and so was his grandfather," she said. "We're talking about more or less two hundred years of Cocuzzos working as carpenters." Fulvio waved us to the workbench at the back of the room, where the tools were made of wood and steel. There was an assortment of hammers, mallets, handsaws, and hand-powered drills. Nothing had a power chord. "Di mio papà," he said.

"Oh, look, these are his father's tools," Delia said.

"Did your father teach you how to use them?" I asked him through Delia.

Fulvio shook his head. Delia translated: "He said his father didn't teach him in the way of a master and an apprentice. He learned from him by staying in the workshop and watching him work; that's how he learned, from watching." He said more about it to Delia. "Yes, there's a saying in San Donato about fathers and sons. The art of the father is already half-learned by the son."

"Half-learned?" I asked.

"Yes," Delia explained. "He said that even if you don't study the art of your father, you will already know how to do half of it because the father's art is already part of the son . . . his father is in him."

CHAPTER 21

The only people who know your story are the ones who helped you write it.

—Unknown

I needed proof, some piece of evidence showing that my great-grandfather was indeed born in San Donato. Sure, there was plenty of anecdotal evidence tying my family lineage to this medieval place—the name carved into the World War II monument, for instance, or the existence of distant cousins like Fulvio and Gaetano—but the journalist in me wanted definitive proof. There was something about getting to the primary sources that felt essential to me. And yes, sure I could plug my information into some genealogy website, but I wanted to walk down the street where my great-grandfather Loreto Cocuzzo was born in 1908. I wanted to see what he saw when he strolled down the piazza every morning. I wanted to know the sights, the smells, the sounds. And I knew just the person to lead me there.

"Ready?" Delia said. "I'll make sure these guys don't give you the runaround. You have those dates with you, right? Of course, you do." We walked passed the Holocaust monument and up the stairs to the town council building. The question of sympathizers still hung over my mind like a dark cloud as we passed the stone star of David. I just couldn't shake it. *What if my family were sympathizers? Or worse . . . Fascists? How could I reconcile with that? What would that mean for my life moving forward?*

The town council building smelled faintly of crayons and ammonia, like a grammar school, and amateurish artwork hung framed on the walls.

"Here's something you should see," Delia said, pointing at a faded certificate in a thin gold frame. "This is from Yad Vashem, the World Holocaust Remembrance Center in Israel. Years ago, they came to San Donato and declared the village Righteous Among the Nations of Israel." I remembered this designation. It was the same honor bestowed upon Cardinal Elia Dalla Costa and Gino Bartali for their heroics saving Jews during the war. "It's quite a thing," she said. "In fact, if you go to Jerusalem today, there's actually a grove of olive trees planted there in honor of the heroes in San Donato. It's true."

Delia toured me through both levels of the municipal building, popping into just about every office and blasting the occupant with a flurry of conversation. As her partner, Suzanne, perfectly described later, going anywhere with Delia in San Donato was like walking the Stations of the Cross. You take five steps, stop, talk to somebody, then take another five steps, stop, talk to somebody—on and on.

"This is Duilio Colletti," Delia said, introducing me to a tall, late-middle-aged man with cropped gray hair and handsome sun-kissed face. "He runs the town's works office, but he also started the skiing and mountaineering club here." The two exchanged another volley of conversation. "Yes, yes, yes . . . he wants to give you something," Delia said. "I told him that you're really interested in the history of San Donato, and he said he has something for you." Duilio reached into his desk, pulled out a paperback book, and handed it to me.

"*Vite di Carta*," I read the title aloud.

"Stories of foreign Jews interned in Italy," Delia translated the subtitle. I flipped through the pages—all in Italian. "This book was written by Maria Pizzutti," Delia said. "She lives in Rome, but she came to San Donato many years ago, and, just like you, she was fascinated by the history, especially how the villagers helped the Jews. Anyway, she ended up researching the lives of the twenty-eight Jews who were interned in San Donato and then wrote this book. Oh, Robbie, you should read the stories of these poor people."

After she wrote the book, Maria Pizzutti continued researching the lives of Jews in Italy during the war, beyond San Donato. She spent years digging through the resources and created a database that Delia thought was somewhere on the internet. "You can find all the names of the Jews who were captured and interned in Italy and those who were sent to the death camps," Delia said. "She became the preeminent scholar on Jews in Italy, and it all began with her research in San Donato. Isn't that something? It's true, it's true."

We continued through the building, where we chatted with the mayor, three old socialists, two local teachers, the director of tourism, and the chief street cleaner. After each interaction, Delia spoke to me in English, sharing her take on the person—good, bad, and ugly. She had a way of encapsulating each character's entire personal history into a single breath, culminating in the most salacious details. I'd never met anybody so thoroughly entertaining to listen to.

By the time we reached the archive office in the basement, my head was spinning. Delia knocked on the door and waited, but it remained closed. She turned the squeaky handle and poked her head in through the doorway. "Salve?" she said. For the first time since I'd met Delia, the person on the other end of her greeting wasn't thrilled to see her. Quite the opposite. The woman glared at Delia over a mess of papers strewn across her desk. "Che cosa vuoi adesso?" she asked impatiently. Her tone told me everything I needed to know: *What do you want now?*

"Allora," Delia said, before explaining who I was and why I was here. I knew exactly what she was saying. I knew exactly why I was here. I wanted to track down my great-grandfather Loreto Cocuzzo's birth certificate and figure out where he lived in this village. My father and I had made such an effort to get here. I needed something tangible that proved my connection to the four-hundred-year history of the Cocuzzos that Fulvio told me about the night before.

The woman heard out Delia's request and sighed dramatically. She looked down at the swamp of papers cresting at her armpits. "Oi, Delia," she muttered, and shot into a long lament. Once again, I didn't really need a translation, but Delia gave it to me anyway. "She says she's incredibly busy. She has no time for this. She says she has no support here. No one helps her. Fucking men! They just dish her the work. And it sounds like she's having some personal problems, some problems at home. Her mother is unwell . . . "

"Oh . . . well . . . I certainly don't want to cause her any more problems," I said. My neck was hot. I wanted this birth certificate more than anything on this trip. "But if there's any way she could just take a look, I would be incredibly, *incredibly* grateful." I felt helpless, desperate, completely reliant on Delia to press my case. She went back on the offense, narrowing her fire hose into a power washer. Delia clasped her hands together as if in prayer and rattled out a rapid-fire litany of petitions at the stone-faced archivist. I didn't hold out much hope, but Delia kept pecking at her.

Finally, the woman cracked: "Nome e data di nascita?"

"What's your great-grandfather's name and birthday?" Delia asked. "Quick, quick."

"Loreto Cocuzzo, 1908."

Delia transferred the information to the woman, who punched it into her computer. I held my breath as she opened folder after folder on her outdated desktop computer and scrolled through lists of names.

"Cocuzzo, Loreto?" she muttered, looking for the name. "Cocuzzo, Loreto. Cocuzzo Loret—no . . . no Cocuzzo, Loreto."

Gut punch.

"Mille novecentotto?" she asked Delia.

"Nineteen hundred and eight?" Delia asked me.

I nodded to both of them. The archivist got up and walked to the back of the room to a series of shelves lined with dusty old books. She ran her pointer finger down their spines until she found the volume she wanted and drew it off of the shelf. Returning to her desk, she opened the handsome book across the stack of papers. She coughed from a bit of dust. Each page was yellow as parchment and written on with a magnificent swooping script.

"These are the *actual* records," Delia gushed. "Would you look at that. Whenever someone was born in San Donato, their parents had to come down here and declare their birth. It was written right here."

The book was painfully old, yet the archivist didn't put on any gloves or seem to handle the pages with any special care. Perhaps she was just too annoyed. Instead, she flipped through the book hastily, running her fingers down the script of each page and searching for my great-grandfather's name. "Cocuzzo, Loreto? Cocuzzo, Loreto? Cocuzzo, Loreto . . . No."

Delia looked up at me with a face of concern. "You sure you have the right date?" she asked, wincing. I was sure.

The archivist pulled down two more of these ancient tomes from the shelf, searched them, and found no sign of my great-grandfather. She flipped through a stack of cards like you'd find in a library's old Dewey Decimal system—still nothing. My heart was in the soles of my shoes. My anxious mind raced with possibilities, none of them good. *Was my great-grandfather even from San Donato? Maybe he was born in a nearby village and then moved here? Or maybe, because everyone in his neighborhood back in Boston was from San Donato, it was just assumed that he was from the village too? And if that was true, what the hell were my father and I even doing here? Had we pedaled all those miles only to discover that our family wasn't even from San Donato?*

As the archivist put away the stack of cards, I saw a thought flash in her eyes. She looked back at the bookshelf for a second, then walked over and pulled out the first book of archives again. She flipped through the pages, ran her finger down the script again, and stopped abruptly. She cleared her throat and announced: "Allora . . . Loreto Cocuzzo, nato otto settembre, mille novecentotto otto a Giuseppe Cocuzzo e Ida Cocuzzo in San Donato in Via Orologio."

My heart shot into my throat. Delia squealed with delight. "She found it! He lived on Via Orologio."

"How'd she find it?" I asked. "Didn't she look at that one already?"

"She says that they had misspelled your last name," Delia said. "With a *U* instead of an *O* . . . C-*u*-c-u-z-z-o."

The woman read from the long script-laden page, and Delia translated: "When Loreto was born, his father was not in the village—usually it's the father who comes to the town hall and declares the birth of his son. He must have been somewhere working away, either in Italy or even outside the country. She doesn't know that." The archivist looked up and said something, which Delia translated: "Because his father was not in San Donato and couldn't declare his birth, the midwife came here and declared the birth of Loreto Cocuzzo."

"The midwife?" I asked.

"Yes, your great-grandfather was delivered by a midwife," Delia confirmed.

The archivist smirked, satisfied with having solved the mystery. She shuffled through the cards again for more information.

"Who would the midwife be?" I asked. Delia turned to the archivist and asked.

"Allora," the woman said, scanning the page.

"She's going to give it to you," Delia said.

"Cardarelli, Carolina," she said. "Carolina Cardarelli."

"That's her name," Delia said. She wrote down the name for me on a scrap of paper.

Cardarelli, I thought. *Where had I heard that name before?*

CHAPTER 22

What would you risk dying for—and for whom—is perhaps the most profound question a person can ask themselves. The vast majority of people in modern society are able to pass their whole lives without ever having to answer that question, which is both an enormous blessing and a significant loss.

—Sebastian Junger

E arlier in the day, Delia had told me about another woman by the name of Cardarelli, a Maria Cardarelli, who was now ninety-five years old and living in Newton, Massachusetts. Along with Brighton and Quincy, Newton was a thriving enclave of Sandonatese immigrants in Massachusetts, many of whom shipped to the United States in the wake of World War II. They came to live in the village of Nonantum, around what was known as Silver Lake. Although the body of water had been filled entirely with cement and rubble by the 1970s, the Italian community in Newton still referred to their hometown simply as the Lake. With the Italian flag's green, white, and red painted as the street lines, residents of the Lake kept their ties to San Donato tight. In 1980 Newton was officially named San Donato's sister city. When my father and I pedaled into the village a few days ago, we spotted a sign commemorating the sisterhood.

The strongest connection between the two places, of course, was found in the people—people like Maria Cardarelli. Delia had visited Maria in Newton. She told me how Maria had immigrated to the United States in 1947 with her mother and sisters. Maria's father had emigrated seventeen years earlier, in 1930, but once he reached the United States, he never contacted his wife and three children again. So it was that Maria and her mother and sisters fended for themselves back in San Donato throughout the horrors of World War II.

After arriving in Boston with no money and unable to speak English, Maria managed to get a job as a seamstress. She had assisted one of the most talented tailors in San Donato, so her skills quickly won her a promotion as a dress designer, earning one hundred dollars a week. Maria eventually married an engineer from Sicily, a man by the last name of Puzzanghero, and had a brood of children and grandchildren. As her grandchildren got older, Maria entertained them with her stories of the Old Country. They reveled in her descriptions of her faraway home village, which she described as "a medieval town perched on a slope way up in the Apennine Mountains."

When Maria's husband died unexpectedly, she spiraled into despair and depression. In an effort to shake their mother out of her sorrows, her children encouraged Maria to attend storytelling events. Soon she was attending conferences across the country with thousands of others. She joined a weekly storytelling group near Newton and shared the tales of San Donato that she had lovingly told her grandkids. One story in particular, about a girl named Katja, regularly drew the group to tears.

AFTER DELIA TOLD ME about Maria Cardarelli, I looked her up online, not expecting to find any digital record of her. To my surprise, I found two books she had written, as well as a recording of her telling the story that Delia had related to me about Katja. In the scratchy audio recording, Maria's delivery is that of a master storyteller, setting the scene in San Donato with riveting imagery and an Italian flare that animated her perfect English. "During the winter, we could hear the howling of wolves coming down from the mountains that circle the town like a protective wall," she began. "Wild animals lived up there." She described living in the village with her mother and sisters during the war, which she said "did not have a face for me . . . until one day a group of Jewish people were sent by the Italian government to my hometown."

Among the Jews sent to the village in 1940 were a couple named Ulla and Mardko Tennebaum; they rented a room from Maria's mother and lived with their family. "Mardko was a doctor and whenever he would hear of people in town in need of medical attention, he would not hesitate to care for them," she remembered. Because the Fascists forbade the interned Jews from working and making money, the grateful villagers would repay Dr. Tennebaum for his medical care with food that he would share with Maria's family. "I was very confused about my government's policy towards these Jewish people, calling them 'Enemies of the Country,'" Maria said. "To me they were the most wonderful people . . . Mardko and Ulla became our family." A couple of years into their internment in San Donato, the Tennebaums welcomed a young girl into the world, whom they named Katja. "Katja was like a living doll for us," Maria said. "We made all the things she needed . . . and when she started talking, she called my mother 'Ma.'" Maria's mother cared for Katja like she was her own daughter.

While listening to the recording of Maria's story, I searched the internet for Mardko Tennebaum and eventually came across an image that had been digitized by the Holocaust Memorial Museum in Washington, DC. In the photo the handsome young doctor has wavy black hair and is looking down upon his cooing young daughter, Katja. He looks contemplative yet strained. What must have been running through his mind at that moment? Here was this defenseless child in his arms, innocent of all wrongdoing, beginning her life as an internee in a foreign land. And here was this man, trained with the gift of saving lives, yet pained by the fact that he might not be able to save that of his own daughter.

"One morning in January 1944, the sun had not yet made it over the mountains," Maria said in the recording. "We heard the rumbling of trucks approaching the town. We held our breath and listened." Coming up from the south, bands of Nazis descended upon the village to round up the Jews. "Panic took over the whole town," Maria said. "Confusion and anxiety reflected on everybody's faces as the people of the town looked out through the smallish windows of their homes as the German Nazis pushed the Jewish people inside their trucks." Sympathizers must have tipped the Nazis off, Maria said, because the soldiers knew exactly where to go. "Otherwise they couldn't have found the Jews so fast," she said. "We all saw the Jews being shoved into these trucks, saw the trucks leave the town . . . and never saw them again."

Somehow, Mardko and Ulla Tennebaum managed to slip out of the village, to escape into the mountains with a handful of other Jews when the Nazis arrived. However, they were forced to leave Katja behind in the care of Maria and her mother. They hid in the mountains for months, "living like nomads," as Maria put it, shivering through the fierce winter and surviving on the food that some villagers covertly carried up to them. Then one day, there came a knock on Maria's door. It was Katja's mother, Ulla. Wracked with fear, Maria's mother yanked Ulla through the doorway. "Ulla, do you realize what you have done?" Maria remembered her mother saying. "You have put your life in danger. You have put your daughter's life in danger and the lives of my daughters as well as mine. And the lives of all the people in the town." After months apart, desperate to see her daughter, Ulla had snuck back into the village in broad daylight.

Thirty minutes later, another knock came pounding on Maria's door. They looked out the window to find two heavily armed Nazis. Ulla hid in the bathroom, while Maria's mother opened the heavy wooden door. The Nazis demanded information about the Tennebaums. They'd been tipped off by a sympathizer, who was standing next to them. But Maria's mother stood stone faced and claimed to have not seen them in months. The Nazis said they'd be back. "It was a miracle that the soldiers and the sympathizer never entered the house," Maria said. "My mother shut the door and fainted. Her knees went first and she started to tremble . . . then I saw her on the floor, lifeless." When she finally came to, Maria's mother told Ulla that she had to leave immediately. Everyone's lives were in danger. Ulla said that she would leave at dark, but Maria's mother demanded they couldn't wait. The Nazis would be back. They needed to get Ulla out of the house and into the mountains immediately.

"My mother and her neighbors were faced with the problem of how to get Ulla out of town," Maria remembered. "So they came up with the idea of putting Ulla in a large harvest basket." A small woman, Ulla curled up at the bottom of the basket and was covered first with a blanket and then with a layer of chicken manure. "Costanza Rufo, a strong woman from the neighborhood, made a donut out of cloth and put it on her head," Maria remembered. "With my mother's help, she hoisted the basket onto her head."

Costanza Rufo then walked down the steep, cobbled streets of San Donato, balancing a full-grown woman on her head. She approached the Nazi checkpoint at the end of the road and told them that she was bringing fertilizer out to the field. Listening to Maria describe the scene, it was hard to fathom the constitution of Costanza, her sheer strength, while she mustered the courage to lie straight in the faces of the Nazi occupiers.

The Nazis let her pass. Safely hidden in the fields, Costanza took the basket off her head and set Ulla free to rush into the mountains. Meanwhile, back at Maria's home, they needed to find a way to hide Katja. Maria's mother dressed the young girl as a peasant and instructed her daughter Sylvia to walk Katja to their grandparents' house to hide until the Nazis gave up their search. "All of this was taking place while the town was being bombarded and shelled by the Allied Forces that were trying to push the German army north," Maria said. "I remember that day. The sun looked as if it transpired [*sic*] through a black veil. The air was heavy. The town feels to be in the grip of an evil spirit . . . I asked myself, 'Are we all going to get killed today?'"

The following day, four Nazis returned to Maria's home and surrounded her house with guns drawn. Maria and her sisters hid under a blanket in the closet. "In the darkness, the fear was unbearable," she remembered. "My mother kept going in and out of the closet all night. She was expecting the Nazis to start shooting and breaking the windows and doors at any moment." But at dawn the Nazis left and never returned to Maria's home.

LISTENING TO MARIA'S STORY, I felt an emotional sense of pride. Although I didn't have a direct connection to those events or to Maria's family—beyond the possibility that one of her "cousins" may have been the midwife who delivered my great-grandfather—the fact that my roots stemmed back to a land of such heroes relieved some of the unease I felt about Italy's role in the war. Many in San Donato were on the right side of history at one of its darkest times.

I wondered, *What would I have done had I been living in the village back then?* Maria's family had nothing to gain and everything to lose by helping the Tennebaums. Maria's mother was caring for three daughters on her own, after her husband had abandoned her. She had every reason to care solely for herself and her family. Yet she put her family's life in danger to help three strangers. *Why? How?*

And what about Costanza Rufo? One second she was minding her own business, the next she was carrying a Jewish woman *on her head* through a Nazi checkpoint. The slightest misstep would have cost her her life. Yet when asked to help a complete stranger, Costanza—a simple woman who had never left the village—snapped into action. *What possessed these women to act so heroically?* I asked myself. *Was it a conscious decision, or were they running on instinct? Did they grapple with whether to act, or was there no question about it? How did they steel themselves in the face of certain death, risking not only themselves but also their little loved ones?*

I had pondered these questions when thinking about Gino Bartali during our ride to San Donato. Now that I was in the heart of such uncommon heroism, I hoped to find answers.

CHAPTER 23

Start with what is right rather than what is acceptable.

—Franz Kafka

Delia led me out of the town council building, past the Holocaust memorial, and into a small courtyard where the shape of Italy was sculpted into the center of a dry fountain. I clutched a copy of my great-grandfather's birth certificate, which the archivist had printed and notarized. A part of me was awakening to a past life, memories I had never personally made but that I now felt somehow intimately connected to.

Until now, my family history had begun with my grandfather. I hadn't been able to see beyond him, especially given how emotionally severed he had been from his own father. Walking around the village of San Donato, seeing my family name carved in ancient stone, and holding proof of my connection to this place, a real sense of belonging took root. Maybe it was all in my head, but it felt physical, as if a chemical reaction was firing off on a molecular level. A voice in my head called out, *Welcome home!*

"I'm so glad the archivist was able to get that for you," Delia said, gesturing to the birth certificate. "That is wonderful to have. So exciting."

"Yeah, I was getting kind of nervous there," I said.

Delia chuckled. But still, a question weighed me down, an anvil clinging to this rising balloon of euphoria. The role of the sympathizers—I just couldn't shake it. As much as I was afraid of what the answer might be, I needed to know which side of history my family fell on. Had they been sympathizers who gave up Jews who were ultimately sent to their deaths?

My great-grandfather had immigrated to the United States in 1915, years before the Nazis occupied the village, but what about the Cocuzzos he had left behind?

I had to find out what I could. "Delia, I don't know if you know the answer to this, but, during the war, do you know what my family did?"

"How do you mean?" she asked.

"I mean, did they . . . did they give people up? Were they sympathizers?"

With compassion in her eyes, I could tell Delia was attuned to the conflict rumbling in my heart and mind. "Oh no," she said. "No, Robbie, no they were not."

My entire being let out a sigh of relief.

"Your family members were not sympathizers," she said. "We know who the sympathizers were . . . some of them still live in San Donato."

I hadn't imagined that prospect. "They do?"

"Yes, they do," Delia said. "But we also know who the heroes were. Some of them are still alive, still living in San Donato. A woman named Pasqualina Perrella, she must be ninety-five years old by now. I met her when I was doing social work, making house visits. When the Nazis occupied the village, Pasqualina forged IDs for the Jews." As I had learned from the story of Gino Bartali, IDs were a vital ticket for survival for many Jews. The act of forging them was regarded as one of the gravest offenses in the eyes of the Nazis, punishable by death. "Pasqualina worked in the archive office," Delia said, referring to the same office where we'd just obtained my great-grandfather's birth certificate.

"Do you think I could meet her?" I asked, now feeling emboldened by my family's apparent innocence.

"I'm sure you can," Delia said. "She runs a little shop down here. Let's go see if she's in. You just never know with these old ladies. They're reaching the end of their road, you know? There's not too many of them left."

DELIA LED ME DOWN from the courtyard and back onto the main road that my father and I had pedaled up just a few days ago when we first arrived at the village. "This road is why the Nazis considered San Donato so effective for interning Jews," Delia explained. "Only one way in and one way out, so the Nazis could put checkpoints on either end." Walking along the narrow road, I admired the ornate knockers on the heavy wooden doors we passed. Delia paused at one of the doors, which was slightly ajar, then pushed it open. "Pasqaulina?" she called.

A wedge of sunlight spread out onto the cement floor of the shop, illuminating specks of dust floating in the air as we entered. Through the darkness I could barely make out displays of merchandise lining the walls. Scarves hung from rafters, boxes of unopened tissues were stacked on the counter along with toys still in their packaging, rolls of wrapping paper jutted out of a bucket, men's dress shirts and babies' bibs were wrapped in plastic, and women's dresses swung on a rack. The miscellaneous items were covered in dust and extended into the far reaches of the room. It looked like an old-fashioned five-and-dime store from back home. At the center of it all was a hearty old woman in a blue dress, sitting in a wooden chair and reading from a prayer book.

"Pasqualina?" Delia repeated, slightly louder. "It's Delia Roffo."

Pasqualina drew the glasses off her face and lowered the book to a tiny folding table by her side, where there was an assortment of religious icons and statuettes. She narrowed her eyes on Delia, allowing them to adjust to the light. "Ah sì, Delia, come va?"

Delia waved me into the room and introduced me to Pasqualina. "Questo è Roberto Cocuzzo," she said. "È di famiglia sandonatese." I took Pasqualina's hand, expecting it to be bony and frail, but instead found a strong, meaty grip that defied the woman's ninety-plus years. Her white hair showed streaks of dark gray and was neatly combed. She had strong features and a broad, welcoming smile. Pasqualina did not look her age. She motioned for us to sit next to her.

"Novantacinque," she said, smoothing out the folds of her dress on her lap.

"She's ninety-five," Delia translated.

"Incredible," I said. "Tell her she doesn't look a day past seventy." Delia translated the compliment, and Pasqualina laughed warmly.

"Do you think she'd be willing to tell me about what happened during the war?" I asked. The topic seemed too heavy, too emotionally charged to abruptly broach with someone I'd just met, but this was a fleeting opportunity. The heroes of World War II—men and women like Cardinal Elia Dalla Costa, Gino Bartali, and Maria Cardarelli—were dying off by the day, taking their stories with them. Sitting before me was a link to that brand of heroism—I didn't want to waste a minute of her time.

"She's happy to answer any questions you might have," Delia said, translating Pasqualina's generous response to my request.

I scanned my mind, which instantly went blank. There was so much I wanted to know, but with so many questions firing in my head, I didn't know where to start. *Start with chronology*, I thought. "When did she start working in the office where she forged the IDs?" I asked.

"Nineteen forty," Delia translated. "Right when the war started, she was eighteen years old. She went to work in the archive office because the two men who were working there were taken out of those positions to go to war. Pasqualina could read and write, so she was called for the job."

"Was she alone?" I asked. I could sense that Delia was enjoying this key role as translator. She exuded such a deep love for the people of San Donato and its history. She understood how rare this conversation was.

"No, she was working with another woman," Delia translated. "Pasqualina wasn't the only one that helped. She really wants you to know that. There were many other people helping the Jews in the village."

"What was it like living here when the Nazis arrived?" I asked.

Pasqualina listened to the question and studied the pattern on her dress. She looked up and answered. "We were stuck in our homes," Delia translated. "We never went out. There was a curfew. Everyone was fearful to come out of their homes. After a certain hour, you couldn't leave."

"How did Pasqualina come up with the idea of making the IDs?" I asked.

"The Jews actually approached her and asked her for them," Delia translated. "She really didn't want to do it at first. She knew she was risking her life. But she knew she had to do it. It was an act of faith that she wanted to protect these people." Delia listened to Pasqualina and translated: "They would come right here to her home, because they were afraid to come out in public."

"This is where she lived?" I asked.

"Yes, in fact, right where you're sitting is where the Jews would meet with her. As you can see, they could come right in off the street. They would come and have lunch at her house. And then after they left, her father would say, 'What are you doing? You're putting our family at risk with this! If the soldiers find out, they're going to shoot us all. We're all going to get shot because of what you are doing!'"

I could hardly imagine the tension that took place in this household. I pictured an eighteen-year-old girl arguing with her father. Except they weren't arguing over curfew or the car keys. Pasqualina had to convince her father to put his family at risk for the sake of others. "So what would she say to her father?" I asked.

Pasqualina smiled. "She'd say, 'They're poor people and we need to help them,'" Delia said. "There's an expression in San Donato: 'Do good and forget about it. But do bad and you'll always remember.' If she did bad and didn't help, she never would have forgotten it."

"How would she make the IDs?" I asked.

"Everything was written by hand," Delia said. "She worked with other resisters who were trying to save the Jews, and they would suggest which names to use for the IDs."

"Where was this all happening?" I asked.

Pasqualina spoke for a while, and Delia's eyebrows nearly shot off her forehead when she heard the answer. "Oh my God, I didn't know this. Pasqualina says she was forging these IDs in the Fascist headquarters, what they called the House of Fascists. They moved all the town hall offices into the headquarters so the Fascists could oversee everything and keep tabs."

Incredible. Pasqualina forged the IDs with the Fascists literally looking over her shoulder. "She's getting goose bumps thinking about it," Delia said.

"How many people did she forge IDs for?" I asked.

"At least thirty," Delia translated. One of the foreign Jews she helped save was named Samuel Berlin. Pasqualina changed his identity to Antonio Bruno, born in Naples. The forged identification kept Berlin from being shipped off to Auschwitz, saving his life.

"Did she know where the Jews were hiding?" Pasqualina listened to Delia's translation and nodded, pointing to the ceiling.

"Yes, some of them hid in her house."

I gasped. "Really?" Pasqualina's family eventually took in Jews, one of whom was a woman named Greta Bloch, the girlfriend of the famous writer Franz Kafka.

"It was said that they had a child together," Delia continued, "but the baby was put up for adoption and died before the war. Greta was born in Berlin and lived in Florence before she was interned in San Donato. She was the most famous of the people interned here."

"Did Pasqualina make her an ID?" I asked.

"No, Greta was too well known. All the Nazis and Fascists already knew who she was, so the ID wouldn't have done anything for her," Delia said. "Pasqualina really loved her, she says. Greta would say, 'Besides the fact that you're a beautiful young woman, you also have a beautiful heart.'"

Apparently the village tried to keep Greta hidden. They moved her from house to house, but the Nazis ultimately found her. They arrested her and sent her to Auschwitz, where she was murdered. Pasqualina's gaze became distant at the retelling, her face flushed with emotion. "She remembers watching them put the Jews in the trucks and taking them away," Delia said. "It was almost at the end of the war. That's when she was most fearful. They would talk to one another, saying that the Nazis were coming for her family next."

Eventually they did. One day, a group of armed Nazis came to Pasqualina's home and demanded her father turn her over or else they'd slaughter the entire family. The trembling girl came out to the street, where they presented her with one of her forged identifications. The Nazis demanded to know if it was her handwriting. She nodded yes, expecting to be shot on the spot, but miraculously they let her go.

Tears welled in Pasqualina's eyes. Delia fought back her own emotion. "'What memories I have,' she's saying. She feels like crying because she thinks about them every day. They were such good people who died. They suffered a lot. They all come back to her in her mind, she says, all the people who she tried to save. When she can't sleep, it all comes back to her. She prays for them." Pasqualina began reorganizing the statuettes of the saints on her side table and looked up at us. "After the war, some of the people she saved actually did come back to see her," Delia said. "They came back and they picked her up and hugged her to thank her. They said, 'You saved our lives. Because of that ID, you saved our lives.'"

As Pasqualina told her story, I reflected on how truly exceptional our conversation was. Here was this woman sitting in a darkened shop for nearly eighty years, quietly reliving these scenes of her past. How easily they could have gone unheard, fading into the ether of time, completely forgotten. There was no plaque outside honoring her contributions to the lives she had saved. Her name wasn't carved in the stone of a monument. Instead, her legacy lived out in the descendants of those she had saved, people who may not know that she ever existed at all.

I wanted to know where Pasqualina found the courage to do all that. Delia translated the question. Pasqualina turned toward me as she answered. A beatific glow surrounded her, the room's clutter fading into the shadows. My whole being was seized by her gaze. "My faith made me courageous," she said, through Delia's translation. "But there's an expression in San Donato. 'The people of San Donato have a terrible tongue—they talk too much—but they have a beautiful heart.'"

Pasqualina was showing me just how beautiful it was.

CHAPTER 24

We shall not cease from exploration
And the end of all exploring
Will be to arrive where we started
And know the place for the first time.

—T. S. Eliot

Dad was sprawled out on the ground like a cat warming himself in the sun. He had his head leaning up against the cafe's cement wall, with his arms and legs flopped to the side on the rock patio. He looked like he had just fallen out of the second-story window. We'd returned from another long ride into the mountains above San Donato, and despite draining two cappuccinos, Dad conked out right in his plastic seat. When I came back from the restroom, I found him flopped on the ground fast asleep, carefree as Tom Sawyer. That is, if Tom Sawyer were sixty-four years old, rocking a scruffy beard, and dressed head to toe in lime-green spandex.

Having grown completely accustomed to my father's bizarre sleeping habits, I thought nothing of his impromptu catnap and continued to spoon the remaining cappuccino foam into my mouth. The usual gang of old men playing cards looked at us with faces of shock or disgust—I couldn't tell which from where I sat.

A few minutes later, Delia burst onto the scene. "What's going on?" she yelped. "I've been getting calls! Where's your father?"

I pointed to the heap of snoring body parts on the ground. His mouth was now wide open.

"What's wrong with him?" she asked. "Everybody has been calling me. They said 'Your friend, he's sick . . . he's passed out in the piazza!'"

Dad's eyes peeled open and he shook himself awake nonchalantly. "What's up?" he said, lifting himself on to his elbows.

"Jesus Christ, Stephen! I thought you had a heart attack or something," Delia said.

"No, but if I have another coffee I just might," he said, chuckling. "You want one?"

"I can't," Delia said, readjusting her bag on her shoulder. "I have to go to Cassino to pay a fucking fine. I was in a car accident not long ago. This bus I was driving behind, it was leaking oil. Anyway, my car hit the oil and skidded off the road."

"Oh my God," Dad said.

"Yeah, yeah, yeah. Well, I was okay, but I was actually planning on suing the bus company."

"So what happened?" I asked.

"Not only could I not sue the bus company, but I also hit a fucking Roman wall. Some ancient wall. I hit this thing and damaged it a little bit, not that bad but enough that they gave me a fucking fine! Can you believe it? Just my luck!"

So Delia was headed to Cassino to try to get out of the fine. "I'll see you guys later in the piazza. Stephen, stay off the fucking ground, would ya?" She threw up her hands and scampered off, stopping to talk to two people on her way. Delia had been one of the most valuable gifts on this journey. Being in her company had opened up this place to us in ways that would have been impossible otherwise.

"So how about it?" Dad asked. "You want another coffee?"

"Sure, why not? What else are we doing?"

"I know," he said. "Don't you just love it? Nothing to do. Nowhere to be." I ordered a couple more cappuccinos and returned to Dad at the table. A warm breeze passed through the piazza and the leaves swayed lazily overhead. "This is the longest I've ever taken off from work," he said, sipping his drink. "The longest vacation in probably fifty years."

"This is just the beginning, Dad," I said. "You should be doing this every year from now on. Taking a couple weeks off here and there." He'd been thinking a lot about it.

"I could really live at this pace. Get up, have a coffee, go for a bike ride, come back, take a nap, then another coffee, spend the rest of the day hanging out in the piazza. Have a big dinner at night. What else is there?"

"Those are entirely feasible retirement objectives," I told him.

"I'd probably drive your mother nuts if I retired."

"As if you don't already?"

"Seriously, I don't know if I could ever *not* work. I don't think I would ever fully retire—maybe just slow down a bit."

"You definitely deserve at least that, Dad."

WATCHING MY FATHER BASK leisurely in the sun, my mind flashed to my teenage years when I got my first job working for him at his hair salon. For most of my early childhood, my father's day-to-day work as a hairdresser and salon owner was completely unknown to me. Apart from coming in to get my hair cut every couple of months, I didn't know what went into his career. That was largely because he rarely told us about it. Every night, he dragged himself through the door like a zombie, wiped down his bike, showered, ate something quietly by himself, and then retreated to the den to watch the Red Sox—all without saying much of anything.

Only when I started working for him on weekends did I come to understand why he was so quiet and reticent when he came home each night. I'd sit on a metal radiator in the corner of his salon, waiting to sweep up hair, run errands, and throw the towels and smocks in the laundry. He paid me thirty dollars a day, not including the five-dollar tips his employees slipped me. From my perch on the radiator, I watched my father in action. His performance was unlike anything I'd imagined.

For ten straight hours, Dad dazzled his clients, entertaining them nonstop as he deftly cut their hair. He was on his feet all day, never stopping to eat or take a break. One after another, his clients took their seat and a new performance commenced. My father met each of them with the same energy and enthusiasm, asking about their jobs, their interests, and their spouses and children—all of whom he knew by name. As much as getting their hair cut, his clients were there to see him. He poured every bit of himself out for each person. His work ethic was something to behold, and I knew exactly where he got it from.

"You worked for Papa growing up, right?" I asked, sipping on my cappuccino, my face kissed by the warm San Donato sun.

"Yeah, started landscaping with him when I was thirteen," Dad said, sliding his chair back to the cafe table. "When I started high school, I used to work the summers, taking care of Papa's clients' properties."

"What was that like?" I asked.

"It was actually kind of fun," he said. "I didn't get paid much. I never remember getting much money. But I loved hanging around my father."

Much like Dad, my grandfather had legions of faithful clients whose properties he tended to for decades, wielding rakes, lawn mowers, and hedge clippers. Up until very recently, Papa still had a handful of properties that he cared for at the same rate he'd always charged. "When did you stop working for him?" I asked.

"I guess when I went to college," he said.

"What did he think of you going to college?" I asked.

"That's the funny thing, with that generation," Dad said, studying the patio's stone mosaic. "School was never important for them. My family never stressed education for me. I mean, when I was in the fifth grade, my grandmother told me to quit school and go work for my father. So I went to school feeling a lot of guilt."

"Papa made you feel guilty?" I asked.

"He did," my father said reluctantly. "I used to feel guilty, especially going away to college. I didn't get a ton of support when I went. He didn't take any interest in school for me."

"Did he ever say anything about it?" I asked.

"You know, he didn't have to. My mother once told me that Papa was jealous of me going to school. Just knowing that made it difficult for me to really get into my studies."

"Do you think that's why you didn't finish?" My father had attended the University of Southern Florida, where he'd majored in special education. With only a semester left, he inexplicably dropped out. Our family never discussed why he didn't finish, especially with only a few months left. I never knew him to quit anything in his life, so his reasons—or lack thereof—for dropping out were always a mystery to me.

"If I had a little more support from him, I'm sure I would have finished," he said. "But I didn't. It was never talked about. If I could do it all over again, I would have gone to art school. I really wanted to go to Mass Art, maybe study to be an architect or something like that."

He ended up at hairdressing school. "What did Papa think about that?" I asked.

"Papa was actually really supportive. He said, 'You're artistic, you'll probably do well.' I just wish he had said that while I was in college." Dad knocked back the last drop of his cappuccino. "That's why for you and your brother, it was a definite: there was no way you weren't going to college."

Listening to my father unpack this story, I reflected on the cause and effect that is being a father to a son. My great-grandfather Loreto was tyrannical to my grandfather, making him feel alienated and unloved. So when my grandfather had my father, he pledged "to do the opposite," as he once put it. Papa did everything in his power to make sure that my father and his siblings were surrounded in a protective shield of unquestionable love. But my grandfather still had an old-world view of education. He put the value of hard work above schooling, and not only failed to support my father as a student but made him feel guilty for pursuing his studies.

When my father had me, he pledged to do the opposite. He and my mom sent me to one of the most prestigious private high schools in New England and then to one of the top colleges in the country. They paid for my tuition in full, despite the fact that it cost more than half of their annual income. My father saw to it that I became the first Cocuzzo in my family to get a college degree. He made sure I graduated without a penny in student loans, giving me the opportunity to pursue my own artistic passions that he never had the chance to pursue for himself.

A heavy sense of guilt blanketed me. Although I never said a word about it to him growing up, or to anybody for that matter, sometimes I felt uncomfortable about what my father did for a living. Growing up, I envied my friends whose fathers were teachers, lawyers, or businessmen. I rarely told anyone that my father hadn't graduated from college or that he didn't wear a suit and tie to work. And now, in this moment, I felt deeply ashamed of myself for having ever thought such things. His decisions weren't wholly his own. But more important, I failed to appreciate that he'd seized the opportunities that were available to him and had become enormously successful in his own right. His talents brought joy to others, while he worked himself ragged to ensure that my brother and I had every opportunity Papa hadn't provided my father growing up. Dad had "done the opposite," as Papa would say, and ultimately I was the beneficiary of the generational cause and effect between fathers and sons, stretching back a hundred years.

"I'LL BE BACK IN a bit," I told my father. He was packing up his tiny backpack one last time. In the morning we were pedaling to Cassino, about twenty-five miles away, to take the train north back to Florence and eventually jump on a flight to Boston. But there was one last thing I wanted to do before I left San Donato.

I strode up through the piazza, past the World War II monument and up the narrow side street where my great-grandfather was born. Like all the walkways in the village, Via Orologio was made up of hundreds of thousands of stones, wedged into the ground and polished by the tides of time. Orologio literally means "clock," on account of the clock tower at the top of the street, but for my purposes this section of stone felt frozen in time. Via Orologio was living evidence of the world my great-grandfather left behind. Although the details of his life remain a mystery to me, I took a small degree of comfort knowing that I had literally walked in his footsteps, if just for a little while.

From Via Orologio, I continued further up into the village as it climbed the mountainside. I followed my gut, taking lefts and rights around one enchanting scene after the next. Ivy crawled up the side of stone facades. A fountain trickled drinking water from the high-altitude springs above.

Ornate knockers, hand-carved doors, and terra-cotta roofs guided my eyes. Through the gaps between the buildings, I made out the valley below with its patches of olive groves. All the roads led to one place at the top—Santuario di San Donato—the namesake church that served as the cornerstone of this remote village.

Unlike most of the gray stone buildings in the village, the Catholic church was painted canary yellow. I entered and found the sacred space completely empty and filled with a heavy silence. Below the church's dramatic vaulted ceilings was a simple altar set behind a statue of Saint Donato. From my back pocket, I drew out the photo I had shown my father when we first arrived in the village—of Papa, my father, and me: three generations of Cocuzzos. On the back of the photo, I penned a short note detailing the journey that had taken place to deliver this photo to this most ancient corner of San Donato. We came across an ocean and up and down hundreds of miles, but the journey had actually taken a hundred years to complete. A century had gone by, but finally these three sons of San Donato had returned to show their faces.

LATER THAT EVENING, MY father and I walked down to the cemetery on the village outskirts. We passed through its wrought-iron gates and high, arched entryway. About the size of a baseball diamond, the cemetery was enclosed in tall white stucco walls and was divided into sections. The bucolic grounds were dotted with trees, giving the cemetery the feel of a botanical garden.

"Here's a Cocuzzo," Dad said. "Carmela Cocuzzo. Born in 1887 and died in 1979."

"1887—that's right around when your great-grandfather was born," I said.

We split up and ambled the grounds, reading the names off the gravestones—Cellucci, Cedrone, Rufo, Roffo, Peligrini. All the names were familiar, especially to my father, who could connect them to people from his neighborhood growing up. Rufo was the last name of one of Papa's best friends. Cellucci was the family name of a former governor of Massachusetts. Although the cemetery was the final resting place for all these people, these were the deepest reaches of the roots that had sprawled across an ocean and germinated a whole new branch of Sandonatesi in the United States. Back home, these roots felt flimsy and theoretical, yet in this cemetery the connection to my ancestors was strong and personal.

The United States is a nation of immigrants. Many Americans have the same story as me. They too could pull at the thread that sewed their family story together and trace it back to the very first stitch. The popularity of DNA testing and the rise of online family tree archives has inspired a growing curiosity among Americans to reconnect with their past. But I'd contend that reading about your family makeup is intrinsically different than walking amid it.

Reaching the back of the cemetery, I turned and spotted my father standing at the top of the stairs near the entrance. He appeared to be admiring the handsome stonework of the arches. I made my way back to him. This trip had become all about discovery. The Tuscan landscape. The depths of my physical endurance. The heroic history of my forebears. But the most dramatic discoveries had come from the person who'd been right in front of me my entire life. I had to cross an ocean and pedal five hundred miles to truly find him. And perhaps it took those lengths as well for him to finally find me.

CHAPTER 25

The way you help heal the world is you start with your own family.

—Mother Theresa

Dad was sitting at the kitchen counter, sewing some pieces of fabric together when I woke up. We were both still on Italian time; it was just past 4 a.m. Of course, my father would have been up at this ungodly hour anyway, with or without the jet lag. I poured myself a cup of coffee and took a seat across from him. I couldn't tell if it was my eyes adjusting to the light, but my father looked oddly different than the night before.

"Did you dye your beard?" I asked.

He laughed. "Yeah."

"Why?"

"*Ugh*, when I saw that photo of myself at the passport thing last night, I just thought I looked so old with that gray beard."

We had landed at Boston's Logan Airport around midnight. Upon arrival, we'd gone through passport control, which used a sophisticated electronic kiosk check-in system. You put your passport into the machine, and it takes an unflattering photo of you that is printed on a paper receipt that you hand to the customs agent. Groggy from the flight, Dad had struggled to figure out the machine and quickly grew frustrated. When the kiosk finally spat out his photo, he was disgusted by the tired face printed on the receipt. "I looked like I was a hundred years old," he said.

"Everyone looks like shit in those photos, Dad," I said. "I thought the gray beard actually made you look pretty distinguished."

"Whatever," he said.

I'd spent eighteen straight days with him, but my father could still surprise me. Sometime in the last four hours, he had dyed his thick, bushy beard as black as shoe polish. Adding his sun-kissed face and tattoos, he looked like a roadie for Guns N' Roses. But what I found even more surprising than the beard was that he actually felt self-conscious about looking old. I mean the guy had just conquered some five hundred miles on a bike, climbing enough vertical feet to reach the summit of Everest, all while keeping up with someone half his age. How could he possibly think of himself as old?

"What are you sewing?" I asked.

"I'm making a scarf."

"Out of what?"

"The blanket from the plane," he said. "I snuck it out in my jacket. I had it threaded though the arms."

"Dad, you didn't have to sneak it out. You could have just taken it. What do they care?"

He put the needle and thread down and raised his coffee for a sip. "So you still want to go for a ride?" he asked.

"Yeah. Looks cold out there."

"Twenty-five right now." His eyes widened. "But it will warm up when the sun comes out and we get moving."

We were both eager to test out the new climbing muscles on the hills at home. Around 6 a.m. we dragged ourselves into the bone-breaking New England cold and mounted our bikes. We glided down the hill that Dad used to take me down as a toddler when I would ride in the plywood baby seat on the back of his bike. We reached Mass Ave., where my father had commuted to work for the past forty years.

"Let's do Park Ave.," he said, when we stopped at the light.

"Sounds like a good one."

Park Ave. was one of the steepest hills in town, rising up for about a half mile. As we mounted the bottom of the hill, we fell into the familiar formation of the past two weeks, me in the front and him in the back. I stayed in the saddle, punching the pedals with the back of my legs, aware of the power reserve I could unleash at any moment. I stared down at my gloved hands and then my feet, hidden under thick neoprene booties. The cold was brutal. Cycling was much more fun under the Tuscan sun.

Dad pulled around the side of me. Standing up in his pedals, he accelerated. Rocking his bike from side to side, he shot past me in a flash and took the lead. Three bike-lengths away, he drove hard on his pedals, gaining more and more ground. I decided not to chase him down, but just watched him go. He looked strong and light. His pedal strokes were swift and deliberate like he was chopping down a tree. One thing's for certain: he definitely didn't look old. After two weeks following my lead, my father was back on his home turf and he was breaking away once again.

DAD AND I DIDN'T talk much during the drive to Papa's. Nor did we feel the need to. We'd become so in tune with one another that we could communicate in silence. He sat in the passenger seat of my car, holding the handle to the right of his head. A light rain collected on the windshield, until I clicked the wipers.

"He's going to hate this," Dad said, breaking the quiet. "There's no way he's going to want to leave."

"Remember what Mom said: we're telling him that this isn't permanent. He's not leaving for good. He's just going to stay with us long enough for him to get his strength back."

"He's going to see straight through that," Dad said.

I knew he was right. There was another long stretch of silence. I watched the hood of my car devour the white dotted line on the highway. It felt weird to be driving a car after depending entirely on my legs to get anywhere for the past two weeks. "Here's what we'll do," I said. "You get him situated with all his stuff and we'll lift him into the wheelchair. Then we'll carry him in the wheelchair down the stairs and I'll have the car right there. We can bring him right to the door. I'll make sure the heat is cranking."

I was terribly nervous about what my grandfather was going to look like when we opened the door. Hospice care had been brought in after we'd left for Italy, and he hadn't eaten much of anything since. The only thing keeping him alive was the few sips of ginger ale he could force down each day.

My mother had told me about the family's plan to move him to my parents' house and I was concerned about transporting him there, an hour and a half away from my grandparents' home on the Cape. But the morning after we landed, Dad and I were sent to bring Papa home.

This role of caregiver to my grandfather couldn't have been more foreign to me and my father. Throughout Papa's life, he refused help from everyone, especially from his children and grandchildren. It wasn't that he was too prideful but rather that he didn't want to inconvenience anyone, especially not his family. Before we left for Italy, Papa became irate when he caught my father taking out his trash. My grandfather struggled to relinquish control, and as a result, we felt inept in taking control.

Getting him from his house, into the wheelchair, down the stairs, into the car, across a hundred miles, into my parents' driveway, back in the wheelchair, up the stairs, and into a chair waiting for him in the living room terrified me. *Would we be able to carry him down the stairs?* I wondered. *What if he needs to go to the bathroom on the ride back? What do we do then?* I decided not to pose these questions to my father; I knew he was already pondering them himself.

Papa was sitting solemnly in his chair when we opened the door. He had his legs crossed and he was staring out the sliding glass doors to the shed, where his Italian flag still hung. The television was off. "Papa!" I called out, putting my hand on his shoulder. His head turned painfully slowly and he fixed his eyes on me. His cheeks had thinned and his eyes were sunken into his skull, but when he recognized me, his face turned up in a smile. I lowered myself to him and draped my arms over his shoulders.

"I didn't think I was going to see you guys again," he said in a labored whisper. I released my grandfather from my embrace and moved to the side for my father.

"Hey, Dad," my father said, his voice caught in his throat.

"Stephen," Papa whispered.

As my father lowered himself to hug Papa, I turned to find my grandmother, who shuffled into the living room. She looked shell-shocked, her hair unkempt and eyes watery. "Oh, Robbie," she said, as I took her in my arms. "It's been so hard. So hard."

"I know it has," I said.

"How do you think he looks?" she asked.

"He looks . . . looks good, Nonnie."

"I just don't know what to do," she said, her voice cracking. "He doesn't eat. Hasn't eaten in weeks. I don't know what to do."

"Well, we're going to help you now," I said.

I walked Nonnie back to the couch, where my father sat with Papa, telling him about San Donato like an excited kid. "Aw, Dad, this place was incredible," he said. "All these buildings were beautiful stone. And the doors, the doors were all hand-carved. Hand-carved by Cocuzzos! Our family are amazing carpenters in the village. We met with all of them. They took us right in. Right in."

Papa tried to stay focused, but I could tell that he was grasping only every other word. He had only one of his hearing aids in, and trying to listen was sapping his energy. "Here, Papa, let me show you," I said. I pulled out my laptop and set it up on the coffee table in front of him. On the flight home, I had put together a slideshow of photos and set it to his favorite Italian love song, "Aldila."

The photos began in Florence with Dad sitting at a cafe table, sipping coffee in the shadow of the Duomo. Then Dad on the Ponte Vecchio looking out to the Arno. Next came photos of us pedaling out of Florence. My father's face of utter despair on the first day arriving in Siena. Then the rolling green hills and canopy of trees of Tuscany and into the frenzied streets of Rome. Then there was the photo with Tulio Rossi after getting the bike fixed. With each photo, Dad looked skinnier, tanner, and more road-worn. His face looked relaxed and at peace.

Finally, the slideshow reached photos of the village. I'd documented walking down through the winding paths, and up to the face of the monument where Cocuzzo was carved. The photos toured through the village, up Via Orologio, where Papa's father was born, and all the way to the namesake church at the top. There were photos of the people: Fulvio, Gaetano, Delia, and all the various characters in the village. There were photos of doors, knockers, and the lush olive groves Papa had imagined. The last photo in the slideshow was of my hand holding out one of the bleached-white rocks from the village.

"Here you go, Papa," I said, handing him the rock from the photo. "Now you have your own piece of the village."

SHORTLY AFTER OUR ARRIVAL at Papa's house, a representative from hospice knocked at the door. "I'm here to pick up a hospital bed and an oxygen tank," he said, reading flatly off his clipboard. "And a wheelchair."

"We're actually going to be using that wheelchair," I said, letting him in. "Can you come and get it later?"

"I'm not supposed to," he said, ruffling the pages on his clipboard. He was more of a mover than a caregiver, and I sensed that his patience for the day was waning. "Let me get going with the bed and I'll see what I can do on the chair." I showed him through the living room to where the bed was. He gave Papa and my grandmother and father a lackluster wave as he passed them. "Alright, this is going to take me twenty minutes," he said, tossing his clipboard onto the bed. "I'll come find you if I need you."

The man went to work haphazardly pulling the bed apart. He flopped the mattress to the floor and yanked metal poles from the bed frame loudly. I returned to the living room, where it was impossible to ignore the racket. As the man made trip after trip to his van parked in the driveway, hauling pieces of the bed, it was difficult not to think that we'd officially given up. Papa stared off, still clutching the rock, and didn't seem to notice the man until he walked by hauling the oxygen tank over his shoulder. "Does he need a hand?" Papa whispered.

For the hospice worker, this was just another day, entering a stranger's house who has days to live. He must have become indifferent to this scene, with its stale air and murmuring voices. "Alright, I just need your signature here," he said, handing me the clipboard.

"Can we keep the chair?"

"I don't need it," Papa piped up. "Have him take it."

Sighing, I turned back to the man and lowered my voice. "If you could just leave it here for the day, we'd really appreciate it. We're transporting him out of here and need it to get him in the car."

"Fine," he said. "I'll let my supervisor know. They'll probably come by and grab it on Monday. After that, you get charged."

With that minor victory, I closed the door behind the hospice worker and turned to my dad, who was sitting vigil next to Papa. I nodded. Dad nodded back. "Alright, Dad, you ready to get a move on?" he said, putting a hand on Papa's bony knee.

I held my breath. Papa let out a long sigh and nodded. He shifted and reached down for his shoes, but even that simple motion exhausted him. He fell back in the chair, shaking his head in frustration.

"Don't worry, Dad," my father said, dropping to a knee. "I got you." He took Papa's foot and guided it into the shoe. He tied the laces in a double knot and reached for the other shoe. Papa put his giant hand on top of my father's head. Dad tied the other shoe in a neat double knot. He got to his feet and reached for Papa's windbreaker. "Here, give me your arm," he said. Papa threaded his arm through the jacket, and Dad pulled it around his back and inserted the other arm. He zipped the jacket slowly up to Papa's chin, and handed him his baseball cap. "Alright, bring the chair over?" Dad said.

But Papa shook his head. "I don't need the chair," he said. "I can walk. I want to walk."

Exchanging worried glances, we took hold of Papa by his armpits and lifted him out of his chair. We drew his arms over our shoulders and shuffled him to the door. "Okay, nice and easy," Dad said, as we reached the threshold. Rain was sprinkling outside. I realized it was probably the first time my grandfather had left the house in at least a month. We guided him down the three steps and slowly walked him to my car in the driveway. Once he was inside, I pulled the seat belt across his chest. "Alright Papa, we're going to grab the rest of your stuff," I said. "We'll be right back."

He patted me on the shoulder and reached up for the passenger-side handle. Dad busied himself schlepping a few of Papa's small bags to the car, while I watched through the window inside. I studied my grandfather looking through the windshield at his house. *What was going through his mind? Was he thinking this was the last time he would see this home?*

The rain began falling harder, and Papa's face blurred behind the water streaking down the glass. Dad popped back into the house. "It's starting to really come down," he said. "We should get on the road." He wrapped his new scarf around his neck. I looked back out the window at Papa. Swollen beads of rain smacked against the windshield. Water was coming down in a thick stream, like a veil across the window. Papa was almost completely invisible, then I saw his giant hand reach back for the handle.

"Alright, let's do it," I said. I picked up the rock from San Donato off the side table and joined my father to bring my grandfather home. We were about to embark on the final leg of Papa's journey. What a privilege it was to be joining him for the ride.

EPILOGUE

Delia burst into the dimly lit restaurant in San Donato. "There you are!" she called over from the doorway. "When did you get in?" Jenny and I had just arrived from Florence and were sitting down to lunch outside the piazza. A year and a half had passed since my father and I had rolled into San Donato on our bicycles. Jenny and I had gotten married and were expecting our first baby. This trip was our babymoon.

"Look at you! *Look* . . . at . . . you. You look so wonderful," Delia said, embracing Jenny and placing her hand on Jenny's pronounced belly. "Isn't that something?" She turned to introduce her partner, Suzanne, to Jenny.

"So wonderful to finally meet you," Jenny said, embracing Suzanne, who had spiky silver hair and a calm, soft-spoken demeanor.

"So, do you know what you're having?"

"Pasta," I said.

"No, the baby!" Delia cried. "Boy or girl?"

"We don't know," Jenny said, laughing. "We're going to wait to find out."

"Isn't that wonderful," Delia said. "People don't do that anymore, they really don't. How far along are you?"

"About six and a half months," Jenny said.

"They let you fly?" Delia asked.

"Yeah, we're right on the cusp, but I didn't even tell the doctor we were going," Jenny said, flashing me a grin. In her own way, she was as bold as my father—intense in her passions, uncompromising in her pursuits. That's part of why I loved her. She was a strong, independent thinker who wasn't afraid to take a risk and dive right in. "If we have the baby in Italy, all the better."

Delia, with more family connections than Don Corleone, said San Donato's town physician was her cousin, so we'd be in good hands. "And Robbie tells me you're raising the baby Jewish? That's just wonderful," Delia said. I'd shared the rich wartime history of San Donato with Jenny right when I got home, including everything I'd learned about the connection between the people of the village and the Jewish people.

"Yes, I'm so grateful to see San Donato with my own eyes, especially for that reason," Jenny said.

"Yeah, particularly before this little one comes," I said, placing my hand on Jenny's belly.

Since returning from the trip with my father, the heroic history of San Donato had stuck with me. I'd spent hours painstakingly trying to translate *Vite di Carta* by Maria Pizzuti, the book given to me in the village that served as the definitive account of the twenty-eight Jews interned there. I discovered that eight of the Jews were like the Tennebaums, originally from Poland, while others like Greta Bloch were from Germany. One was from Hungary, one from the Ukraine, one from Slovakia, two from Italy, and five were from Vienna, Austria—the birthplace of Jenny's great-great-grandfather, who had been a Jewish tailor for the Austrian king.

Although we couldn't tie ourselves directly to these individuals, the stories of my so-called "people" trying to save the lives of Jenny's "people" bridged the gap between our faith traditions in my mind. Gazing at her belly, I envisioned myself telling my baby about Italian heroes like Pasqualina and brave Jews like Mardko Tennebaum. These stories would serve as the basis to form our own family traditions, melding each of our backgrounds into something uniquely our own. That my Jewish child was now in the village of San Donato, albeit in the womb, struck me as a fitting chapter in my family's long history here. And as fate would have it, our baby was due the day after my great-grandfather Loreto's birthday.

AFTER FINISHING LUNCH, JENNY and I followed Delia and Suzanne up to the piazza. Nothing had changed. The same old men sat in the same seats, wearing the same outfits. The cafe owner lingered at the table behind them, smoking a cigarette. Delia greeted them all in a flurry as Jenny and I studied the monument, scanning the names until we arrived at COCUZZO at the top.

"Are you okay to walk a little bit?" Delia asked Jenny.

"Yes, absolutely," she said. "We've been sitting in the car all afternoon, so it will be nice to stretch my legs a bit." We walked around the monument and up one of the side streets into the courtyard by Delia's apartment.

"This is where Fulvio had his Passion of the Christ performance," she said. "They wanted Robbie to play Jesus!" she laughed. "Can you believe that? He wanted a blond-haired, blue-eyed Jesus, for Chrissakes!"

"How did that go?" I asked.

"Oh fuck, it was a cold day, and the guy Fulvio got to play Jesus was up there on the cross yelling down in Italian, 'I'm fucking freezing up here, get me off this thing!' It was good though. It was. Real nice."

Delia led us around the corner of her apartment and pointed to a polished plaque at the top of one of her neighbor's staircases. "They just put that in," she said. "It was for my cousin who was caught helping the Allied Forces. He was sent to the concentration camp in Dachau. They did a big ceremony here for him. It was really something." The town council had added a number of these plaques around town. You could now walk around and see the houses where some of the Jews lived when they were interned in San Donato.

"They're doing a much better job at celebrating the history of this place," Suzanne said.

"Fulvio must be happy about that," I said.

We continued through the courtyard and up another narrow side street. Trudging up the stone walkways, we were all breathing heavily in the June heat. Delia stopped to catch her breath and pointed to a stone building to our left. "This is where I was born," she said. "Can you believe seven of us lived in that little place?"

A spiderweb of cracks ran across the facade. "What's the damage from?" I asked.

"That's from the Allied Forces bombing the village," she said. "That's shrapnel. My father wanted to fix it but the town said no, they didn't want to erase that history." During the Nazi occupation, the Allied Forces bombed San Donato, in an effort to drive the Germans back north. Delia said, "It was only a few weeks after the Nazis shipped all those poor Jews to Auschwitz that the Allied Forces finally broke through and liberated the village."

Slowly, slowly, we ambled our way up the stone streets, past one ornate vignette after another, until we reached the Church of San Donato at the top of the village. Delia pulled open the door and we followed her in. "See, they have the patron saint out," she said, pointing to the statue of Saint Donato to the left of the altar. "Legend is that an Allied pilot was flying over San Donato about to drop a bomb on the village. But right before he was going to release the bomb, he saw a face staring back at him and he stopped and turned away. Many years later, that pilot returned to San Donato and came to this church. He said that the face he saw was that face." Delia gestured to the statue. "That's the legend anyway."

As Delia toured Jenny and Suzanne through the church, I lingered at the back. I couldn't remember where I'd left it. I ran my hand along the top of the confessional box and under the pews, but it wasn't there. I looked behind the statues by the altar, but found nothing. *It must be gone*, I thought. *Priest must have found it and tossed it out.* I walked to the back corner, where a statue of Joseph stood. I reached up and ran my hand around the dusty base by his feet—and there it was.

"Hey, babe," I called over to Jenny. "I want to show you something. Real quick."

She met me beneath the statue. I reached again to the ledge and grabbed the photo. "Check this out," I said. "I left this here." It was the photo of Papa, me, and Dad. She turned it over and read the inscription I'd penned more than a year earlier. "Oh, he would have loved that," Jenny said, handing the photo back to me. I gave it another long look and then slid it back into its secret hiding spot.

"Someday I'll bring my son here and show him that photo," I said.

Jenny smiled. "Or your daughter."

"Right . . . or my daughter."

MY GRANDFATHER PASSED AWAY a little more than a month after my father and I moved him into my parents' house. We'd set up a bed for him in the living room where family and friends could sit and visit. Uncle Joe, Aunt Nancy, and Aunt Jodi—Dad's younger siblings—moved in for days and weeks at a time to help take care of him, along with my grandmother, the hospice nurses, and my parents. Papa had actually remodeled the room himself decades earlier, so it was appropriate that he'd spend his remaining days in the space that he had built for my father.

For most of the day and night, Papa lay in a deep slumber, his two giant hands folded across his chest, rising and falling. He went more than a month without eating. A few sips of ginger ale and water were all that sustained him. Occasionally his eyes would flutter open, and he'd raise his hands to the ceiling as if he were reaching for the pearly gates themselves.

We each took turns sitting with him. Most of the time, he was sound asleep, but occasionally he'd wake up and be completely lucid for a few minutes. During those fleeting moments, I told him how much I loved him and how grateful I was for everything he had done for me in my life. "I'm going to try to be like you, Papa," I told him. "I'm going to try and be a good father and husband." He placed his big hand on the back of my neck and pulled me in close. "You just be good," he said. Those were his last words to me.

My grandfather had held our family in his hands. Powerful hands that knew how to shuck a cherrystone, frame a house, slice an eggplant, hit a hole in one, edge a hedge, plant a geranium, and hold a baby. He was a towering man whose stature wasn't so much in size but in sheer presence. Charisma wafted off his every move. The dainty way he adjusted his glasses with thumb and pointer finger. The gestures he waved through the air as he told a story. The bellowing laugh that made you feel good and warm and safe down to your bones. He did everything for everyone. Never a complaint. Never a question. He had a sweet tenderness that betrayed his man's man persona. His heart was huge, and he had a capacity to love more than anyone I've ever known.

In the end, cancer and the cold onslaught of age tried to strip my grandfather of everything that made him who he was. Seemingly overnight, he became a tiny old man who could barely lift his head off the pillow. For the first time in his life, he depended entirely on others to perform the most fundamental tasks. But in his decline he gave our family the one gift he wasn't able to provide throughout his life. Papa finally gave us the chance to take care of him.

Dad quietly struggled through those final weeks of his father's life. The role reversal of caring for my grandfather seemed to overwhelm him, and he relied heavily on my mother's direction. Part of me wished my father knew instinctively how to help, but another part of me felt just as helpless. Whenever my aunt or mother needed to bring Papa to the bathroom or change his clothes, I darted out of the room. I couldn't handle the indignity of it all. Although Papa wasn't totally aware of who was around him at any given time, I knew that he would never want me to see him like that. Perhaps my father felt the same way.

I pondered how or if I would be different than my father in the years to come. When he becomes old and frail, how will I respond? Taking care of him on a bike ride through Italy was one thing, but what about when he couldn't perform the most fundamental functions? I didn't know the answer to that question. Perhaps I won't know until I'm tested.

I realized that the same could be said of being a father. From the moment that pink line appeared on Jenny's pregnancy test, the calibration of my life began to shift dramatically. As her belly grew bigger, and as we navigated hurdles and juggled unfamiliar stresses, I began to appreciate the true gravity of what it was to be a father. And with that, I appreciated my own father with brand-new eyes. He was my age when he had me. He had grappled with the same worries and realities of supporting a family.

Considering my childhood memories with these fresh insights, I marveled at what an astounding parent my father had been—and that he still was. I'd spent most of my adult life resisting becoming too much like him. I had tried to suppress the little eccentricities of his that I'd occasionally find myself doing. Yet when it came to raising my own child, I could only hope that I inherited his fatherly gifts and would be able to build a similar relationship with my son or daughter.

EVEN AFTER MY GRANDFATHER was laid to rest, his life still felt unresolved in my mind. I'd traced his roots all the way back to the soil where they first sprouted, but I still couldn't find where the disconnect had happened with his own father. Days before he passed away, Papa's older sister Jennie came to his bedside. They'd been estranged for most of his life after his falling out with his father. Jennie held his hand dearly and called him by his childhood name, "Joe-Joe." I was sitting at the foot of his bed, utterly wracked with grief. Papa hadn't been conscious in two weeks. Jennie ran her hand across his brow tenderly. Apart from occasions that I was too young to recall, this was my first encounter with my grandfather's sister. She turned to me and whispered, "He looks just like my father."

Two years later, I visited Jennie in her home in Brighton. I had been putting off meeting with her for reasons I really couldn't put my finger on. Perhaps I was subconsciously nervous to finally discover the truth of Papa's relationship with his father. Huddled in her living room, Jennie paged through a tattered photo album and shared her memories of growing up in the Yard. She was about to turn ninety years old, but was as sharp as can be. "There's Joe-Joe," she said. "Boy was he handsome . . . and what a rascal." Papa looked to be in his early teens in the photo and wore a hint of a smile on his face. "He was the nicest kid. Just the greatest guy you ever wanted to know. He's a lot like your father."

She continued flipping through the old album and stopped on a photo of two men standing on the bow of a ship. "That's my father right there," she said. "He was beautiful. Blond with blue eyes."

"Really?" I said. "I always thought he had dark features."

"Oh no, he had light eyes and hair just like you. It runs in the family, you know." Jennie told me how her father came over to the United States at the age of nine with her grandfather. He went to the same high school as my father had, before becoming a car mechanic. "Oh, he was a doll," she said. "Just a doll . . . and he loved his little Joe-Joe." Both statements took me by surprise. She painted an entirely different portrait of her father than Papa had. "He was one of the best men. Everybody loved him," she said. "He never swore, he never lied . . . he drank, I'll admit that, but I'd never seen my father drunk." My mind raced to reconcile this beatific portrayal of my great-grandfather with the tyrant Papa and my father told me about. "He loved Joe-Joe," Jennie continued. "I never understood why Joe-Joe hated him so much. It broke my heart."

Jennie shared her theories for their feud. She thought her father might have pressured Papa to grow up and get married too early, and he always resented him for that. My grandfather had never mentioned that to me, but it was plausible. Still, none of her explanations offered a clear breaking point in their relationship. Jennie had moved out by then and was working three jobs and raising several children. She cherished the memory of her father in a way that was completely inconsistent with the stories I'd heard. "I know you're probably thinking I'm sticking up for him, or making too much of him, but I'm just telling you how he was," she said. "My mother would dig into him, they would fight, and I think she'd confide in Joe-Joe. Maybe he resented him for that."

As we reached the end of the album, it was clear that I would be leaving Jennie's living room with more questions than I'd had when I arrived. There was no resolution. Just like my grandfather, my father, and me, Jennie had her own stories she was telling herself to preserve her past in a way she could live with. To draw our conversation to an end, I asked her how my great-grandfather passed away. She explained that he died of cirrhosis of the liver at the age of sixty-three. "When your father was nearing the end, did my grandfather, Joe-Joe, go to visit him?" I asked.

Emotion flooded Jennie's face. Recalling the memory, she took a couple of wheezy breaths and swallowed dryly. She told me how after her father was given two years to live, he was hospitalized in Brighton, right up the street from my grandfather's house. Months, then years passed by, but Papa never visited. At the very end, my great-grandfather was moved to a different hospital for hospice care. Jennie called Papa and told him that if he wanted to see his father again, now was the time. "Joe-Joe drove up there. He had a bag of cherries with him to give to my father," Jennie said, tears now rolling down her cheeks. "But when he looked up to his hospital window, the nurses were just pulling down the curtain . . . Joe-Joe didn't make it in time to see him alive."

As I left Jennie's home to return to my own Jenny, that's all I could hang on to, the fleeting nature of time. Whether looking forward or back, time can seem so abundant. Only when we hold it up against the finality of life do we realize how little we're actually given. I couldn't make up for what had happened in the past, couldn't mend the relationships that were broken, or live the dreams that were left undone. All I could do was glean the lessons of my forefathers, and honor their memory by pedaling hard with the time I had left.

ACKNOWLEDGMENTS

As should be obvious to anyone who has read the preceding pages, the first person I must thank for making this book possible is my father. Dad, thank you not only for embarking on this adventure with me but also for having the courage to share your story. From the moment I put pen to paper, you trusted my instincts, candidly shared your thoughts, and never questioned how I was going to tell our story. I hope this book serves as a testament to what a remarkable father you've been and what an extraordinary human being you are.

Thank you most especially to my wife, Jenny, for your wholehearted support during this endeavor. I'll forever cherish the countless nights you and I spent reading this entire manuscript to our baby girl, Vienna, while she was in your belly. I'm inspired by you every day and cannot wait to raise our child together.

To the first woman in my life, Mom, the success of our family is a credit to you. You have always served as our moral compass, bringing balance to the many ups and downs of our family unit. Just as with Dad, I thank you for your courage and trust in allowing me to share the intimate details of our family.

And when it comes to family, I thank my brother and best friend, Mark. No one knows the journey of these pages quite like you. For all the times you jogged my memory about the events of our childhood and for always finding places for us to laugh, even when the stories weren't all that funny, thank you.

Thank you to my grandmother Nonnie, Uncle Joe, Aunt Nancy, Aunt Jodi, and to all my aunts, uncles, and cousins. And to the newest members of my family—Carol, Hillary, Zack, and Arthur—I'm so grateful to be part of your tribe.

Thank you to Delia Roffo. This project never, *never* would have happened without you in my corner. You opened every door to me in San Donato and were boundlessly generous with your time and wisdom. I'm also grateful to your partner, Suzanne, and your brother, Sergio, and his wife, Debbie, for their support and friendship during this endeavor.

Thank you to all my friends and mentors who encouraged me to take on this project, especially Charlie Kravetz, for giving me the nudge I needed to jump on this project, and Guido Vitti, for insisting that I take on this particular project as my baby book. I'm also grateful to Lydia Tanner and *Bicycling* magazine for publishing a shorter version of this story that helped me get the wheels turning on writing this book. Thank you to Chris Brown who went above and beyond in proofreading all the Italian (and English!) in this book.

To my team at *Nantucket Magazine*—Bruce Percelay, Emme Duncan, Kit Noble, Brian Sager, Paulette Chevalier, Leise Trueblood, and Brian Maranian—the months of writing this book were undoubtedly some of the most stressful in my life, and I'm so grateful for the patience, support, and friendship you've shown me during that time and all the times before.

Thank you to the good folks at Mountaineers Books who jumped enthusiastically right on board with me. In particular, thank you to Kate Rogers, Mary Metz, and Amy Smith Bell for helping me tell this story in the clearest voice possible, and to Jen Grable for creating a cover that reflects that voice.

Thank you to the people of San Donato for welcoming two long-lost sons of the village back into your warm embrace and making us feel at home. Most especially, thank you to Fulvio Cocuzzo and Gaetano Cocuzzo.

Last but not least, thank you to my late grandfather Joseph Cocuzzo. As I hope I captured in these pages, Papa represented everything it means to be a good father, husband, and man. I hope this book honors his memory and serves as a small encapsulation of the love and joy he brought to our entire family during his rich life.

ABOUT THE AUTHOR

ROBERT COCUZZO lives in Boston with his wife, Jenny, and daughter, Vienna. He is the author of *Tracking the Wild Coomba: The Life of Legendary Skier Doug Coombs*, as well as the longtime editor of *N Magazine* and a contributor to numerous publications. Prior to beginning his writing career, Cocuzzo studied at Boston College High School, the College of the Holy Cross, and St. Andrews University in Scotland. After graduation, he became a US Coast Guard–certified charter captain and traveled extensively around the world. When they're not in the city, Cocuzzo and his family split their time between Jackson, New Hampshire, and the island of Nantucket.

MOUNTAINEERS BOOKS

recreation · lifestyle · conservation

MOUNTAINEERS BOOKS, including its two imprints, Skipstone and Braided River, is a leading publisher of quality outdoor recreation, sustainability, and conservation titles. As a 501(c)(3) nonprofit, we are committed to supporting the environmental and educational goals of our organization by providing expert information on human-powered adventure, sustainable practices at home and on the trail, and preservation of wilderness.

Our publications are made possible through the generosity of donors, and through sales of 700 titles on outdoor recreation, sustainable lifestyle, and conservation. To donate, purchase books, or learn more, visit us online:

MOUNTAINEERS BOOKS

1001 SW Klickitat Way, Suite 201 • Seattle, WA 98134
800-553-4453 • mbooks@mountaineersbooks.org • www.mountaineersbooks.org

An independent nonprofit publisher since 1960

OTHER MOUNTAINEERS BOOKS TITLES YOU MAY ENJOY

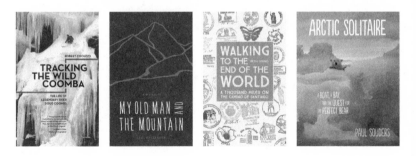